Dedication

To my loving family and Rascal the dog

ABOUT THE AUTHOR

Dr. Myles H. Bader (known as The Wizard of Food) has been interviewed on more than four thousand radio and television shows in the United States and Canada and is an internationally recognized leader in the preventive care and wellness fields. Recent media appearances have included *The Oprah Winfrey Show, Crook and Chase, America's Talking, The Discovery Channel, Trinity Broadcasting, QVC,* and *Smart Solutions*.

Dr. Bader received his doctoral degree from Loma Linda University and is board-certified in preventive care. He has practiced weight control, nutrition education, fitness, stress management, and cardiac rehabilitation for twenty-three years. He has established prevention and executive care programs for numerous safety departments, civic organizations, and Fortune 500 companies.

Current books that Dr. Bader has authored include *10,001 Food Facts, Chef's Secrets & Household Hints, The Wellness Desk Reference, 2,001 Food Secrets Revealed, To Supplement or Not to Supplement,* and *8,001 Food Facts and Chef's Secrets*.

Recently, Dr. Bader has formulated a number of unique products that will be a part of a special weight management program called "Do It My Weigh."

THE WIZARD OF FOOD

REVEALS

5,001
MYSTERIES OF LIQUIDS
&
COOKING SECRETS

(Plus 100 World-Class Recipes)

THE FIRST BOOK EVER PRINTED
SPECIFICALLY ON LIQUIDS AND SEMILIQUIDS

BY DR. MYLES H BADER

A BADER CORPORATION AND FRIEDMAN/FAIRFAX BOOK

© 1999 by The Bader Corporation
1818 Industrial Rd. Ste. 209
Las Vegas, NV 89102
(702) 383-8511
Order line only: (800) 717-6001
www.wizardoffood.com

ISBN 1-56799-945-X

Illustrations by: Paulette K. Bader, Deborah Rose Peek

1 3 5 7 9 10 8 6 4 2

For book trade sales:
Friedman/Fairfax Publishers
Attention: Sales Department
15 West 26th Street
New York, New York 10010
212/685-6610   FAX 212/685-1307

Visit our website:
www.metrobooks.com

CONTENTS

Introduction

This book is intended to provide you with information about liquids and semiliquids of all types. Every day we either drink or cook with liquids, but we rarely think about these liquids and the effects some of them may have on our bodies. The body needs liquids to survive; without an adequate supply we can live for only a short period of time. There are also many factors that relate to cooking with liquids, including the changes that occur when they are heated or frozen, how they interact with other liquids and foods, and whether they are healthy or unhealthy for our bodies.

Our bodies, however, are subjected to utilizing a number of liquids that do not really benefit our health. The extent to which we drink or use some of these liquids in our foods may have a definite impact on our overall health and subsequently our level of health and even our longevity. Continuing to consume a large quantity of poor-quality liquids takes its toll on your body.

If you have ever wondered what is in a particular liquid, how it is produced, or just how good or bad it really is, this book will provide you with the information. How a liquid will act when you cook with it, freeze it, or heat it and whether certain liquids are good for you or leach needed nutrients from other foods or your body are included. This book contains recipes that will provide the best preparation methods and the most flavorful type of that particular liquid or semiliquid. In many instances the chemical makeup will be discussed, as well as how small changes in a recipe can make a major health or taste difference in a particular dish.

This book will provide you with general information regarding almost every kind of liquid or semiliquid you consume. It is not a health book, but one that will assist you in understanding each different liquid, its nature, and its relationship to food. Since the book covers almost every kind of liquid, it is really an encyclopedia of liquid facts of which every person who cooks or drinks any kind of liquid needs to be better informed. The more knowledge we gain in regard to the elements we put into our bodies, the longer we will live and the healthier we will be. The information in this book is 100 percent accurate and can be used by everyone. It is information that is not easily found without extensive research through thousands of newsletters, books, computer files, and scientific papers.

5,001 Mysteries of Liquids and Cooking Secrets is a book everyone will use and enjoy.

and can utilize efficiently. The human body is between 60 and 70 percent water, which is found in all cells, organs, tissues, urine, perspiration, and blood.

Water is an excellent lubricant and keeps nutrients moving throughout the body. We do get water from some of the foods we eat, such as juices, milk, and soups; however, the best source for the body is pure water. A number of other liquids such as coffee, tea, and most carbonated beverages may act as diuretics and cause our water supplies to be depleted.

However, it is possible to damage the body or even kill yourself if you drink too much water. Drinking 11/2 to 2 gallons of water within a one-hour period will short-circuit the body's systems, may cause serious illness, and could kill a very young child.

The following is the breakdown of the average adult annual liquid consumption. You may not be drinking the amount mentioned in each category, but someone else is making up for it.

- Soft drinks: . . . . .46.7 gallons
- Water: . . . . .43.1 gallons
- Coffee: . . . . .28.6 gallons
- Beer: . . . . .27.8 gallons
- Milk: . . . . .19.8 gallons
- Tea, juice, liquor, and wine: . . . .25.3 gallons

BOTTLED WATER

Sales of bottled water have never been higher due to the number of incidences of contaminated water-supply scares in the United States. Many wells in all parts of the country have been found to be contaminated from industry dump sites, abandoned mines, and animal or human sewage, and there has even been natural mineral contamination. Most U.S. water treatment systems were developed before 1915. Estimates are more than $125 billion to update our present water purification systems, as well as taking more than eighteen years to complete the project. It is a sad commentary that many bottled-water companies just sell us back our own local tap water after they clean it up for us.

Bottled water is still the fastest-growing beverage sold in the United States. In 1998 we consumed about 2.2 billion gallons of it. The quality of bottled water is regulated by the Food and Drug Administration (FDA), which considers bottled water a food product. Most water bottlers are members of the International

Chapter 1

Water, Water, Everywhere (But Is It Safe to Drink?)

Water seems to be getting more complicated with each passing year. It used to be simply water! However, commercially that was just too simple, and water now has to be flavored, colored, oxygenated, caffeinated, softened, filtered, carbonated, fluoridated, ginsenged, and vitamin- and mineral-enriched. New studies now say that we should drink water with minerals for a healthy heart, while other studies say that we should filter as much as we can from the water. I don't know how our grandparents lived to a ripe old age without all these newfangled preparations and filter systems.

There is, however, a lot of truth in the fact that our drinking water has become somewhat polluted from the contamination of ground waters all over the United States. Drinking bottled water or partially filtered water is in my opinion the safest way to go. Presently, about one in every five Americans is being exposed to possible harmful levels of a variety of toxic elements in our water supplies.

Water assists the body in the elimination of wastes and is a constituent of every living cell. The average adult consumes approximately 191 gallons of liquids annually; unfortunately only about 38 percent is a liquid that the body prefers

Bottled Water Association (IBWA). The bottled-water business is a $3.6 billion industry.

States also regulate water bottlers and are analyzing and inspecting facilities on a regular basis. States must also inspect the laboratories that perform the water testing. Approximately 75 percent of all bottled water originates from springs or wells, while the other 25 percent is usually from tap-water sources. If the water is from a municipal water company source, it must be labeled as such.

If the water is labeled as purified, then it must be distilled, deionized, demineralized, or run through a reverse osmosis system. If this is done then the water does not have to be labeled "tap water" even if it comes from that source. Most bottling companies have in-house testing capabilities and stringent controls. IBWA members, which include almost all twelve hundred U.S. bottlers, must also have unannounced inspections by National Sanitation Foundation International inspectors.

Source inspections are also performed on a regular weekly basis, especially for microbacterial contamination. Additional information can be found on the IBWA web site at www.bottledwater.org or by calling (800) WATER-11.

FLOURIDE

This tooth decay–fighting mineral will not be found in high levels in bottled water. If you prefer a higher level then check the label, since there are a few bottled-water companies that do add additional fluoride. Fluoride has been proven effective, especially in children, in reducing the risk of cavities, and it promotes increased mineralization even into adulthood. Fluoride supplements, however, are available at most health food stores.

CRYPTOSPORIDIUM

While there are many bacteria and other contaminants that may affect our water, cryptosporidium, a disease-carrying parasite, is one of the more common contaminants. This parasite lives in animals such as goats, cattle, rabbits, squirrels, wolves, and raccoons and is passed into the water through their waste. The eggs of the parasites have been the cause of gastrointestinal problems in a number of areas of the United States. Flulike symptoms may materialize; the infestation may be fatal to those with poor or underdeveloped immune systems, such as the young, the elderly, and especially people suffering from HIV.

When you are hiking or camping in a forest, it is always wise to bring water with you or at least use a water purification tablet or boil the water. Mountain streams, lakes, rivers, and ponds are easily contaminated.

Well water or deep spring water for the most part is free of this contaminant. Surface water is usually the culprit. Filtration systems in bottled-water companies remove organisms such as cryptosporidium very effectively.

One of the most serious outbreaks of cryptosporidium water contamination was in 1993, when 110 people died and more than 400,000 people became ill in Milwaukee, Wisconsin. Animal waste contamination or a sewage leak likely caused this problem.

ADDITIVES

Bottled water must not contain any form of chemical additive or preservative, not even a sweetener. It can, however, contain a natural extract derived from fruit or spices. Bottled water must contain no calories and be sodium-free, and even natural flavors, when added, must be less than 1 percent of the weight of the finished product.

STORAGE

There is no dated shelf life on bottled water. It can last forever if stored in a cool, dry location away from any solvents or other household chemicals that may produce fumes.

TYPES OF BOTTLED WATER

▽ SPRING WATER

This water is usually found in underground springs, which flow close to the surface. Usually this water is labeled with the name of the spring. Whether the spring water comes to the surface or is drilled for, the water must have the same physical properties and be tested before bottling. One of the purest spring waters is found in Iceland and comes from the Hesjuvalla Spring. This has been a pure water source for more than one thousand years.

▽ ARTESIAN WATER

This is water that is bottled from a specific underground water source called an aquifer. The source may be a well or body of water found in a layer of rock. Artesian water is one of the purest natural waters.

☐ MINERAL WATER

This water that must have at least 250 parts per million of dissolved solids. It must contain a specific level of minerals and trace elements when it is harvested from its source. Bottled-water companies must not add minerals to this water product. Recent studies show that drinking lightly mineralized water may be beneficial for your heart.

☐ SPARKLING WATER

Sparkling water is naturally carbonated by nature with carbon dioxide. Bottled-water companies may recarbonate the water if it has lost a percentage of carbon dioxide, but only to the original level. Seltzer is not considered bottled water, is not regulated by the IBWA, and can contain sugar and calories. Seltzer, soda water, tonic water, and the like are considered soft drinks and are regulated as such.

☐ PURIFIED WATER

Purified water is produced through distillation. This process removes all contaminants and minerals and is the purest water. If this is your water of choice, it is wise to take a mineral supplement. This water may be labeled as distilled water.

TAP WATER

It will probably be a long time and take billions of dollars to clean up all the tap water in the United States. The studies that have been done all report similar findings, which conclude that millions of Americans are taking either a small risk or a major risk from drinking tap water. This will not come as a surprise to anyone since the television shows and articles are numerous on the subject.

Many of the risk factors are right in our own backyards and are not the fault of the water companies' purification methods. In older homes the water pipes may be deteriorating, allowing the metals contained in the pipes to leach into our drinking water. If the water has a slight acid/base upset, this could easily come from these metals. If you live in an older home, you may have lead pipes; if so your tap water should be tested at least once each year. The tap water flowing into more than 80 million homes in the United States may contain carcinogens.

Even if your home has copper pipes, they may have lead-soldered joints, which could also leach lead into your water supply. The levels of possible carcinogens found in tap water by the Environmental Protection Agency (EPA) was a real eye-opener. The list included most of the major cities in the United States, the worst being Tampa, Florida; Houston, Texas; Oklahoma City, Oklahoma; and Charleston, South Carolina.

SOFT WATER

Soft water contains very few minerals; in most areas of the country, tap water is high in mineral content and needs to be softened. Softened water is high in sodium, which is not healthy to drink, especially for those with high blood pressure or kidney problems. Soft water may also leach lead out of pipes in older homes.

Water softeners utilize a method of ion exchange to remove hard minerals, such as calcium and magnesium, while replacing them with sodium. Sodium then creates a softening effect on the water, creating more soap suds. This makes the water more efficient for doing laundry, bathing, and washing dishes.

The medical community has issued a health alert regarding the use of potassium-based water-softening units or the use of a salt that is high in potassium. Drinking water that is high in potassium can be a health risk to people who suffer from high blood pressure, diabetes, and kidney disease. High potassium levels may lead to muscle weakness, heartbeat irregularities, and even heart failure. Most products that are sold come with a warning label regarding the risks of the potassium-based units and products.

HARD WATER

Hard water contains different minerals than soft water does. The mineral content will usually depend on the area of the country where the water is found. High mineral content causes residues of calcium and magnesium to form in plumbing fixtures. These two minerals may protect women against heart disease.

OXYGENATED WATER

A number of companies are now producing oxygenated water. Some of the drinks are being marketed as breath fresheners due to the increased level of oxygen, which improves the oral ecology and has a cleansing effect. These beverages have oxygen dissolved into the drink under pressure, similar to the carbonation process of placing carbon dioxide into a beverage.

The drinks are sold in both glass and plastic containers. The glass container may be more efficient in retaining the level of oxygen since plastic containers tend to lose the oxygen at a faster rate. The higher the concentration level of available oxygen in the drink, the more effective a breath freshener the drink may be. This effect is derived from the oxygen increasing the level of good bacteria, the ones that are called aerobic bacteria and need oxygen to survive and multiply. The anaerobic bacteria are usually responsible for causing bad breath and do not require oxygen to survive.

Oxygenated beverages may be a natural solution to eliminating bad breath in some individuals and are a better alternative than using a mouthwash that contains alcohol, which is effective for only a short period of time. Other mouthwashes utilize chemicals that may only mask the offensive odor for a short time. When you inhale oxygen, you obtain a small level that mixes with saliva to keep your mouth moist. However, a thin film may easily form on your tongue, allowing the anaerobic bacteria to multiply and cause odors. Oxygenated water consumed on a daily basis will increase your oxygen level to about seventy parts per million (ppm) of pure oxygen compared to only seven ppm pure oxygen in the air you breathe.

Quality mouthwashes should contain chlorine dioxide, which is an effective killer of anaerobic bacteria. If you drink an oxygenated beverage and you are using a chlorine dioxide mouthwash, the beverage should increase the effectiveness of the mouthwash.

The majority of oxygenated beverages do not contain any sweeteners, preservatives, calories, or artificial flavorings. There is no limit to the number of drinks you can consume per day since it is a natural beverage. If you prefer drinking the beverage over ice cubes or just cold, this will not reduce the effectiveness.

LIFE O2 SUPER OXYGENATED WATER

This drink contains ten times the oxygen level (72mg) found in standard bottled water. The company claims its water will increase the amount of oxygen in your blood. The beverage is supposed to provide increased energy levels with no after-taste. It contains no artificial ingredients and may be worth a try during an exercise period or sports activity. It is one the best oxygenated waters on the market.

GINSENG SPRING WATER

This new water has only recently been introduced into the United States and contains about 100 milligrams of the herb ginseng. Ginseng has been a popular energy-related herb for hundreds of years. Most drinks are very tasty and refreshing.

CAFFEINATED WATER

A number of beverage manufacturers are now producing caffeinated water, which provides an alternative to drinking coffee to acquire caffeine. Most of the drinks have a very poor taste, though they do provide an adequate level of caffeine that may assist you in staying awake longer. Unless they figure out how to improve the taste, I do not foresee this drink being around too long.

ACIDULATED WATER

This is a mixture of water and an acid—usually a citrus acid derived from lime, orange, or lemon. It is commonly used on fruits or fruit salads to prevent them from browning when exposed to the air. Oxidation, which takes place very rapidly in many fruits and vegetables, vitamin C is lost in the brown areas. To prepare acidulated water, just use one part of the citrus fruit to five parts of pure water.

WATER PURIFICATION METHODS

There are numerous methods of home water purification systems. If you decide to purchase a system, be sure to investigate the different types and the availability of service for that particular system. A number of units produce only a minimal quantity of pure water, which is insufficient for many families, while other units do not provide the level of desired filtration.

ACTIVATED CHARCOAL FILTRATION UNITS

A number of the more popular units filter the water through activated charcoal filters. This method is very efficient in filtering out insecticides, pesticides, chlorine, and organic matter. However, this type of filter is not very effective in filtering out bacteria and undissolved metals, such as lead, copper, iron, and manganese. Filters need to be checked regularly and changed or the system will be useless. If you do choose this type of unit, be sure it does not contain silver to neutralize bacteria. Silver is not that effective and a percentage may end up in your drinking water.

CHLORINATION

Systems that utilize chlorine to kill bacteria usually produce water with a somewhat "off" taste and odor to the water. The system must be functioning properly at all times or there is the possibility of the chlorine forming a dangerous element.

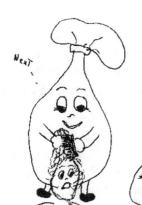

MULTISTAGE FILTRATION

These units are one of the most effective and are usually recommended above most other units. They utilize a number of filtration methods such as a prefilter, which will remove iron, rust, dirt particles, and sediments as small as 5 microns. They also have a lead-activated carbon filter, which removes lead and chlorine, as well as a carbon block filter to improve the taste and remove chlorine, odors, and most organic impurities.

MICROSTRAINERS

This is a good method of filtration, though it is unable to remove most nitrates and nitrites. It will remove almost all chemicals and bacteria.

REVERSE OSMOSIS

This is one of the most popular units sold in the United States and utilizes a duel sediment filter system. The system is effective in removing up to 90 percent of the minerals and inorganic matter. The system works by forcing water through a thin membrane, which removes the inorganic metals. Most units store only 5 gallons of water or less. This system produces only 20 percent drinking water and discards 80 percent as waste.

Commercial systems are used to remove salt from seawater to produce drinking water.

DISTILLATION

Distillation is one of the most effective methods of filtration. Water is boiled to produce steam, which is then cooled to produce water vapor, which is then trapped. However, certain gases are not removed through this method. The more efficient distillers utilize activated charcoal filters as an additional organic-material remover. Be sure to descale your distiller regularly or its efficiency will be greatly reduced.

AERATION

Radon gas is a continuing water-contamination problem, especially in the Midwest. An aeration filter is the most effective type of filter to resolve this problem. A survey conducted by the EPA estimated that more than 8 million people are at risk from radon contamination.

ULTRAVIOLET RADIATION PURIFIERS

These types of filters are very effective in filtering out bacteria and are normally installed on wells in conjunction with other types of filtration units. This system does require a constant electric voltage, and does not remove cyst contamination.

OZONATORS

These filters are being used more extensively than ever before and are frequently found on swimming pools built after 1992. They utilize activated oxygen that is capable of purifying and removing bacteria without chlorination. They are recommended more for swimming pools than for drinking water since the systems may produce bromate, which may be related to tumors of the kidney.

CARBON FILTERS

These filters utilize carbon to attract the contaminants, which then adhere to the carbon. They are useful in removing odors, improving the taste of water, and eliminating organic chemical compounds. Their drawback is that they do not remove heavy metals.

MAGNETIC WATER CONDITIONERS

Since all home appliances or equipment that use water build up scale over a period of time, these conditioners are a must for the homeowners who wish to protect their investment with a minimum of repairs from water-scale damage. These systems do not affect water purity; however, they condition the water magnetically, altering the physical characteristics of waterborne minerals. The mineral will no longer be able to cling to the insides of the water pipes and no scale can be formed.

CHECKING YOUR OWN TAP WATER

The following hints will help you evaluate your own tap water for possible contamination or problems:

• If your sink has a dark reddish stain, it may be the result of rust in your pipes.
• If your sink has a greenish stain, it is probably from copper leaching from the pipes.
• If you notice a rotten egg smell, it's probably hydrogen sulfide produced from bacteria.

- If the water is cloudy, it can be from dirt particles, iron, or bacterial contamination.
- Cloudy water can also result from small air bubbles forming when the water is under pressure as it leaves the tap and soon dissipates. This is harmless and no need for concern.

COMMON CONTAMINANTS IN TAP WATER

※ COPPER
Usually more of a problem in older homes stemming from the metal leaching out of the pipes.

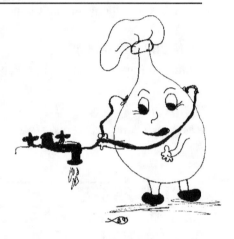

※ FLUORIDE
Water companies add fluoride to reduce the incidence of tooth decay. While fluoride does reduce the incidence of cavities, it is also a very toxic chemical and must be carefully controlled.

※ CHLORINE
Sometimes added as a disinfectant. People who frequently swim in pools that are chlorinated have reported arthritis and immune system disorders.

※ LEAD
Leached into tap water from older pipes.

※ CHLOROCARBONS
If chlorine is present, it may react with organic compounds to produce a harmful contaminant.

※ ORGANIC MOLECULES
Includes hydrocarbons, gasoline, and cleaning solvents.

※ PVC
Plastic materials from water pipes.

※ RADON
A naturally occurring contaminant.

※ MINERALS
Sodium content of some water may be too high.

※ PESTICIDES/FERTILIZERS
Filter through the ground and end up in our water supplies.

※ MICROORGANISMS
Include fungi, bacteria, and parasites.

※ NITRATES
Residues from fertilizers.

HEALTH FACTS

DEHYDRATION

A 1998 survey of three thousand Americans showed that a significant number are suffering from dehydration brought on by drinking too little water and too many cups of coffee and soft drinks. Remember that you can't fool Mother Nature! The following are a few good tips to staying well hydrated and healthier.

• When you exercise, remember to drink sixteen ounces of water for every pound you lose through perspiration. Keep a water bottle handy and drink regularly.

• For good health drink eight glasses of water each day, especially when you are ill. The body dehydrates more easily when you have a cold or fever.

• Never wait until you are thirsty before you drink water.

• Remember that coffee, soft drinks, tea, and alcoholic drinks have a diuretic effect. Caffeine especially is an excellent diuretic. Your body must find 8 ounces of water to break down 1 ounce of alcohol.

• If the weather is hot, cool water is the best fluid and will be more easily absorbed and utilized by the body.

WATER AND AGING: A SERIOUS PROBLEM

As we age, dehydration becomes a serious health problem due to the fact that our body's thirst mechanism is not working as well and does not tell us when our body requires more fluid. We don't know why our bodies tend to lose this ability, but it is common among seniors and leads to dehydration. Remember that our body is about 70 percent water, and the cells, joints, and tissues that protect our organs all rely on a good water supply.

Many seniors worry about fluid retention; however, if your body is functioning normally, your body will not retain excess fluids. Adequate water helps the kidneys function more efficiently, which helps alleviate fluid retention and improves waste disposal. Lack of adequate water may also cause the heart to work harder, and if it is already weak, dehydration can lead to heart failure.

WATER AND ATHLETES

There are numerous studies that discuss the need for adequate water relating to the efficiency of an athlete. If the body is dehydrated by 5 percent, physical performance may be reduced by as much as 25 percent. When working out or performing a sport at an average pace, the body can lose up to 1 quart of water every hour.

The average 150-pound adult should drink about 100 ounces of water daily if he or she takes part in an active sport or exercise on a regular basis. If you plan on a strenuous exercise regimen, you should drink about 2 cups of water two hours before starting. To replace water losses through perspiration, you need to drink about 1 cup of water every fifteen minutes.

If you allow your water level to get too low, you may develop headaches, lightheadedness, dizziness, and nausea. Since water is used to cool the body, a number of increased–body temperature problems can occur, especially heatstroke. Depending on the duration and intensity of the activity, a sports drink may be best.

WHERE IS YOUR WATER FROM?

If your water is from a surface water source, such as a lake or a river, the water can be exposed to acid rain, storm water runoff, fertilizer and pesticide runoff, or industrial waste residues. Exposure to sunlight will cleanse the water to some degree, but you should have it checked regularly. If your water supply is from a well or a public water company, it takes longer to become contaminated, but should still be checked at least every six months.

RISK OF DYING FROM PESTICIDES IN WATER SUPPLIES

The risk of getting cancer from drinking pesticide-contaminated water is about one in 1 million if you drink eight to ten glasses per day. The chances of getting cancer from smoking cigarettes (one pack per day) are about eighty thousand in 1 million.

WET FACTS

IT'S A FACT

The human body loses the same amount of water when sleeping as when awake.

WATER WEIGHT

Sometimes a recipe mentions the weight of water. The weight of 1 tablespoon is ½ ounce and the weight of 2 cups is 1 pound of water.

ARE YOU STILL THIRSTY?

When you drink twelve ounces of pure water, you will absorb only about 8 ounces of water during a fifteen-minute period. If you drink a regular soft drink that contains about 10 percent sugar, your body will absorb only about 1 ounce of water.

OH, THE WEATHER OUTSIDE IS GLOOMY

A person requires the same amount of water in cold weather as in hot weather.

COOL, CLEAR WATER

Symptoms that are associated with dehydration or low water intake include skin irritations, itching, dry skin problems, lack of alertness upon arising, or the midday blues (energy loss). More serious symptoms may include blood pressure problems, digestive upset, and even poor kidney function.

ARE YOU AMONG THE FEW, THE HEALTHY

Statistics show that only one in every eight Americans drinks the required eight glasses of water daily.

UP, UP, AND AWAY

On the average day, the human body can lose 32 ounces of water. This will increase significantly if you exercise or are otherwise active, or if the weather is very hot.

TOP OF THE HEAP

The top water bottlers are Evian, Perrier, Black Mountain Spring Water, Calistoga, Clearly Canadian, NAYA, Water Joe, Earth 20, Aqua Penn Spring Water, and Saratoga.

THE LATEST COUNT

There are still more than fifty thousand identified dump sites in the continental United States that are contaminating our water and have not been cleaned up yet. These exist from poor refuse disposal sites; old manufacturing companies, most of which have gone out of business; and mines that have closed.

RISKY WATER AREAS

Approximately 15 million Americans may be drinking water that is below EPA standards. Higher-risk cities include New York, Portland, West Palm Beach, New Orleans, Cleveland, San Diego, Denver, Houston, San Francisco, and Chicago.

IT'S A WONDER WE DON'T SLOSH WHEN WE WALK

A 180-pound adult contains more than 100 pounds of water. The brain is 76 percent water, and the lungs are 86 percent.

GOING UP, BUBBLE LEVEL

When water boils, the bubbles that come to the surface are just pockets of water vapor that originate on the bottom of the pot. As soon as the bubbles absorb enough energy to overcome the weight of the liquid and the atmospheric pressure, they rise to the surface.

STOP BOILOVERS COLD

When you add pasta or other food to boiling water, the food contains a percentage of organic matter, especially protein, that is released into the cooking water. These elements accumulate on the surface and disrupt the surface tension that has been created by the boiling water. When this occurs, foam is formed and mixes with the water, causing the bubbles to be somewhat stronger and not burst as easily, thus flowing over the top of the pot. To avoid this problem, just add a small amount of oil to the water, which does not mix well with the water and will form tiny droplets on the surface. The oil droplets act as "bubble breakers" prevent the bubbles from becoming large and the pot from boiling over.

HIDDEN DANGER

Never drink tap water first thing in the morning or if the water has not been run for about three hours. The risk of contaminants is very high from water that is allowed to rest in the pipes. Always run the tap for at least one minute before drinking or using the water for cooking. The hot water tap is even guiltier than the cold water tap.

WATER AND SEA LEVEL

The normal boiling point of water at sea level is 212°F. For every 500 feet over sea level, the boiling point of water decreases by 1°F.

DON'T HARM THAT ICEBERG

Most of the fresh water on earth is in glaciers. However, if we melt them, we'd better all grow gills and fins. Only 3 to 4 percent of the fresh water is available for human consumption and to grow crops. It would be best if we learned more efficient methods of desalinization.

ADDING SALT TO WATER—DO MICROSECONDS REALLY COUNT?

When sugar, salt, or almost any other solid is added to water, the boiling point is raised and the freezing point lowered. If you add 1 ounce of salt to 1 quart of water it will raise the boiling point 1°F. For example, if you live at an elevation of 1 mile you would have to add 8 ounces of salt to water to reach 212°F. The molecules of salt and sugar interfere with the natural breakdown of the water molecule.

Adding salt to water to cook pasta faster is a waste of time, since the amount needed would be too much to fit into the pot. If you added 1 tablespoon of salt to 5 quarts of boiling water to cook 1 pound of pasta, it would raise the boiling point by only seven one-hundreths of 1°F. Cookbooks that advise you to add salt to the cooking water of pasta should advise you that it is done only for flavoring. However, other studies tell us that adding salt sometimes makes certain pasta tough.

BRING A BIG CANTEEN

If you're planning to climb Mount Everest, bring a good supply of water, since the higher the altitude, the more water the body requires. Water will evaporate much faster as you climb higher. The increased rate of breathing also has a lot to do with it.

DID CAESAR DRINK PERRIER?

The source of Perrier Sparkling Mineral Water can be traced back about 130 million years with the first known record dating back to Roman times. The first bottling of the water took place in 1863, and it has been imported into the United States since around 1900. The water is the result of rainwater flowing down hillsides in southern France and being filtered through limestone, sand, and gravel deposits. During the natural filtration process the water acquires certain minerals that give it a unique flavor. Geothermal activity deep underground provides the natural carbonation. The water rises to the surface at a constant pressure and at 60°F.

Since the demand for the water worldwide was too much for the springs to supply, the French collected the water and the gas separately and brought them to a bottling plant and combined the ingredients there to increase production.

RAINDROPS KEEP FALLING...

Rainwater may contain a number of contaminants and minerals. Acid rain is a good example of how we can even contaminate the clouds.

HOT, COLD, OR TEPID

The temperature of drinking water does make a difference to our bodies. Cold water will quench our thirst faster. Hot water tends to open the cells in the intestines and may allow allergens to enter. Tepid or room-temperature water is best tolerated by the body and utilized more easily.

A WORD TO THE WISE

When in any foreign country, try not to drink tap water, brush your teeth with tap water, use ice cubes, or drink any beverage with ice cubes, noncarbonated locally bottled water, or mixed-alcohol drinks.

WATER VS. IRON AND OIL

Just a bit of interesting trivia! Water is capable of absorbing a large quantity of energy to raise its temperature. For example, it takes ten times more energy to heat 1 ounce of water 1°F than to heat 1 ounce of iron 1°F. A pot of water will take twice as long to heat than the same pot of oil to the same temperature.

WATER CONTENT OF BUTTER

Butter is made up of 59 percent water, 40 percent fat (mostly saturated), and only 1 percent protein.

STOP SCALDING YOUR HANDS

When pouring off boiling water from a pasta pot or vegetables into the sink, try running the cold water in the sink while you are pouring to prevent the steam from burning your hand.

WHERE, OH WHERE, HAS THE WATER GONE?

- To produce food for one year: . . . . .1 million gallons
- To grow one large potato: . . . . .18 gallons
- To produce one pat of margarine: . . . . .85 gallons
- To produce one loaf of bread: . . . . .56 gallons
- To manufacture one pint of whiskey: . . . . .110 gallons
- To produce 1 pound of flour: . . . . .350 gallons
- To produce 1 pound of beef: . . . . .4,850 gallons
- To grow one ear of corn: .61 gallons
- To produce a lettuce dinner salad: . . . . .6 gallons
- To grow one tomato: . . . . .3 gallons
- To produce one cola soft drink: . . . . .10 gallons
- Taking a bath: . . . . .30 gallons
- Watering the lawn: . . . . .200 gallons
- Brushing your teeth: . . . . .1 gallon
- Washing a car: . . . . .100 gallons

COOKING WITH WATER

WHAT TEMPERATURE IS SIMMERING?

A simmer at sea level at a normal barometric pressure is around 195°F. A high simmer is 210°F and a low simmer is about 180°F. The simmer temperature can be important when the recipe asks for a specific type of simmer. Keeping a thermometer handy in the kitchen will improve the quality of your cooking.

WHEW! TURN DOWN THE STEAM

When water turns to steam, it must expand to sixteen hundred times its original volume. Steam is an important leavening agent for baked goods. This is especially important for pie crusts and puff pastry. The more rapidly the steam develops, the better the product will turn out; therefore, the higher the starting baking temperature, the better.

SPECIAL WATER FOR RECIPES

When a recipe calls for water, the water should be between 60 and 80°F. For the best results, allow the water to stand at room temperature for about thirty minutes before using it.

I'M BOILING—THERE GOES MY OXYGEN

When boiling vegetables or meats, allow the water to boil for about two minutes before adding the food. This will allow a percentage of the oxygen in the water to be released. Oxygen has the ability to reduce the percentage of available nutrients found in the food. The shorter the cooking time for vegetables, the more nutrients that will be retained. Leaving the skin on also helps.

TO SALT OR NOT TO SALT

It is okay to salt the water for foods that have a short boiling time, such as vegetables. Never salt the water when cooking corn or it will toughen the corn; instead add 1 teaspoon of sugar to the water to sweeten it. When cooking foods for a prolonged period of time, never salt the water, especially for stews, stocks, and beans. Beans especially tend to get tough. The safest way to use salt for many foods is to salt them just before they are finished cooking.

BOILING POINTS AND ALTITUDE

As the altitude increases, the atmospheric pressure decreases, placing less pressure on the water you are trying to boil. When the pressure decreases, the water molecules are released more easily and it takes less time and a lower temperature to boil water. For every 1,000-foot increase in elevation the temperature of boiling goes down about 2°F.

ALTITUDE (FEET)	BOILING POINT
0	212°F
1,000	210°F
2,000	208°F
3,000	207°F
4,000	205°F
5,000	203°F

BLANCHING FOODS

There are different methods of blanching or parboiling foods. The following are two of the more popular methods:

• Place the food in a bowl, then pour boiling water over the food and allow it to stand for thirty-to sixty seconds. Drain off the water and immediately place the food into ice cold water to stop the cooking action.

• Place the food in a large pot of boiling water, add ¼ teaspoon of salt; and boil rapidly for one minute. Immediately drain and plunge the food into ice water.

Soft vegetables such as tomatoes do not need to be boiled for one minute to be blanched. Tomatoes require only fifteen seconds in the boiling water. Cabbage and spinach require only thirty seconds. Use your judgment depending on the hardness of the food when blanching or parboiling.

POACHING

Both poaching and simmering are methods of cooking that require a large amount of water or stock. The liquid should be very hot, but not to the point of boiling. If the food is accidentally allowed to boil, it may fall apart. The cooking pot may be covered or uncovered. This method is mainly used for softer foods such as fruit, eggs, fish, and shellfish. Tougher cuts of meats and stewing chickens can be also be tenderized using this method. Poaching is commonly used to cook and tenderize corned beef in delicatessens. When chefs wish to poach fish they will frequently place the fish in cold water and bring the water up to a gentle simmer, remove the pot from the heat, and allow the fish to cook from the heat.

When poaching fruit, the best method is to use sugary syrup with a spiced wine. If you are going to poach a whole fish, the recommended technique is to wrap the fish in a small towel and lightly tied so that it will not fall apart. This will also make it easier to handle when removing the fish from the pot.

I'M TOO HARD FOR BAKED GOODS

When preparing dough for baked goods, hard water may cause a problem since too high a mineral content may result in the gluten not being able to develop properly, which will make the crust tough.

MY FOOD IS IN A BAIN-MARIE

This is a French term used in cooking to denote that a dish of food has been placed in a shallow pan of water and cooked in an oven. The food is continually cooked by the moist heat. Delicate dishes, the most common being mousses and custards, are usually cooked using this method, which allows them to set without breaking or curdling.

WATER SUB

When you are making bread and the recipe calls for water, you can substitute milk, which will make the texture softer and the crust darker. The milk should be scalded first to improve the volume.

STORING WATER FOR EMERGENCIES

The following information is important to your entire family in case of an emergency. You can live without food for a long period of time, but you cannot live without water

TYPE OF WATER TO STORE

There are two basic types of water: commercial and tap. Bottled water is safer to store for drinking purposes and emergency storage. However, the bulk of your water supply will probably be tap water due to the difference in cost.

QUANTITY OF WATER TO STORE

We require a minimum of 2 gallons of water per person per day to survive reasonably comfortably: 1 gallon for drinking and 1 gallon for cooking and washing. Two people will require 56 gallons of water to survive for two weeks. Forget the daily showers.

CHOOSING THE PROPER CONTAINER

Be careful not to choose a container that will leach chemicals into the water. Glass is excellent and plastic is fine as long as both are thoroughly cleaned before being filled. Camping jugs are okay, as are empty soda bottles. A 2-liter soft drink bottle can hold about 2 quarts of water.

EMERGENCY PURIFICATION

If you are unsure of the water or need to use suspect water in an emergency, place ten drops of liquid chlorine bleach into 1 gallon of the water. Adjust the number of drops for smaller containers. Boiling the water is always preferred if you have heat available.

EMERGENCY WATER SOURCES

Water can be used from a waterbed, pond, pool, or hot tub, but should be purified before drinking. These sources may be best used for toilet flushes. The water in your hot-water heater or commode tank (not the toilet) may be used for drinking after purification. If you suspect a water shortage, clean the bathtub until it is spotless and fill it with cold water.

ROTATE YOUR WATER

Stored water should be rotated at least every six months. The containers should be emptied and cleaned thoroughly before you refill them.

NUMBERS TO REMEMBER

* Safe Water Drinking Hot Line: (800) 426-4791 (ask for a free booklet)
* Greenpeace International: (202) 462-1177

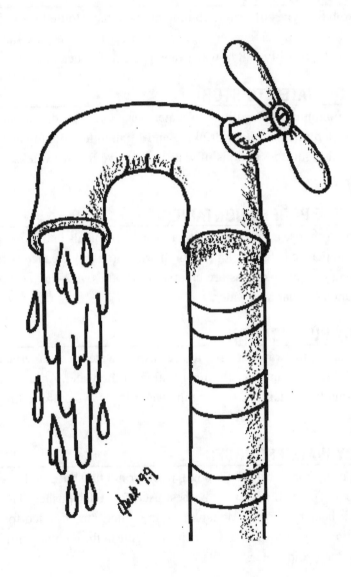

Chapter 2
Carbonated and Noncarbonated Beverages

A SHORT HISTORY OF CARBONATED BEVERAGES

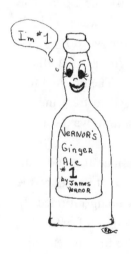

THE FIRST SODA IN THE UNITED STATES

In 1866 James Vernor invented Vernor's Ginger Ale, which was one of the most popular soft drinks of the 1800s. The extract to produce the ginger ale was aged for four years in an oak cask before it could be used. This aging process was continued until the 1980s. Ginger ale was the most popular soda until the 1920s. During Prohibition, dry ginger ale was introduced as a mixer and became very popular, and ginger ale was associated with alcoholic beverages as a mixer, which reduced the sales and popularity of the golden ginger ale produced by Vernor's. Vernor's is presently owned by 7 UP; the real Vernor's is very difficult to find and sold only through select distributors.

THE SECOND OLDEST SOFT DRINK

In 1884 a soft drink called Moxie was introduced by Dr. Augustus Thompson of Union, Maine, and was originally sold as a nerve tonic. The soda was formulated using the root of the yellow gentian plant, which was thought to calm frazzled nerves.

THE THIRD OLDEST SOFT DRINK

Dr Pepper was manufactured in the United States in 1885 in Waco, Texas. Pharmacist Charles Alderton at Morrison's

Old Corner Drug Store invented this new drink, which first appeared at the 1904 World's Fair in St. Louis and was a big hit. Dr Pepper dropped the dot after the _r_ and made its first slogan "King of Beverages" in 1910. Diet Dr Pepper is presently the number one–selling diet noncola in the United States.

COKE CAME IN FOURTH

Dr. John Styth Pemberton in Atlanta, Georgia, invented Coca-Cola in 1886. In 1891 Asa G. Candler purchased control of the company for $2,300. In 1915 the company patented the contour bottle. In 1919 the company was sold to Ernest Woodruff's investment group for $25 million. In 1992 more than 685 million servings of Coca-Cola products were consumed per day worldwide.

INGREDIENTS: 7 OUNCES—MUST BE 7 UP

The original name for 7 UP was Bib-Label Lithiated Lemon-Lime Soda. The soda, invented in 1929, may have contained seven ingredients and was sold in 7-ounce bottles. The name was changed to 7 UP in 1936 since the word _Lithiated_ was confusing the public. The inventor of 7 UP may have named the soda after a cattle brand or a popular card game of that era called Sevens Up. The original formula contained a small amount of lithium, a mineral now used to treat mental patients. The drink was popularized during the 1920s when it was sold to speakeasies as a drink mixer to compete with dry ginger ale.

During World War II the beverage became very popular since it could continue production at a high level due to the low level of sugar need to produce the drink. Other soda companies needed more sugar, which was being rationed. In recent years, due to the competition, 7 UP has found a new method of extracting their flavorings, providing their product with a new crisp taste to compete with similar products.

KVASS

During the early 1900s many immigrants brought recipes with them for a number of unusual carbonated beverages. One of these beverages was kvass, which originated in Russia. It is only slightly carbonated and has a very small alcohol level. The ingredients to produce kvass included black bread, sprigs of peppermint, boiling water, sugar, ale yeast, and sultanas (in the raisin family). Occasionally, rye bread is substituted for the black bread. Kvass is sometimes used as stock for soups.

A BROOKLYN ORIGINAL

One of the tastiest chocolate-flavored sodas ever produced was the Egg Cream. Louis Auster, who owned a candy store in Brooklyn, New York, invented the Egg

Cream in 1890. The beverage was so popular that he opened five stores to handle the business. In 1928 a large independent ice cream company made Mr. Auster an offer for his recipe that was too low, and he refused. The company official then used a racial slur, and Mr. Auster stated that he would take the recipe to his grave. All the members of his family were sworn to secrecy, and no one has ever revealed the secret formula.

There are a number of companies today that sell bottled egg cream soda, and most are very good. To make an egg cream, use a 12-ounce glass and fill it ¾ full of seltzer water, then add 1½ ounces of chocolate syrup and 2 ounces of whole milk.

THE HISTORY OF THE SODA FOUNTAIN

MINERAL WATER

Mineral water is produced by water percolating to the surface through layers of magnesium and calcium and other minerals. The water also passes through layers of carbon dioxide gas, which attaches to the minerals and is held in suspension.

The origination of the soda fountain really had its start in Europe, probably in the 1500's. Diseases were commonplace and the more affluent escaped to the countryside for cleaner air and a change of pace. They frequently went to spas where they drank water that was coming from natural underground sources and had a high mineral content and naturally carbonated in many instances.

The water made people feel better and seemed to improve their health and was eventually bottled and sold in the cities as mineral water. The carbonation seemed to neutralize acidic conditions and that really made the drink popular. The cost unfortunately was high having to haul water great distances and a method was needed to carbonate local water.

THE ARTIFICIAL CARBONATION OF WATER

Dr. Joseph Priestley in Leeds, England, produced the first glass of carbonated water that was drinkable in 1767. In 1770, Swedish chemist Torbern Bergman improved on Dr. Priestley's work and invented an apparatus that produced carbonated water using chalk and sulfuric acid. He also dissolved a number of minerals commonly found in popular mineral waters to make his product more closely related to the spa water. Since the spa water sources dried up at different times of the year, this was a significant development. Another plus was that the taste was always uniform.

As the years passed, the method of producing the carbonated water improved and larger volumes of the water could be produced. In 1807 a patent was issued to Henry Thompson of Tottenham, England, for impregnating water with carbon dioxide gas and minerals. The first U.S. patent for soda water was issued in 1810 to Simons and Rundell of Charleston, South Carolina. Mass production of carbonated mineral water was now in full swing.

In 1832, however, the first carbonic acid gas and carbonating machine was built by John Mathews, the "father of american soda water," who was granted a number of patents. He invented the method of liberating carbonic gas from marble dust and was able to produce 25 million gallons of soda water from the marble scraps left over from the construction of St. Patrick's Cathedral in New York City and from tombstone makers. Originally carbon dioxide was released from bicarbonate of soda, from which the name _soda_ is derived. The word _pop_ originated from the sound made when the corks were removed from soda bottles. A common word also used when referring to soda was _seltzer_, which originated from the German spring Brighton Seltzers. The bottles used to sell the spring water were called seltzer bottles.

THE FIRST CARBONATED WATERING HOLE

In 1808 Professor Silliman opened a business that sold carbonated mineral water in New Haven, Connecticut. In 1809 a pharmacy in Philadelphia started selling the water and in 1810 a similar business was opened in New York City. Most establishments in the 1800s that served the soda water were men's clubs and pharmacies. Pharmacies were more like meeting places, and the drink was served to the upper crust of society for the most part.

It wasn't until 1825, when a French immigrant named Elié Magliore Durand opened a high-class pharmacy in Philadelphia, that artificial mineral water was sold as a soda beverage. Since the beverage was regarded as a health-related drink, other pharmacies soon copied Durand and started selling the mineral soda water. The water was sold to overweight people, who were told to drink a glass twenty to thirty minutes after every meal to lose fat.

The area of the pharmacy where the water was sold was called a soda fountain. The word _fountain_ and its relationship to carbonated mineral water originated when fountains of soda water were to be exhibited at City Hall in New York City. The first true soda fountain was not used until 1863.

A FLAVORFUL CHANGE IN SODA WATER

A perfume dealer in Philadelphia in 1838 named Eugene Roussel, who sold soda water in his shop, decided to add lemon juice and sugar to the drink. Lemonade was very popular at the time and he thought that he could improve his sales with a new drink. He found that adding lemon juice and sugar did not work well because the stirring needed to place the sugar in suspension lost most of the carbonation.

He then prepared syrup made of lemon juice and water, then added the sugar to the syrup. The syrup dissolved more easily, and he had invented the first flavored carbonated beverage. The popularity of the beverage was phenomenal, and bottling plants sprung up in Philadelphia almost overnight. By 1843 a number of bottling plants opened in New York City. The only flavor that was available until 1850 was lemon soda. After 1850 the flavors came fast and furious, with vanilla leading the way and strawberry, raspberry, and pineapple following close behind.

The only other close relative to soda water during this period, which had been around for a few hundred years, was sarsaparilla. Sarsaparilla was produced from beer that did not ferment well; sugar was added, turning it into probably the closest relation to soda pop as far back as the 1500s. Both root beer and sarsaparilla are related to beer as their originator.

THE REAL SODA FOUNTAIN ARRIVES

The first soda water dispenser was invented in 1819 and looked like a beer keg with a curved spout. Next came an urn-shaped device that sat on a counter. In 1858 another urn-shaped device was invented that dispensed the soda water with the addition of syrup. The "real" soda fountain dispenser, invented by G.D. Dows in 1858, was part of a marble box with one arm to dispense the soda and eight syrup dispensers as well as a shaved ice unit to provide cold soda pop. He patented the soda fountain in 1863, and it became the industry standard for fifty years.

The person to really commercialize the soda fountain industry was James W. Tufts of Somerville, Massachusetts. He invented an easily produced soda fountain unit that he patented in 1863 and established a factory in Boston. He patented a number of significant improvements to the fountain and dominated the industry, producing and selling more than twenty-five thousand "Tufts Fountains" by 1893. In 1876 Tufts paid $50,000 for the exclusive right to sell soda water at the Philadelphia Centennial Exposition with a 30-foot-high soda machine, the most elaborate ever built.

One of the most popular drinks other than soda pop sold at the soda fountain was the ice cream soda, which was invented in 1874 by Robert M. Green. Mr. Green was selling sodas that required cream, and when he ran out of cream he substituted ice cream. A number of customers would not wait for the ice cream to melt and took their drink with the ice cream in a somewhat solid state. The customers were excited about the taste of the drink and Mr. Green increased his income from $6 per day to $600 per day selling ice cream sodas.

THE SODA FOUNTAIN MOVES FORWARD

Until 1902 soda fountains were all designed to be functional only against a wall and supported by a refrigeration unit and work spaces. In 1903 a literal revolution occurred with the design of a new soda fountain sold by the American Soda Fountain Company. New syrup pumps were incorporated into the new unit that delivered measured amounts of syrups. The units were placed in a counter, which a person could stand in front of and dispense the products more easily. This forced owners of all the older units to upgrade as fast as the units could be produced and increased their business, since they were now able to handle a larger volume of traffic.

Another great innovation occurred in 1908 when L.A. Becker invented an "iceless" soda fountain. This new type of refrigeration unit that did not require ice to cool the soda water. Another giant move forward was in 1928 when Jacob Baur invented a method of liquifying carbonic acid gas. This eliminated the production of gas onsite using sulfuric acid. All that was needed was to purchase a tank of carbon dioxide from the Liquid Carbonic Company.

Eventually, food was served at the soda fountains, and many were called luncheonettes. By the 1930s it was a common occurrence to go to a pharmacy or diner for a meal, not just a soda.

THE SODA FOUNTAIN CALL—AN AMERICAN ORIGINAL

Taking an order for food was one thing, but having to write it down was considered a waste of time since the soda dispenser was too busy. The dispensers developed a code system that was funny, which made it even easier to remember the orders. These calls are a part of American history and unique to the United States.

The first recorded instance of a soda fountain call was in 1880, when Preacher Henry Ward Beecher ordered food from a soda fountain drink dispenser. The first order ever recorded was when Beecher ordered two medium eggs on a piece of toast. The dispenser promptly called out to the cook to make one "Adam and Eve on a raft." Finding this interesting, Beecher changed his order to scrambled eggs, and the dispenser called out, "And wreck 'em."

Some customers would order a laxative and did not want the other patrons to hear what they were ordering, so the dispenser would call out for a "Mary garden."

The following is a list of the more common calls that were used at soda fountains from the 1880s through the 1930s:

THE CALL	THE MEANING
Bucket of mud	Large scoop of chocolate ice cream
Jerk a bridge through Georgia	Four chocolate sodas
("Jerk" was the term for an ice cream soda, "bridge" was four, and "through Georgia" told the dispenser to add chocolate syrup.)	
Ninety-five	Customer leaving and not paying their bill
Fix the pumps	Check out the girl with the large breasts
Dog and maggot	Cracker and cheese
Black and white	Coffee and cream
Filet one and mode mode	Fudge cake with two scoops of vanilla ice cream
Filet one all the way	Fudge cake with chocolate ice cream
Lacy cup	Hot chocolate
Eighty-one	Glass of water
Eighty-two	Two glasses of water
Shoot one	A small glass of Coca-Cola
Shoot a left	Glass of Coca-Cola with lemon
Burn a crowd of van	Three vanilla milk shakes
(A malted milk was referred to as a "burn," "a crowd" is three, and "van" refers to vanilla. If the call was just "burn a crowd," it would mean three chocolate milk shakes.)	
Shoot one through Georgia	Coca-Cola with chocolate syrup
Shoot one and stretch it	Large glass of Coca-Cola
Mug of murk	Black coffee
Hail a crowd in the air	Three large glasses of ice
Bucket of hail in the air	Large glass of ice
Draw some mud	Coffee with cream
Sinkers and suds	Doughnuts and coffee
Eye-opener	Castor oil in sarsaparilla
Two cents plain	Carbonated water
Black cow	Chocolate milk
Oh gee	Orangeade
Squeeze one	Orange juice
Patch	Strawberry ice cream
Burn it and let it swim	Chocolate ice cream float

THE CALL	THE MEANING
Fish eggs	order of tapioca pudding
Nervous pudding	Jell-O
One all the way	Chocolate soda with chocolate ice cream
Tune in one	tuna sandwich
Chewed fine with a breath	Hamburger with onion
Ground hog	Hot dog on a bun
Bellywash	Soup
Cackle berries	Eggs
Hen fruit	Eggs
Whistle berries	Beans
hounds on an island	hot dogs and beans
Fly cake	Raisin cake
Red paint	Ketchup
Rabbit food	Lettuce
Skid grease	Butter
Sand	Sugar
Dog biscuit	Cracker
Dough well done, cow to cover	Toast with butter
Cream de goo	Milk toast
Graveyard stew	Milk toast
Cackle berries on slice of squeel	Ham and eggs
Sea dust	Salt
Wart	Olive
Looseners	Prunes
Shake one in the hay	Strawberry milk shake
Black stick	Chocolate ice cream cone
Houseboat	Banana split
Bovine extract	Malted milk
Birdseed	Grape nuts cereal
Bossy in a bowl	Beef stew
Twelve alive in a shell	One dozen oysters
Choker holes	Doughnuts
Twins	Salt and pepper shakers
Fourteen	Special order
Gravel train	Sugar bowl

THE CALL	THE MEANING
Lumber	Toothpick
Salt water man	Ice cream mixer
Souvenir	Stale egg
Eighty-six	Don't have the item
Echo	Repeat the order
Pittsburgh	Toast is burning
Saturday night special	Easily dated girl
Pest	Assistant manager
George Eddy	A nontipper
Thirteen	One of the big bosses around
Let it walk	Take-out order
Spike it	Add lemon flavor
Break it and shake it	Add eggs to a drink
Slab of	A piece of the item
Load of	A plate of the item

BY THE NUMBERS	THE CALL
One	Just one
Two	A pair
Three	A crowd
Four	A bridge
Five	A handful
Six	A handful plus one
Seven	A handful plus a pair
Eight	A handful plus a crowd
Nine	A handful plus a bridge
Ten	A real handful

THE DEMISE OF THE SODA FOUNTAIN

Soda fountains managed to hold on until the late 1950s, but there were too many factors that hastened their demise into the history of Americana. The soda fountain and luncheonette provided the public with somewhere they could go for lunch and get a relatively fast meal before heading back to work. With the coming of fast-food restaurants, Coca-Cola manufactured a soda machine that could be placed in any restaurant or theater. Home refrigeration units and the loss of teen patronage created another problem. The teens were going home to watch television or hang out at the mall, making inevitable the end of an era.

Also, cars were becoming more readily available and the public was not providing foot traffic, which the drugstores depended upon. To top it all off, the supermarkets started carrying soda and ice cream.

CARBONATED BEVERAGES IN THE 1990S

Carbonated beverages in 1998 accounted for more than 30 percent of all beverages consumed in the United States. The majority of these drinks were soft drinks, with sales over $56 billion and 15.7 billion gallons. Coca-Cola is one of the largest sugar purchasers in the world. Almost 20 percent of all two-year-old children drink soft drinks on a regular basis. Baby bottles are now being sold with soft drink labels, and some are in the shape of the actual bottles.

Both adults and adolescents are encouraged to drink more soft drinks by offering the larger-size drinks at a discount. Carbonated beverages are the number one source of sugar in the American diet, providing seven to eight teaspoons per day. Soft drinks are presently providing about 6 percent of the total adult caloric intake. In teens soft drinks provide about 9 percent of their calories every day. Dr Pepper has had increased sales by almost 60 percent over the last five years.

Presently, the natural soda market is coming on strong; two of the major brands are New York Seltzer and Clearly Canadian.

THE TOP TEN SODAS IN THE UNITED STATES

1. Coca-Cola
2. Pepsi-Cola
3. Snapple
4. 7 UP
5. Dr Pepper
6. Jolt Cola
7. Surge
8. Shasta
9. Jones Soda
10. A&W Root Beer

ADVERTISING BUDGETS OF SOFT DRINK COMPANIES

* Pepsi-Cola: . . . .$112.2 million
* Coca-Cola: . . . .$82.4 million
* Sprite: . . . .$50.7 million
* Dr Pepper: . . . .$37.7 million
* Mountain Dew: . . . .$29.8 million
* Diet Coke: . . . .$21.6 million
* 7 UP: . . . .$15.2 million

CAFFEINE CONTENT OF SOFT DRINKS (12 OUNCES)

* Jolt: . . . . .71.5 milligrams
* Sugar-Free Mr. . . . . .Pibb: 58.8 milligrams
* Pepsi One: . . . . .55.5 milligrams
* Mountain Dew (regular and diet): . . . . .55 milligrams
* Kick Citrus: . . . . .54 milligrams
* Mellow Yellow: .52.8 milligrams
* Surge: . . . . .51 milligrams
* Tab: . . . . .46.8 milligrams
* Coca-Cola (regular and diet): . . . . .45.6 milligrams
* Shasta Cola (regular and diet): . . . . .44.4 milligrams
* Mr. Pibb: . . . . .40.8 milligrams
* Sunkist Orange: . . . . .40 milligrams
* Dr Pepper: . . . . .39.6 milligrams
* Storm: . . . . .38 milligrams
* Pepsi-Cola: . . . . .37.2 milligrams
* Aspen: . . . . .36 milligrams
* RC Cola: . . . . .36 milligrams
* Barq's Root Beer: . . . . .23 milligrams
* Diet Rite: . . . . .0 milligrams
* 7 UP: . . . . .0 milligrams

As a comparison, the average cup of coffee contains 120 milligrams of caffeine, the average cup of tea 50 milligrams.

CALIFORNIANS ARE HEAVY DRINKERS

More than 12 billion soft drinks are consumed by Californians every year. The good news is that 9 billion containers made of aluminum, plastic, and glass are recycled in California annually.

ATHLETES AND CARBONATED BEVERAGES

Studies are under way to determine if carbonated soft drinks will impair an athlete's physical ability. The premise is that the carbon dioxide may overload the body and interfere with carbon dioxide utilization. To date there is insufficient evidence to support this claim.

HOW TO PRODUCE THE WORLD'S BIGGEST BELCH

A new soda pop has been released that is supposed to appeal to consumers between the ages of five and seventeen. The drink is double-carbonated and is called Belcher's soda. However, the drink is finding its way into adult bars, where burp contests are being scheduled. The Belcher Company has two soda pop drinks in distribution, Gastro Grape and Loogie Lime.

ARTIFICIAL SWEETENERS MAY CAUSE BITTERNESS

If you purchase a soft drink that uses Nutrasweet as the artificial sweetener, the drink should be consumed within a three-month period. After three months the sweetener may start to break down and impart a bitter taste to the soda.

WE ARE SETTING A WORLD RECORD

In 1998 Americans set an all-time record for soft drink consumption: an average of 525 sodas per person, which equals about 50 gallons per year. That amounts to a 240 percent increase over 1958.

SOME USELESS FACTS

The National Beverage Corporation has stated that their annual usage of labels, if placed on a roll, would extend the combined length of the Nile, Mississippi, and Amazon Rivers—twice. They manufacture enough cans to circle the earth five times. If one year's total number of bottle caps were placed on top of each other, they would be 740 times higher than Mount Everest.

DO THE DEW

Mountain Dew originated in 1940 and was marketed as a lemon-lime soda to be used as a bar mixer. Since the name was related to the hillbilly slang term for moonshine, the soda was called the "zero proof hillbilly moonshine." In the late 1950s Mountain Dew was altered from the original lemon-lime formulation, and in 1964 the rights were sold to Pepsi, making it the company's second best–selling soda.

The new slogan for Mountain Dew, "Do The Dew," and thirty vehicles hit the road in 1998 in an advertising blitz centered around skateboarders, snowboarders, roller bladers, and sky surfers.

NEW SWEETENER

Diet RC Cola was the first carbonated beverage to use an FDA-approved, no-calorie sweetener, Sucralose.

PEPSI-COLA HITS THE SPOT—DIRT THAT IS

If you add one bottle of Pepsi to a load of really dirty clothes along with your detergent, the clothes will get really clean.

GRANNY SMITH SODA?

There is a new soda due to appear that tastes like Granny Smith apples. It is an all-natural soda with no preservatives, no sodium, and natural flavor. The Elder Beverage Company of Bloomington, Minnesota, is producing the soda.

WANT TO DRINK A SHRUB?

This is a sweet drink made from fruit juice, sugar, apple cider vinegar, and carbonated water. The early colonists drank the Shrub to keep cool when the weather became hot.

ESPRESSO SODA—WHAT'S NEXT?

A new carbonated beverage called Rageous Cool Bean Espresso Soda contains a very strong coffee flavor. The taste is similar to a double or triple espresso with a fairly pleasant honey flavor. It is a coffee lover's dream soda.

THE BEST ROOT BEER

At a recent food show, Virgil's Root Beer beat out all contenders for the title of the best root beer. Virgil's contains all-natural ingredients and is slow-brewed to bring out the flavor. The product is pasteurized to give it excellent shelf life and uses no preservatives. The sweetener is derived from pure unbleached cane sugar.

The list of the ingredients includes anise, licorice, vanilla, cinnamon, clove, wintergreen, sweetbirch, molasses, nutmeg, pimento berry oil, balsam oil, and cassia oil.

THE ORIGINAL ROOT BEER

Made in the United States by the colonists in the 1600s, the first root beer included sassafras root, water, sugar, and a small amount of ale or bread yeast placed in warm water. However, in recent years, studies have shown that laboratory rats can develop cancer from consuming safrole, the active ingredient in sassafras. The FDA has now banned sassafras from being sold other than as a raw food product by health food stores.

ROOT BEER WITH CAFFEINE?

Twelve ounces of Barq's Root Beer contains about 23 milligrams of caffeine. A flavoring agent must be added to counteract the bitterness of the caffeine.

THE TOP OF THE SODA POP HEAP

Yacht Club Ginger Ale is one of the highest-quality soft drinks produced in the United States and is manufactured by Yacht Club Bottling Works in Providence, Rhode Island. The company was founded in 1915 by Harry Sharp, who was so fussy about the water to be used that he drilled his own artesian well 170 feet deep. The water tied with Perrier as one of the best sparkling waters in the world. The purity of the water has remained since the original well was drilled. The company uses only pure cane sugar and will sell the product only in glass bottles. Their carbonation process utilizes dry ice, which they feel gives the soda its excellent flavor.

Their Golden Ginger Ale is different from the ginger ales sold in supermarkets, which are produced and used as mixers. It has a darker color, more sweetness, and a more pronounced ginger flavor. Their White Birch Beer is similar in flavor to root beer but is clear.

WHAT'S IN A NAME?

New sodas are arriving daily, and it is almost impossible to keep track of them. The following are a few of the new names reaching the market:

- Keg Orange
- Thai Lemongrass
- Vermont Maple Ale
- Peruvian Passion Flower
- Honey Lemon Soda
- Hazelnut Flavor Twisted Bean
- Vanilla Bean
- Raven
- Lemon Beer
- Siberian Sun Ginseng Brew
- Venetian Creame
- Brainwash Blue
- Black Lemonade
- Brainalizer
- Wizard
- The Drink
- Dusk Til Dawn
- Nestle Cosmo
- Mega Melon
- Hypnotonic
- Mental Trick

TONIC WATER

This carbonated beverage is usually flavored with fruit extracts, sugar, and quinine, which is a bitter alkaloid. It is normally sold and used as an alcoholic mixer.

THE GREAT BRAZILIAN SODA POP

One of the most popular sodas in South America is Guarana, which is sold under a number of different names. The flavoring is difficult to explain but very appealing. Guarana is also known as Brazilian Cocoa, and the soda made from Guarana is produced and sold by the Crystal Beverage Corporation in the United States. Their product is called Guarana Brasilia and is an excellent-tasting soda.

Guarana is actually a seed of the plant _Paullinia cupana_, which is high in caffeine (guaranine). The seed contains almost three times as much caffeine as a coffee bean. The soda contains about 55 milligrams of caffeine. The plant grows in the Amazon rain forest and has been a staple of the Indians living in that region for more than five hundred years. The vines of the plant may reach to 60 feet when climbing up a tree, and the berries from which the seeds are removed may be found at the highest elevation.

Guarana also has the reputation of being one of the world's most effective aphrodisiacs.

CARBONATION LASTS LONGER IN COLD SOFT DRINKS

The two most popular acids that are used to produce carbonation in soft drinks are citric acid and phosphoric acid. The carbon dioxide that is formed expands more in warmer beverages, and more of the gas escapes, reducing the level of carbonation.

BEGONE FIZZING UP

To eliminate the fizzing up of soda pop when it is poured over ice, just wash the ice cubes for ten seconds in cold water first. This will change the surface tension of the ice and reduce the carbonation level of the beverage.

JUST THE FACTS

In a twenty-four-hour period, Coca-Cola is consumed 195 million times in thirty-six countries. Four caffeinated sodas will supply a child with the caffeine equivalent of two cups of regular coffee. Children prefer a soft drink over milk 75 percent of the time.

THE NEW ICE CRYSTAL BEVERAGE

A number of companies are now producing a beverage cup with a walled separation that contains a liquid that will easily freeze. The cups are to be stored in the freezer so that they will be ready to use and are perfectly safe. However, when you pour a liquid in, ice crystals tend to form, which have an effect on the flavor and aroma of the beverage. A standard cup kept in the freezer will not produce the same effect on the beverage.

PUNCH

GREAT PUNCH TIPS

* On a mild-temperature day, a guest will drink about two or three cups of punch.

* One gallon of punch will make about thirty-two servings.
* Prepare a number of batches of punch and store them in 1-gallon containers.
* Use a block of ice, not ice cubes. If possible, freeze some of the punch in a ½ gallon milk container to use in the punch bowl.
* Sweetness should be adjusted with sugar syrup, which is more easily absorbed.
* Chill the punch bowl.
* Never float too many pieces of fruit in the punch. This makes it hard to scoop out the punch, and most people don't like the fruit.
* Always add champagne or any other carbonated beverage last, since the carbonation will only last effectively for about thirty minutes at the most.
* Never place a hot punch in a glass bowl; always use metal.
* Prepare any mixed liquors or flavorings beforehand and store.

I NEED SOME LIVENING UP

If your punch is too bland, try adding nutmeg, cardamom, or rosemary. Just dissolve 1 teaspoon of any one of these herbs in ½ cup of any hot fruit juice, then allow it to cool to room temperature before adding it to the punch.

Orange Sherbet Punch

If you have ever tasted an orange Creamsicle, then this punch will bring back memories of that great taste treat. Your guests will not be able to get enough of it. The recipe can be reduced or increased at your discretion depending on the number of people you wish to serve. The following recipe will serve approximately 20 people.

8 cups cold orange juice (without pulp)
2 cups whole milk
6 ½ tablespoons granulated sugar
3 ½ teaspoons finely grated orange peel from a very fresh orange
¾ teaspoon ground nutmeg
2 quarts quality orange sherbet (not low-fat)
3 cups club soda

Combine the orange juice, milk, sugar, orange peel, and nutmeg in a large bowl. Blend until well mixed and the sugar is fully dissolved. Cover and refrigerate for 2 days to allow all the flavors to mingle. When ready to serve, place the sherbet into a large punch bowl. Pour the club soda into the refrigerated mixture and stir until blended well, then pour the mixture over the sherbet.

The carbonation will not last long, so it will be best if served immediately.

NONCARBONATED BEVERAGES

Since there is a segment of the population that would prefer a soft drink that is noncarbonated, a number of companies are capitalizing on this trend. The leader in this area is Snapple, with Coca-Cola's Frutopia and Pepsi's Lipton Tea trying to play catch-up. Snapple, however, is the market leader in this area by leaps and bounds. In November 1994, the Quaker Oats Corporation purchased Snapple for a cool $1.7 billion. The original name of the company was the Unadulterated Food Products Company and was started by Arnold Greenberg, Leonard Marsh, and Hyman Golden on New York City's Lower East Side in 1972.

FRUITOPIA

This soft drink was introduced to the public in March 1994 and was manufactured by Coca-Cola to compete with Snapple's $6 billion market in noncarbonated beverages. Frutopia is composed mainly of corn syrup and 5 percent fruit juice, and it's not that exciting a drink. Coca-Cola improved the drink and introduced two "lighter-tasting" fruit flavors in November 1994.

Each bottle contains 20 fluid ounces and 225 calories. It is mainly a fruit-flavored sugar water with preservatives and artificial coloring. The only redeeming quality is that it contains 100 percent of the required daily allowance (RDA) of vitamin C in each serving. The taste leaves a lot to be desired; some flavors leave an aftertaste. This could not be classified as a very nutritious or satisfying drink. Frutopia contains eight times the sodium content of Snapple.

JMJ JOOSE

This noncarbonated soft drink contains 10 percent real fruit juice and sugar water. It states "all natural" on the label but doesn't mention the fact that it contains the colorings yellow number 6 and red number 40. It has an excellent taste and is sodium-free.

SNAPPLE

Snapple combines 5 percent natural juices with water and sugar. It is a satisfying drink that uses no preservatives and has all-natural flavor extracts. It is a low-sodium drink but does not contain any significant vitamin content.

PEPSI LIPTON TEA

Lipton Tea is a water and sugar drink that contains a small amount of instant tea. It also contains citric acid, phosphoric acid, and five times more sodium than Snapple. It does not contain any fruit juice or vitamins of any consequence. It does, however, contain FD&C red number 40; the National Cancer Institute reported that _p_-credine, a chemical used in the preparation of red number 40, was carcinogenic in animals.

KOOL-AID

Edwin Perkins of Hendley, Nebraska, invented Kool-Aid in 1920. The original product was a soft drink syrup called Fruit Smack that was sold in 4-ounce glass bottles. The original flavors were grape, orange, cherry, root beer, and raspberry. Perkins started to sell the flavorings dehydrated in small packets, as this made shipping less costly and resulted in a lower price for the product. In 1928 he changed the name to Kool-Aid. The product was a big hit, so Perkins gave up all other products and concentrated on selling the concentrated powdered flavoring.

Kool-Aid sold for 5 cents in 1933, a price that remained stable for thirty years. In 1953 Perkins sold the company to General Foods, which merged with Kraft Foods in 1988. Additional Kool-Aid products that are presently available are Kool-Aid Slushies, Kool-Aid Pops, Kool-Aid Bursts, and Kool-Aid Splash. The annual world wide consumption of Kool-Aid is about 565 million gallons.

Today's Kool-Aid is a powdered flavoring to be added to water and sweetened with either sugar or an artificial sweetener. It contains preservatives and dyes such as red number 40. The vitamin C content is only 10 percent of the RDA. The sodium content is low.

❧ BUBBLY KOOL-AID

If you want to have a different type of Kool-Aid, just use club soda instead of water. It doesn't add calories.

O'SIPPIE

This is an excellent-tasting, all-natural drink that has been pasteurized for a longer shelf life. It does not use yellow numbers 5 or 6, red number 40, or blue number 1. It is caffeine-free; uses the purest water available, making it sodium-free; and is sold in four flavors—root beer, orange, black cherry, and vanilla cream. For information call (888) 99-SIP-ME.

LEMONADE AND LIMEADE

Lemonade and limeade are prepared from concentrate. These are high-calorie drinks that contain a high degree of sweeteners to counteract the sour nature of the fruit. They are not good sources of vitamin C, since the average glass provides only about 15 percent of the RDA unless the product has been fortified. Drinking too much can lead to sensitive teeth and even enamel corrosion. Lemonade and limeade prepared from a powdered mix have a high sugar content and will end up having less than 5 percent actual juice.

✎ THE OLD-FASHIONED WAY

To prepare "real" lemonade or limeade, just squeeze the juice from enough lemons or limes to make 1/3 cup. Add 1 cup of water and 5 teaspoons of sugar or a sugar substitute. Mix together and pour over ice.

FLAVORED DRINKS

These drinks are usually sold in cans and may be called any one of a hundred different names, the most popular of which is Orange Drink. These drinks are usually a diluted and sweetened form of the original juice and contain only a small amount of the real fruit. A number of orange drinks may also contain a percentage of orange peel, which has been known to cause allergic reactions in susceptible individuals.

DRINKS DESIGNED FOR CHILDREN

KIDZ WATER™

This new water is flavored and contains 1 milligram of fluoride per liter. The drink is designed to appeal to children so that they will drink more water and get the fluoride to reduce the incidence of tooth decay.

TROPICANA BURSTERS

Tropicana has produced juice drinks that are bottled to appeal to children and contain all-natural ingredients. They are 100 percent juice and are a great alternative to soft drinks. They are packaged in convenient six-packs of 8-ounce bottles and reasonably priced. Most of the other juice drinks for children have only 5 percent real juice. For more information, Tropicana's web site is *www.bursters.com*. Chilled multipack children's drinks have grown in sales by more than 139 percent since they were introduced in the mid-1990s.

COLORED SUGAR WATER

General Mills has a new drink for kids called Sqeezeit®. It is advertised as a fruit drink and contains only 1 percent fruit juice.

RIP IT, SIP IT, AND SLURP IT

The Children's Beverage Group, Inc., is patenting a new type of packaging for children. It is a self-contained fluid-dispensing system called the "rip it sip it™" system. Wal-Mart will be one of the first companies to sell the new packaging.

NUTRITIONAL CONCERNS REGARDING SOFT DRINKS

There are two main carbonating agents used in soft drinks: phosphoric acid and carbonic acid. There have not been too many studies showing any significant risk factors in the use of carbonic acid other than an article in the _Pennsylvania Medical Journal_ a few years ago relating an increase in nearsightedness to overuse of the carbonating agent. Other studies may show that it is also related to reducing the effectiveness of certain vitamins depending on the number of sodas consumed per day.

However, the medical community is becoming more concerned about phosphoric acid. It would be best if you read the label of your favorite soft drink and at least be aware that consuming too many drinks that have phosphoric acid may upset the phosphorus/calcium ratio in your system. The concern is that if the ratio is upset this will result in a calcium deficiency, which is especially significant in middle-age women who may be at risk of osteoporosis. Kidney stone problems may also be related to excess intake of phosphorus.

The average American has a dietary phosphorus intake of about 1,500 to 1,600 milligrams per day. The RDA of this mineral is 800 milligrams per day. Soft drinks are a large contributor of this excess.

SOFT DRINK	MILLIGRAMS OF PHOSPHORUS PER OUNCE
Coca-Cola	69.9
Pepsi-Cola	57.2
Diet Cherry Coke	55.7
Diet Pepsi	49.3
Dr Pepper	44.7
Tab	44.4
Kool Aid (lemon flavor)	31.6
Hires Root Beer	22.4
Hawaiian Punch (lemonade flavor)	16.7
7 UP	3
Canada Dry Ginger Ale	3
A&W Root Beer	3

EXTRACTS

Extracts are a relatively inexpensive method of making your own soft drinks at home. They are excellent flavorings, and the cost is about 60 percent less than the supermarket brands. The homemade sodas will also contain less sugar, and the use of yeast will add a number of B vitamins. The formula is simple: all you have to do is add the extract, water, sugar, and yeast following the recipe to the letter.

The mixture is then bottled, and two days later you have a carbonated soft drink. Hires Root Beer extract is one of the oldest extracts in the United States and was one of the most popular for many years. Check the Yellow Pages for a home brewer's supply house, or just purchase the extract at the supermarket or health food store.

BEVERAGE GLOSSARY

BURDOCK ROOT

A traditional ingredient used in American root beers. Burdock root has been used as a blood cleanser for hundreds of years. The herb is common to most of the United States.

CINNAMON BARK

Cinnamon sticks are commonly used to flavor beverages, especially soda pop. They are harvested from the bark of the cinnamon tree and look like a curly stick.

CITRUS RIND

The zest or flavorful extract from citrus fruits that has been used to flavor drinks for hundreds of years.

EXPLODING BOTTLE

When carbonated beverages are home-brewed and not stored in a cold environment, the carbonation increases to a level that will cause pressure to build up, and the bottle will explode.

GINGER ROOT

An herb used in many soft drinks that provides a strong flavor and should be used only in moderation if other flavors are desired.

GUSHING BOTTLE

When a drink is allowed to sit at room temperature for too long, it can become overcarbonated. Cooling the drink in the refrigerator before opening should help alleviate the problem. A bottle will gush mainly when you are home-brewing. Poor sanitation of home-brewed beverages will also cause this problem.

LICORICE ROOT

An herb that tends to impart a sweet, pleasant flavor to soft drinks. It is usually found only in health food stores or at a home brewer's supply house. It is not a native plant to the United States.

LITHIATE

A salt of lithic acid.

MAPLE SAP

A number of root beers were produced with maple sap instead of water. The sap is more diluted than maple syrup and does not add too strong a flavor to the soft drink.

NO CARBONATION

A problem almost always associated with weak or dead yeast. The yeast must be placed into a lukewarm water solution with sugar.

SARSAPARILLA ROOT

An herb commonly used in soft drinks. The species that is used is found only in South America. Sarsaparilla grown in the United States does not have a strong enough flavor.

SASSAFRAS ROOT

An herb that was used as the main flavoring for root beer until the FDA placed it on the unsafe food list. Though it is no longer used in products produced in the United States, it is still used in small amounts in drinks in South America.

WEAK CARBONATION

This usually occurs when carbonated beverages are bottled at home and not allowed to remain at room temperature long enough before refrigeration. Poor stoppers are another cause.

WILD WINTERGREEN LEAVES

If you would like a different flavor in your soft drink, try adding one or two small wintergreen leaves to the glass. This works best with drinks that do not have a strong flavor, such as 7 UP.

WINE YEAST

A specially developed yeast that can be purchased from a home brewer's supply house. This yeast is one of the best for preparing soft drinks.

YEAST

A block of yeast is composed of millions of one-celled fungi that will multiply at a fast rate, especially when given their favorite food—sugar—and a moist, warm environment. Yeast turns the sugar into glucose, which in turn produces alcohol and carbon dioxide. Yeast should be tested before being used to be sure it is alive and active. To test yeast, just mix a small amount in ¼ cup of warm water with ¼ teaspoon of sugar. The mixture should begin bubbling within five to seven minutes. If this does not occur, the yeast is either dead or too inactive to be of any use.

Chapter 3
All About Brew

Beer is really just a generic name for any beverage produced by fermentation of extracts of a cereal grain, usually barley. Words such as _beer_, _brewing_, and _lager_ originated in Germany.

The brewing of beer can possibly be traced back about nine thousand years from drawings made that showed the coarse milling of a prehistoric grain called emmer. The oldest record that verifies the brewing of beer goes back about six thousand years, when the Sumarians who lived in southern Mesopotamia discovered fermentation. It all started with a piece of bread that was forgotten and got wet.

The Babylonians took over and produced more than twenty varieties of beers. The Egyptians and the Romans also brewed beer. The Germans started brewing beer about 800 B.C.; at the time, the task was done only by women.

In the Middle Ages, beer was an important beverage and was brewed at monasteries. Monks found beer to be a nutritious drink that was inexpensive to produce. Monasteries sold beer in monastery pubs, which provided many a monastery with considerable income.

GERMANY LEADS THE WAY

The Beer Purity Law of 1516 decreed that beer produced in Germany must be made only from barley, hops, and pure water. Later, approval was given that allowed the use of yeast. Beers imported to Germany needed to state on the label that they did not comply with the Beer Purity Law. Germany was the leader of beer manufacturing for many years.

In 1765 the steam engine was invented, bringing industrialization to the beer industry. Steam beer breweries were now producing beer more efficiently than ever. Temperature problems were still affecting the production of beer until the invention of refrigeration by Carl Von Linde. The next giant step was pasteurization, which provided beer with a reasonable shelf life and eliminated harmful microorganisms.

The purity of the fermentation process took a giant step forward when Danish scientist Christian Hansen isolated a single yeast cell and was able to cause it to reproduce in an artificial medium.

JAPAN

Originally, beer was introduced to Japan from the Netherlands around 1725. However, beer did not become a popular drink until William Copeland of America established the first brewery in Yokohama, Japan, in 1876 called the Spring Valley Brewery. The first Japanese-owned brewery, the Sapporo Brewery (Dai Nippon Brewery), opened in 1906. Kirin, which purchased the Spring Valley Brewery in 1907, is the largest brewery in Japan and controls 50 percent of the beer market.

Japanese beer was not exported to the United States until 1963. This was accomplished by the largest distillery in Japan, the Suntory Company.

Today, almost all beer produced in Japan is pilsner beer, which has a light taste and tends to go well with seafood and rice, the staples of the Japanese diet. The strength of the beer is somewhat stronger than the average American beer, since Japanese beer producers use more hops. The alcohol level of Japan's pilsner beer is about 5 percent. Rice is often used in the beer production and gives the beer a somewhat "crispy" taste. The most popular brands of Japanese beer sold in the United States are Sapporo, Kirin, and Asahi. Beer is available from vending machines in Japan, the country that is presently ranked as the fourth largest beer consumer in the world.

SAPPORO

This is a very smooth beer that will appeal to the average American. It is a high-quality beer with an excellent, authentic Japanese taste.

ASAHI

This is a very dry beer that is produced by using corn, rice, and yeast. With these additions, the beer tends to ferment more completely, resulting in less sweetness.

KIRIN

This beer, ranked number one in Japan, has a somewhat more bitter and stronger flavor than most other beers.

KIRIN ICHIBAN-SHIBORI

All liquids used in the production of this smooth beer must be filtered, which allows the beer to retain a high percentage of the ingredients' original flavor.

YEBISU

This beer is one of the oldest beers in Japan and is distributed by Sapporo. It is sold in cans and brewed using a formula that makes it one of the more authentic beers.

JAPANESE FLAME-THROWER BEER

The latest craze in Japanese beer is a "hydrogen beer" called Suiso, which is produced by the Asaka Beer Corporation. The carbon dioxide normally used to carbonate beer is replaced with hydrogen. The harmless hydrogen is lighter than air and has similar properties to helium, causing sound waves to be transmitted more rapidly and giving a person's voice that same high pitch. This provides the customer with an edge when he or she enters a karaoke contest.

Another side effect to drinking the hydrogen beer is that hydrogen is very flammable; when a person belches and holds a cigarette lighter in front of their mouth, a flame appears. If you exhale rapidly after drinking the beer you can actually shoot flames across a room! This is a new contest in Japan—the farthest flame and the best color win prizes. People have been injured drinking too many hydrogen beers and shooting fireballs across a room.

I'LL HAVE A SAKE

Sake is sometimes called rice wine, but it is really more of a beer than a wine. Sake is produced from grain, not fruit, and similar to beer it undergoes a process of converting starch to sugar. The best sake is Junmaishu, made from rice, water, and koji, which is rice that has been injected with a mold that is capable of dissolving mold. The rice used to produce sake has a higher starch content than dinner rice and is highly polished to about 70 percent alcohol instead of the 95 percent for the average dinner rice. Sake is about 15 to 17 percent alcohol.

Sake is not carbonated like beer, and the flavor is closer to wine. It is not a distilled beverage and therefore not related to gin or vodka. It takes about a month to brew, then six months to age. Sake can be stored for about six months if kept in a cold, dark location. There should be a bottling date on all bottles. A brew date of 9-4-23 would relate to April 23, 1997. The year 10 in Japan is 1998; if the label starts with 11 it refers to 1999. Sake is free of sulfites and does not contain any of the congeners that usually cause hangovers.

The better grades of sake sold in the United States sell for $35 to $70 for a 1.8-liter bottle. Never purchase dark sake; it is probably a very low quality or has been left in the light for too long. There are about ten thousand different varieties of sake. The United States has seven breweries that produce sake compared to seventeen hundred in Japan. There are sixty-five different varieties of rice that can be used for producing sake.

AMERICAN BEERS

JACK DANIEL'S OAK AGED PILSNER
Has a good taste of hops and good body. A tasty quality brew. Jack Daniel's American Ale is also an excellent beer.

SAMUEL ADAMS GOLDEN PILSNER
An excellent-tasting beer, with a smooth flavor of fresh hops.

RED WOLF AMBER ALE
A smooth, great-tasting beer.

ABITA AMBER
Has a malty, sweet taste and is a favorite in Louisiana.

ENGLISH AND IRISH BEERS

GUINNESS DRAUGHT
One of the finest beers. It has a somewhat creamy, bitter-roasted taste. Usually ranks as one of the best beers in the world.

CALDERS CREAMY ALE
A creamy, highly carbonated, and very smooth beer. Ranks right up there with the best.

BEAMISH IRISH STOUT
An excellent stout with a rich flavor.

SWISS BEERS

LTTINGER KLOSTERBRAU

A light amber beer that is perfectly blended with hops. One of the finest beers in Switzerland.

WEIZENTRUMPF

Has great wheat flavor and a somewhat limelike taste. An excellent, satisfying beer.

MEXICAN BEERS

CORONA

A pale beer that is not highly rated even though it is one of the best-selling beers. Corona does not have the traditional bitter beer taste and is best when drank with lime to add flavor. Not one of the better-tasting Mexican beers.

DOS EQUIS XX

An amber-colored beer that seems to lack some taste but is one of the better Mexican beers.

NEGRA MODELO

An excellent, creamy, well-balanced, sweet beer. One of the better Mexican beers.

TECATE

One of the worst-tasting beers.

TYPES OF BEER

ALE

Mainly a generic term for all beers that are top-fermented. These beers tend to ferment at a warmer temperature (50 to 70°F) than bottom-fermented beers such as lagers. Ales are the oldest known beers and one of the strongest. They are occasionally brewed from rice, grass, or corn and may be brewed without hops. The taste may be somewhat bitter.

BOCK

A beer brewed by bottom fermentation that is usually dark, full-bodied, and somewhat sweet. Traditionally brewed in the spring, it has an alcohol content of 5.5 percent. Originally a German beer, the name means "goat" and originated when drinkers acted like young goats after consuming the brew.

BROWN ALE

A top-fermented beer, originally from England, that is only lightly hopped, then flavored and roasted.

LAGER

A bottom-fermented beer that utilizes yeast which is less active and takes a longer time to ferment. It also ferments at a colder temperature (33 to 55°F) and has a lower alcohol content than ale.

MALT LIQUOR

A beer that has an alcohol content above 5 percent.

MEAD

One of the first beers ever brewed. It is normally produced from yeast-fermented honey water; fruit, herbs, and special spices may be added for flavor.

PORTER

A somewhat bitter, dark, top-fermented beer. The dark color is derived from the use of black malts instead of roasted barley.

STEAM BEER

Produced using lager yeast but is fermented at the warmer ale temperatures. It had its origins in the California gold fields in the mid-1800s, when ice was too scarce to use for beer production. The name may have originated from the hissing sound made when the kegs were tapped, reminding the miners of the steam engines.

STOUT

A standard ale produced with a higher percentage of roasted barley or malted barley. The degree of the roasting will result in a variety of flavors. The beer becomes darker as the roasting time increases. Stout beer is usually sold black; therefore, the darkest roasted grains are used. Stout is classified as either dry, sweet, imperial, or specialty. The finest dry stout in the world is Guinness. Guinness is 10 percent roasted barley, giving it a strong flavor.

Sweet stout utilizes oatmeal to impart a sweet flavor. The finest sweet stout in the world, produced by the McAuslan Brewery of Montreal, is called St. Ambroise. Imperial stout does not use the highly roasted grains and was called barley wines at one time. Specialty stouts were born in America, and cherries, other fruit, and even chocolate were added to the stout.

WHEAT BEER

A top-fermenting beer produced using at least 40 percent malted wheat in the grist. It normally has a somewhat tart taste and is highly carbonated.

RATINGS OF BEERS

Ratings were acquired from a number of people I consider to be professional beer drinkers. Needless to say the ratings are somewhat altered by their individual preferences and tastes. However, since the information was taken from many sources, the accuracy of the ratings is good and should pertain to the majority of the population.

THE TWENTY BEST

1. Guinness Extra Stout, Ireland
2. Ipswich Stout, USA
3. Heineken, Germany
4. Lucky Ace's Love Bites Bitter, USA
5. Triple Grimbergen, Belgium
6. Cascade Premium, Australia
7. Liberty Ale, USA
8. Samuel Smith's Oatmeal Stout, England
9. LaTrappe Dubbel, Holland
10. Longshots Black Lager, USA
11. Best Bitter Ale, USA
12. Sierra Nevada Pale Ale, USA
13. Newcastle Brown Ale, England
14. Lindemans, Belgium
15. Cooper Black Crow Ale, Australia

THE TWENTY BEST(continued)

16. Maccabee Beer, Israel
17. Steinlager Premium Lager, New Zealand
18. Union Premium Beer, Slovenia
19. Boag's Tasmanian Lager, Tasmania
20. Dead Guy Ale, USA

THE TWENTY WORST

1. Icehouse
2. Lowenbrau Dark
3. Mallard Bay Red Ale
4. Pyramid Snow Cap Ale
5. Rogue Shakespeare Stout
6. Rowdy's Perfect Lager
7. Slo Brewing Company
8. Fosters
9. Coors
10. Busch
11. Miller Genuine Draft
12. Naked Aspen Brown Ale
13. Maisell's Weisse
14. Singha Thailand Beer
15. Winter Red Hook Ale
16. Hair of the Dog Old World Ale
17. Hannen Alt Ale
18. Dogday Golden Ale
19. Mickey's Ice
20. Rattlesnake Beer

BEER CONTAINERS

I'M HAPPY—LEAVE ME ALONE

Beer should not be moved to other locations once it is stored. The slightest temperature change can alter the taste of a good beer.

BEER BARRELS HAVE RETIRED

The old big beer barrels were retired about thirty-five years ago since they were too difficult to handle. The largest barrel or keg as they are now called, is called a ½ keg and holds 15 gallons of beer, which is equal to seven cases. A ¼ keg can hold 7.5 gallons, and a beer ball can hold 5 gallons.

MINI KEGS

These small kegs are available in most beer supply houses and are designed for home refrigerator use. They hold 1.3 gallons of beer, are reusable, and are portable. A mini keg utilizes a 16-gram carbon dioxide, which regulates the dispensing pressure through the built-in tap.

BOTTLES ARE BETTER THAN CANS

Aluminum cans have very thin walls, and when you hold a can there is enough heat transfer to raise the temperature of the beer. A bottle is much thicker, making it difficult to transfer heat. Beer will stay colder for at least double the time in a bottle. The same is true when it comes to choosing to drink a cold beer from a can or a glass. The glass is a poor conductor of heat from your hand, while the aluminum is a good conductor and will warm the beer faster.

DECODING BEER LABEL DATES

All beer bottles contain two dates—the bottling date and the expiration date. The following information will assist you in decoding some of the more popular beer labels. From the following information you should be able to figure out almost any coding system.

ANCHOR

One of the most complicated coding systems. The code gives only a number and two letters. The number is the last number of the year; for example, 9 is 1999. The month is second and coded with letters that may not relate to that month. The twelve months are J, F, M, A, Y, U, L, G, S, O, N, D. The first to twenty-sixth days of the month are coded A to Z, and days twenty-seven to thirty-one are coded using the last digit of the day. For example, 9YL would be May 12, 1999.

BECK'S, COORS, GORDON BIERCH, SAMUEL ADAMS, AND ST. PAULI GIRL

Clearly indicate the date on the label.

GUINNESS

Uses a code giving the date, month, and year. The month is related to a letter of the alphabet; for example, D is April. The year is the last digit and is signified by the last digit of the year. For example, 12D9 would be April 12, 1999.

HEINEKEN

Uses a four-character dating system. The first digit is the year, and the other three pertain to the day of the year using a 365-day year. For example, 9312 would be the 312th day of 1999.

LOWENBRAU, MILLER, AND RED DOG

Use a five-digit expiration code. The first two digits are the month, the next is the day, and the last two are the year. For example, 05299 is May 29, 1999.

MOLSON

Uses a four-digit code system. The first is a letter that pertains to the month using the alphabet; for example, January is A. The next two digits are the day, followed by the last digit of the year.

BEER INGREDIENTS

There are only five main ingredients used in the production of beer. These are grain, malt, hops, yeast, and water.

GRAIN

The best grain for the manufacturing of beer is called brewing barley. A specific variety is grown that contains fat, vitamins, and minerals, and must be low in protein and high in complex carbohydrates. The barley is cleaned and then soaked in water until it starts to germinate. The fertilization of barley is limited as much as possible so as not to alter the flavor. The growing of quality brewing barley is a team effort between the farmers and the brew masters.

MALT

Malt is always produced naturally by soaking barley or wheat in water to produce germination. When this is done, the cellular structure of the malt is broken down, releasing enzymes that are activated and utilized in the next stage of brewing. This broken-down malt, called green malt, is then dried in special kilns, which control the humidity and temperature and stop the germination. This process produces the needed brewing malt and reduces the moisture content to about 3 or 4 percent, which makes it easy to store.

The malt is never subjected to direct contact with combustion gases so that there is almost no production of nitrosamines, which are a known carcinogen and capable of producing free radicals (abnormal cells) in the body. The germinated malt is dried utilizing heated air.

HOPS

A member of the nettle or mulberry bush family, hops are used to flavor the beer and give it its characteristic taste. Hops also make beer more easily digestible. Only female hop plants are harvested. The part of the hop that is used contains the ethereal oils, which impart the taste and are called catkins or cones. Unfortunately, catkins have a very short shelf life and lose their potency relatively fast. Since beer cannot be brewed without catkins, they are made into a hop extract or powder, which is easily stored and retains the bittering and flavors.

YEAST

A yeast is a single-celled organism that is needed to ferment the wort and convert it into alcohol and carbon dioxide in about seven days. The strain of yeast varies from brewery to brewery, and a process of continual microbiological inspection is needed to ensure the quality of the final product. Beer yeast is also called top-fermenting yeast.

WATER

The water that is used in beer must be of the highest quality possible. If there is an excessive amount of minerals, the water must be treated before it is approved for use. Breweries that have access to a natural pure low-mineral spring or artesian well may produce the finest-tasting beer.

THE MANUFACTURING PROCESS

STEP ONE: THE MASH TUB
This contains a mixture of ground malt and water. The mash is heated in a brewing kettle until the starch is converted into sugar.

STEP TWO: THE PURIFICATION TUB
The sugar-liquid is then filtered in the purification tubs. The remaining liquid after filtration is called wort, which flows to the wort kettle.

STEP THREE: YEASTING
The wort is then boiled and hops are added to give the beer its bitter flavor. The remaining hops and protein residues are removed. The wort is then cooled and sent for yeasting.

STEP FOUR: ALCOHOL CONVERSION
The yeast is added and the mixture is converted into alcohol and carbon dioxide. This process takes about seven days to complete. The beer is then sent to the lager tanks, where it is aged for three to five weeks at 32°F. During this process the alcohol percentage increases to about 5 percent. The carbon dioxide is trapped in suspension and provides the carbonation and foamy head.

STEP FIVE: PURIFICATION
The final step is to high-pressure-filter the beer, which removes any debris and thus reduces the cloudiness. The beer is then packaged and sent to market.

HOME BREWING SUPPLIES
* Wholesale Suppliers: (800) 780-7837

NUTRITIONAL INFORMATION
Beer is produced from all-natural ingredients. There is no scientific evidence linking beer drunk in moderation to any specific disease process, especially since the nitrosamine content has almost all been eliminated.

Beer has been related to the fattening of male America, which is really giving beer a bad rap. The only near-truth to that statement is that beer does have the ability to stimulate the appetite due to the combination of the hops, alcohol, and carbon dioxide.

Current studies indicate that one to two drinks per day may reduce the risk of heart attacks, which is accomplished by the effects of the alcohol relaxing the individual and relieving stress. Studies have also shown that moderate amounts of alcohol will increase the good cholesterol (HDLs), slow the deposition of arterial plaques, and improve coronary blood flow.

One quart of pilsner beer contains the following RDA of B vitamins all contributed by the malt: riboflavin (B2) 20 percent, pantothenic acid (B3) 25 percent, pyridoxine (B6) 36 percent, and niacin 46 percent. Beer also contains a number of minerals, such as phosphorus, chloride, potassium, calcium, magnesium, sodium, copper, manganese, zinc, and iron.

SENIORS ARE CHEERING UP

Some nursing homes in the United States have started having "beer pub hours." Most nursing homes serve a light beer, which has fewer calories and a somewhat lower alcohol level than regular beer.

ALCOHOLIC AND CALORIC CONTENT OF COMMON BEERS

BEER	ALCOHOL CONTENT –%	CALORIES –12 OZ
Amstel Light	.4	.101
Anchor Steam	.4.6	.212
Anheuser Busch Natural Light	.4.1	.112
Asahi Draft	.5.2	.148
Ballantine Premium Lager	.4.8	.155
Ballantine XXX Ale Falstaff	.4.8	.166
Bass Ale	.5.5	.162
Beck's Beer	.5.1	.151
Big Barrel Australian Lager	.4.7	.140
Black Horse Draft	.4.7	.162
Blatz	.4.9	.155
Bud Light	.3.9	.119
Budweise	.4.8	.144
Busch	.5.2	.155

BEER	ALCOHOL CONTENT –%	CALORIES –12 OZ
Carling Black Label	4.4	140
Carte Blanca	4	130
Colt 45	6.1	176
Coors	5	148
Coors Light	4.4	108
Corona	4.8	162
Dos Equis XX	4.8	155
Foster's Lager	5.3	151
Genesee	5	155
Grolsch	5.2	158
Guinness Extra Stout	4.3	155
Hamm's	4.5	144
Heineken	5.2	173
Killian's Irish Red	5.6	176
Kirin	6.9	191
Labatt's 50	5.3	155
Lowenbrau	5.1	162
Michelob	4.8	162
Michelob Light	4.5	140
Miller High Life Genuine Draft	5	155
Miller Light	4.4	104
Molson Golden	6	173
Molson Light	2.4	83
Moosehead	5.1	155
Old Milwaukee	4.5	148
Old Milwaukee Premium Light	3.8	115
Pabst Blue Ribbon	5	155
St. Pauli Girl	5	140
Samuel Adams	4.9	173
Schlitz Light	4.3	112
Schlitz Malt Liquor	6.3	187
Sierra Nevada	5.3	173
Stroh's	4.7	151
Stroh's Light	4.5	126
Tecate	4.5	148
Tsingtao	4.8	155

NONALCOHOLIC BEERS

NEAR BEER	ALCOHOL CONTENT –%	CALORIES –12 OZ
Bass Barbican	0.1	54
Elan Swiss Brew	0.5	90
Kingsbury Nonalcoholic Brew	0.1	50
Metbrau All-Natural Draft	0.5	76
Moussy	0.1	58
O'Doul's Amber	0.1	52
Saint Michael's	0.73	61
Wurtzburger Hofbrau	0.1	108

COOKING WITH BEER

When you cook with beer, the heat will cause the alcohol content to evaporate, allowing the flavoring agents to remain intact. The acid, however, will react with certain metals, so it is recommended that you do not use aluminum or iron pots to prepare dishes that contain beer. The best cookware to use is glass or an enameled pot. If your pot gets discolored, just boil a small amount of rhubarb juice in the pot to remove the stain.

Ultimate Chili

This recipe is by far one of the best chili recipes you will ever find. The taste is out of this world.

The beans should be soaked overnight with 1 tablespoon of fennel seed and ½ teaspoon of baking soda in the water. This will reduce the possibility of unwanted flatulence and will help soften the beans. Drain the water, add 1 tablespoon salt, cover the pot, and simmer the beans until they are just tender. Check the beans regularly to make sure they don't overcook and become mushy.

Ultimate Chili continued from last page

2   pounds ground beef
1   cup red onions, diced
¼   cup granulated sugar
3½ tablespoons chili powder
4   cloves garlic, chopped
½   tablespoon dry mustard
30 ounces Samuel Adams beer
2½ pounds dried kidney beans
12 ounces tomato paste
8   ounce can whole tomatoes
¼   cup sliced black olives
½   cup red bell pepper, diced
½   cup celery hearts, diced

In a separate pot, brown the beef and onions, then drain off the fat. Add the sugar, chili powder, garlic, dry mustard, and half the beer. Cover and simmer (do not allow to boil) for 30 minutes.

Add the beef mixture to the beans. Add the tomato paste and whole tomatoes. Stir gently, then add the rest of the beer, olives, red bell pepper, and celery hearts. Allow to simmer (not boil) for another 30 minutes.

White Cheddar Beer Soup

The following soup will have a very mild beer flavor. However, it will retain enough of the flavor to be an appealing soup you will make over and over.

2   tablespoon unsalted butter
½   tablespoon canola oil
½   cup can peas
1   cup sliced mushrooms
1   cup carrots, diced
½   cup celery, diced
½   cup onions, diced
¼   cup all-purpose flour
1   teaspoon salt
½   teaspoon black pepper
½   teaspoon dry mustard
4   cups chicken broth, defatted
1½   cups finely grated white cheddar cheese
12   ounces quality English ale

Heat the butter and the canola oil in a frying pan, then sauté all the vegetables just enough to soften them slightly. (The canola oil should eliminate the problem of the butter breaking down too early and smoking.) Add the chicken broth. Mix the flour, salt, pepper, and dry mustard, then add the mixture to the vegetables and broth, and simmer (do not boil) for about 7 minutes.

Add the cheese and beer, mix well, and allow to simmer for 5 minutes before serving.

Spicy Beer Soup

1	cup quality dry mustard
1	cup pure water
3	cups stout
4	cloves garlic, finely chopped
3	large red onions, chopped
2	cups apple cider vinegar
1	teaspoon dried tarragon
1	teaspoon dill seed
2	tablespoons finely grated horseradish or 1 tablespoon prepared
1	teaspoon fresh ginger, grated

Blend the mustard and water in a large bowl to make a paste. In a large pan, cook the stout, garlic, onions, vinegar, tarragon, and dill seed over medium heat. Stirring occasionally, bring to a light boil and cook for 30 minutes. Strain the mixture through a fine mesh strainer and place into the top of a double boiler. Add the mustard paste and cook over the boiling water to reduce the mixture for about 1 hour, stirring occasionally. Add the horseradish and ginger, stir for 1 to 2 minutes, and remove, allowing the soup to cool before refrigerating it for 2 to 3 days. This will allow the flavors to blend.

REMEMBER

When cooking with beer, pale lager can be used to thin a batter; lighter ales or lagers and some water can be used for steaming mussels; Scottish ales can be used as a substitute for chicken or beef stock; light- or medium-bodied lager beer can be used for marinades; beer can be mixed with soy sauce; and full-bodied lagers or ales can be used for strongly flavored marinades.

STORAGE OF BEER

PHOOEY, COLD BEER

The colder the beer, the less flavor it will have. In Germany you will never be served a cold beer unless you force the issue.

DRAFT VS. BOTTLED

A knowledgeable beer drinker will always order a draft beer over a bottle or canned beer. All beer is subject to a degree of spoilage by microorganisms; therefore it must be pasteurized or it will not have a good shelf life. Draft beer is not pasteurized and retains most of the flavor that the heat from the pasteurization process removes. Draft beer should be consumed within twenty to thirty days or it loses its taste.

ATTENTION!

Always store beer in an upright position, whether it is in a can or a bottle. When beer is allowed to rest on its side for any length of time, a larger percentage of the beer is exposed to the oxygen in the container. The more oxygen it is exposed to and the longer the duration, the less flavor the beer will have.

THE FORMULA FOR SKUNKY BEER

If you want to taste "skunky" beer, just leave a bottle of beer in the sunlight for an hour or so. The sun's wavelengths will react with the hop resin humulone, which will then react with the sulfur-containing molecules, producing isopentenyl mercaptan. The smell will be that of rotten eggs or hydrogen sulfide.

PLEASE TAKE MY TEMPERATURE

Since draft beer is not pasteurized it must be kept at 38°F. If the temperature rises above 45°F, the beer may become cloudy, sour, and skunky.

FUN FACTS ABOUT BEER

SOUTH OF THE BORDER, DOWN MEXICO WAY

In 1998, Corona increased sales by 10 million cases and surpassed Heineken as the number one imported beer sold in the United States. A number of U.S. companies will soon be producing a pale lager beer. The first may be Anheuser-Busch, which is going to market Azteca.

IT'S THE WATER

Just over 1 gallon of water is required to produce 1 quart of beer. Water is needed for cleaning, malting, and cooling.

BOTTLEMANIA

Most large modern beer-bottling plants are capable of filling 100,000 beer bottles per hour.

TRYING TO REMAIN NUMBER ONE

The U.S. brewing industry has reported annual sales of about $50 billion. The craft brewing industry is moving fast with $3 billion in sales in 1998.

THE YOUNGER, THE BETTER

Beer does not need to be aged to give it a better flavor. Beer should be drunk while it is fresh for the best taste.

I'M GLAD I HAVE SUNGLASSES ON

Beer bottles are normally made of dark glass to protect the beer from the sunlight, which can affect the taste. Fluorescent lights in a supermarket can also have a negative effect.

THE BIGGEST GUZZLING STATES

It is probably no surprise that Nevada leads the way with more than 5 gallons of booze consumed per person annually. Washington, D.C., is just behind, followed by New Hampshire, Alaska, and Vermont. Utah is at the end with only 1½ gallons per person. However, about 10 percent of the U.S. population consumes 50 percent of all alcoholic beverages sold.

OCTOBERFEST YEAR-ROUND

Germany consumes more beer than any other country in the world.

CHEF'S BEER SECRETS

FATTY FILM BEGONE

When eating foods that leave a fatty film in your mouth or on your teeth, just drink a beer that has a high acidity level such as a pilsner or an American pale ale. The acid will cleanse these fatty particles away and refresh your palate.

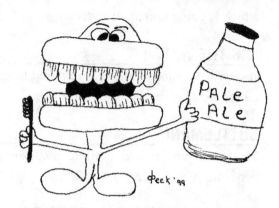

FOUR-ALARM FIRE—BEER TO THE RESCUE

Drinking a malty beer that is high in alcohol content may neutralize capsaicin, the spice in hot peppers. The hot pepper chemical is literally dissolved by alcohol. Water will not do the trick, but dairy products will temporarily reduce the discomfort.

SUSHI BEER?

The beer that is most recommended by sushi chefs is Kirin Ichiban-Shibori lager. It has a mild, sweet taste that complements the sushi without detracting from the flavors.

LET'S PAIR BEERS

Honey ale goes with lamb, India pale ale with soups (especially if they contain cheeses), brown ale with chicken dishes, and a smoked beer with appetizers.

BE STILL AND KEEP IT LIGHT

When preparing any recipe with beer, chefs will always use a light beer and allow it to remain open at room temperature for fifteen minutes. You do not want to add the carbonation when it is too active.

BEER GLOSSARY

ABBY BEER

This refers to a beer that has been brewed in the style of the Trappist monk beers.

ALPHA ACID

The most important compound found in hops. It provides the beer with the bittering flavor.

AMYLASE

An enzyme that converts carbohydrates to malt sugars. They are released from the germination of the barley and assist in the breakdown of the wort.

BEER BARREL

A stainless steel container that holds 31 gallons of beer.

BEER CLASSIFICATIONS

The classification of beers varies from country to country. Some of the more popular ones are pilsner, alt, lager, stout, and draft. The color of beer is commonly pale or dark. Dark beers have grain that is roasted at higher temperatures than pale beers. Depending on the variety of yeast, the beer may be either top- or bottom-fermenting.

BEER FOAM

Also called head. It is formed when the carbon dioxide is released. The amount and type of hops and proteins used in the production of the beer will determine how long the foam will last.

BOCK

A top-fermented beer is sold either dark or pale. The name was derived from a German town called Einbeck.

BODY

The thickness of beer perceived as its mouthfeel. The level of carbonation can affect the body.

BREWPUB

A restaurant that contains a brewery and sells its beer onsite. The beer is brewed, stored, and dispensed from its own tanks.

BULK HEADING

The pressurizing of beer storage during the secondary fermentation process, which results in the desired level of carbon dioxide that is dissolved in the beer.

BUNG

The hole in a keg of beer used for filling and emptying. Also called a bunghole.

CANNED BEER

Originated in the United States in 1935. All canned beer in the U.S. is pasteurized to increase shelf life.

CARBOHYDRATES

Grains used for beer production contain a complex form of carbohydrate that must be broken down into a simple carbohydrate such as sugar. The sugar is then converted into alcohol and carbon dioxide through fermentation.

CARBON DIOXIDE

A gas that is produced when sugar is fermented under pressure. It combines with water and forms carbonic acid. It is the pressure of the carbon dioxide gas that helps beer maintain its freshness.

CLARIFICATION EQUIPMENT

Centrifuges are used to speed up the clarification of beer. This is normally done during the secondary phase of fermentation when the yeast cells sink to the bottom. When they sink, they trap and carry with them the haze-producing factors such as proteins and hop resins.

COARSE-GRINDING

Gristmills are used to crush and grind the malt before it can be mixed with water.

COLLOIDS

Proteins and tannins that produce a haze in beer and need to be removed. Stabilization compounds are added to the mixture, which attach to the colloids and make it easy to remove them.

CREAM ALE

An American beer that has a high level of carbonation. Usually fermented with both ale and lager yeast.

DIACETYL

Produced from the metabolism of yeast during the fermentation process. It must be removed by the last stage of fermentation or it will impart an unwanted flavor and odor.

DOPPELBOCK

An extra strong beer. Also called a double bock, strong ale, or malt liquor.

DUNKEL

Means "dark" when referring to a German dark beer.

EXTRACT

A compound that is withdrawn from a liquid. In beer production, the extract is malt extract and is taken out during the process of mashing. When it is dissolved in water, it is then called wort.

FASTING BEER

What monks in the Middle Ages called their beer so that it would be part of their fast.

FERMENTATION

The process by which yeast converts malt sugar into alcohol and carbon dioxide.

FERMENTATION HEAD

The foam layer that accumulates on the surface of fermenting beer. It is formed by bitter compounds and protein.

FLAVOR

Determined by the quality and variety of the grains, water, hops, and yeast used by the brew masters as well as the fermentation controls and aging.

FORCING TEST

A method of determining what the shelf life of a beer will be. It employs a method of artificial aging using specific alternating temperature changes.

FUSEL OIL

A poor-tasting, oil-based liquid that is produced during fermentation and consists of amyl alcohol. If the concentration is not kept to a low level, it will alter the overall quality and will make the beer difficult to digest.

GAMBRINUS

The patron saint of brewers.

GREEN MALT

Barley after it has been soaked in water, which creates swelling and germination, then dried in kilns.

GRIST CHARGE

The quantity of malt used for one brew.

KEG

A sealed metal barrel that holds 15 gallons of beer. Also referred to as half a barrel or a pony keg.

KRAUSEN

The white foam that appears on the top of beer that is fermenting.

LAGERING

The cold fermentation process at almost-freezing temperatures.

LAUTERING TANK

Where wort is separated from residues after the mashing process is complete.

LEES

Sediment that may be produced by the yeast and should be filtered off.

LIGHT BEER

A beer that is produced with lower caloric content by reducing the alcohol level.

LOW-ALCOHOL BEER

A beer that contains approximately 1.5 percent alcohol.

LUPULIN

The most important compound found in a hop catkin. This is actually a resin that contains the flavoring and essence of the bitter.

MALT BEER

A top-fermented dark beer that has a high extract content of about 12 percent using caramelized sugar. It is higher in calories than most beer and contains only 1 percent alcohol.

MALT GRIST

Just-crushed malt that has been ground up in a gristmill before it is mixed with water during the process of mashing.

MALTING BARLEY

The finest barley that is preferred for the brewing of beer. Also called two-rowed nodding summer barley. The quality of barley is determined by the aroma, size, and shape of the grain, glume, and endosperm. Another important factor is how efficient the barley will germinate.

MASH

Coarsely ground malt mixed with water. When boiled all the insoluble carbohydrates (starches) are dissolved in the malt grist.

MASH TUN

A large pot where the cracked malt combines with water, resulting in the production of wort.

MATURING

After beer is fermented for the first time, it is stored for several weeks and allowed to further mature, at which time the secondary fermentation takes place and the carbon dioxide content increases.

MICROBREWERY

A brewery that produces less than fifteen thousand barrels per year. These outlets normally sell directly to the public through onsite tap rooms, direct carryout, or brewery restaurants.

REGIONAL BREWERY

A major brewery that has the capacity to brew between twenty thousand and 2 million barrels.

SACCHARIFICATION

The process by which malt starch is converted into sugar by enzymatic action.

SLUDGE

The protein particles that are simmered out of the malt solution during mashing. These must be removed before fermentation.

SPIKE

Germans prefer their beer at room temperature. To accomplish this and to caramelize some of the sugar in beer, a red-hot spike is placed into the container.

STEEPING

Soaking grains in water to start the process of germination.

WORT

A liquid that has a high sugar content produced by mashing malted barley in hot water. After it is cooled, it is then fermented into a distiller beer.

ZYMASE

An enzyme found in yeast that produces fermentation in monosaccharides (simple starches).

WEB SITE FOR ADDITIONAL BEER INFORMATION

* bbc.bloomington.com

Chapter 4
The Fruit of the Vine

FROM GRAPES TO WINE

Wine is fermented grape juice and can also be produced from a number of fruits, herbs, berries, and flowers. All wines must be fermented, a process that changes sugar into alcohol. The yeast used is only able to provide wine with a maximum of 16 percent alcohol before the yeast dies. A high alcohol level can be achieved only through distillation.

The finest grape is the European *Vitis vinifera*, which has the perfect balance of acid and sugar. It is capable of creating an excellent fermented wine without the addition of sugar or even water.

Weater can affect the quality of the grapes. There must be enough hot days to allow an adequate amount of sugar to be produced. If rain occurs and the grapes cannot be harvested on time, the sugar content will be reduced. Wine grapes must be picked at just the right time.

Grapes are normally crushed with a machine that will also remove the stems. The skins and seeds remain in the juice for a period of time—from two hours to two weeks depending on the color desired. A bladder press is then used to squeeze the grape juice and leaves behind all the residues. The grape juice is then placed into a vat with yeast, which produces fermentation and turns the sugar into alcohol and carbon dioxide. A number of different strains of yeast are used during processing, the most common being *Saccharomyces*. As the yeast does its job, it may produce heat, which is carefully controlled.

THE CHEMISTRY OF WINES

Wine is composed of water, alcohol, various pigments, esters, vitamins, minerals, acids, and tannins. It does not remain in a constant state and is continually changing.

THE MORE POPULAR WINES

CABERNET SAUVIGNON

This is a red wine that contains a large amount of tannins. This indicates a long aging process, which gives the wine a bolder taste. If the cabernet is produced from grapes that are not completely ripe, you may notice an aroma that is similar to asparagus. This wine is usually enjoyed with meat dishes.

CHAMPAGNE

Champagne is considered a "sparkling wine." A true wine is made from one of three grapes: chardonnay, pinot meunier, or pinot noir. Champagne is produced through a number of fermentations. The first lasts about two to three weeks; the wine is placed in heavy bottles with a temporary cap that will withstand the extreme pressures created. The sugar and yeast then create a new fermentation, which produces a high degree of carbon dioxide. While the carbonation is developing it also creates sediment in the bottle, which needs to be removed.

Removing the sediment is a special process and requires that the bottles be stored at a forty-five-degree angle pointing downward. Each day the bottles are turned a small amount and the angle is increased to allow the sediments to fall toward the cap. This process takes six to eight weeks, after which the bottles are frozen. When the bottle is opened, the pressure forces the sediment out in a process called disgorgement. Wine mixed with sugar is then added to fill the bottle to the top.

The English actually invented sparkling wine forty years before the French introduced it. The English invented the cork stopper that could be used to seal bottles with cork from Spain. The French were still using hemp steeped in oil, which was not very efficient at keeping the carbonation in the bottle. The French bottles always leaked, while the corked English bottles didn't.

CHARDONNAY

This grape produces a white burgundy wine called chardonnay in most restaurants in the United States. Most chardonnay in the United States is produced from "lesser" grape varieties.

DESSERT WINES

Dessert wines are produced from grapes that have an exceptionally high sugar content. The wines usually have a deep golden color. The most popular dessert wine is French sauternes, which should be aged at least fifteen years for the finest flavor to materialize. Another excellent dessert wine is eiswein, which is produced by allowing the grapes to remain on the vine until they start to become raisins and until they actually freeze.

The lower-priced sweet dessert wines may be made by just adding sugar to a dry wine and are sometimes referred to as "skid-row wine."

PORT

An after-dinner wine that is somewhat sweet, port is produced by adding grape alcohol to the wine as it is in the process of fermentation. The name came from the city of Oporto in Portugal, and the wine was originally called porto wine. Wines produced in that area are still called porto wine. The most expensive and highest-quality port is called vintage port, whihc is always produced from grapes of a single vintage and usually bottled within a two-year period. The best of the vintage ports are called late-bottled vintage ports and may be aged as long as fifty years.

Tawney ports are produced from a blend of grapes, possibly from different vineyards. A lower-quality port is vintage character port, and the lowest grade is called ruby port. Wineries in America have been bottling port since the early 1970s.

REISLING

This is a light, somewhat floral-smelling wine often served as a dessert wine.

SHERRY

The finest sherry is produced from the palomino and the pedro ximenez grapes from Spain. The soil must contain a high chalk content. It takes about ten days for the first fermentation of the sugar to take place, forming alcohol in a very intense seething and frothing of the liquid. The second fermentation process allows the balance of the sugar to relax and complete its conversion, resulting in an excellent-tasting dry sherry. The wine is then placed into barrels to age. Cream sherry is produced from the dry grape olorosos, which is sweetened with aged wine made from the pedro ximenez grapes.

ZINFANDEL

This wine, produced mainly in California, has a high degree of fruit characteristics. A large percentage of zinfandel is made into white zinfandel, a somewhat sweet wine more popular with people who are not true wine drinkers.

HOME WINE MAKING

The following is a step-by-step process of making wine at home. The process does take considerable time and expertise and a lot of patience. This summary does not give you the in-depth information you will need, but only attempts to explain some of the steps in the wine-making process.

Locate a wine-making supplier in your area in the Yellow Pages to purchase the necessary equipment and to give you advice. The equipment you purchase will be sanitized with oxygen-based caustic solutions, rinsed with water, and sterilized with an antibacterial substance and a sulfite solution. The equipment is rinsed with water for the second time and then assembled.

The "wine pack" that is purchased should include the fermentor label, which will keep track of the processing information, such as the type of wine, your name, the type of yeast used, and the beginning specific gravity of the must (juice used). The label will also contain information regarding the type of cask and any other additive. A sugar such as lactose may be suggested.

The must is mixed with ultralow-chlorine water to bring the total volume to about 6 gallons. Readings are recorded to be sure that the sugar content is high enough for you to obtain a high enough alcohol percentage. A hydrometer is used to be sure that the proper specific gravity is achieved.

The yeast is rehydrated to activate the dry yeast, and the must solution is inoculated with the yeast solution. The primary fermentor is now sealed so that air cannot get to it and oxidation cannot take place. The holding environment needs to be kept at about 76°F.

After seven days the wine must be siphoned to another container, a process known as racking. White and blush wines are racked on the fourteenth day. The wine is siphoned again to separate it from the sediments, which would eventually destroy the wine. Oak chips may be added for flavor and bentonite added to attract and cause the balance of the residues to fall to the bottom and form a lees deposit. The wine is racked again after a number of days.

The wine is mixed to remove excess carbon dioxide, clearing agents are added, and the wine is finally ready for bottling after about forty-five days. The bottles must be sterilized and the wine taken to the shop for bottling in a vacuum atmosphere. The wine is taken home and aged.

CONTAINERS AND CLOSURES

SIZING THEM UP

The following are the standard bottle sizes used for wines other than champagne:

- split: . . . . .187.5 milliliters
- half bottle (fillette): . .375 milliliters
- bottle: . . . . .750 milliliters
- magnum: . . . . .1.5 liters

The following are the bottle sizes for champagne:

- split: . . . . .200 milliliters
- half bottle: . . . . .375 milliliters
- pint: . . . . .400 milliliters
- bottle: . . . . .800 milliliters
- magnum: . . . . .1.5 liters

BOTTLE SHAPES AND COLORS

Bottles from the Burgundy region of France have shoulders that tend to slope, while bottles from Bordeaux have high shoulders. German bottles that are tall, slender, and brown are from the Rhine. If the German bottle is green it comes from Moselle or Alsace. If you purchase wine in a clear bottle it should be consumed shortly after purchase. Darker bottles contain better-tasting wine if stored for a short period of time before opening.

MY BOTTOM IS INVERTED—WHAT NEXT!

The indentation on the bottom of a wine bottle (also called a push-up or punt) is necessary to increase the strength of the bottle and support the pent-up carbonation. It is also a handy location for the sediments to reside.

STORAGE

ROLL OUT THE BARREL—OAK OF COURSE

For fine-wine storage, oak is the only wood used to make a barrel. Red wines stored in oak barrels will develop richer color and stability and a more complex aroma. The oak is composed of a variety of chemical compounds that contribute a uniqueness and flavor to both red and white wines. The chemicals in oak may even improve the mouthfeel of wine. The variety of oak, how the tree is cut down, and how the slats are prepared will all have an effect on the final product. Barrel making is an art. The logs used must be hand-split and cannot be sawed.

If you can identify the smell of vanilla in a wine, the chances are it is a quality wine that was aged in an oak barrel.

PUT A CORK IN IT!

Since cork is becoming expensive, a number of wineries are replacing the corks with alternative materials. Plastic is frequently used, but whether it will be a source of contamination if allowed to remain for a number of years has not yet been determined. Plastic corks may be marketed under the name Cellukork and made from ethylene vinyl acetate. Screw caps are being used more and more; however, the thought of purchasing a fine wine with a screw cap has not gone over well with wine connoisseurs.

The average wine cork contains more than 700 million cells and is a natural vegetable tissue with closed air cells. The cork acts in a suction-cup manner to seal the bottle and does not allow for leakage. Cork is mainly composed of suberin, which is a very elastic fatty acid. Cork is harvested from a member of the evergreen oak family and is found only in the western Mediterranean. It takes twenty-five years for a tree to mature and can take up to fifty years for the cork to obtain the proper size and density that will be acceptable for use in a wine bottle. Almost 50 percent of all cork produced comes from Portugal.

CAN'T GET THE CORK OUT

Some really stubborn corks may take 100 pounds of pressure to remove, while the normal pressure to remove a cork is only 25 pounds.

IT'S ALIVE, IT'S ALIVE

When wine is ready for storage and has not been pasteurized, it is still considered to be "alive" with microorganisms. The wine needs time to mature slowly and must be corked to limit the amount of oxygen available so that the aging process can proceed at a somewhat controlled rate. Too porous a cork may result in the bottle being allowed to remain upright, which will sour the wine. If the cork is made from a material that is nonporous, such as metal or plastic, the wine will not be allowed sufficient oxygen and the desired quality will not be obtained. A moist high-quality cork that is made for that specific wine is best.

Pasteurized wines such as inexpensive jug wines do not have this problem since the microorganisms have been destroyed by the heat. Therefore, it makes no difference what kind of stopper is used.

A CHILLING SOLUTION

Champagne should always be stored in a cool location on its side to keep the cork damp. Champagne will deteriorate if stored too long and will not improve with age. Two or three years should be the maximum storage time. Never place a bottle of champagne in the freezer to chill it; it may explode. Champagne can easily be chilled by placing the bottle in the refrigerator for two hours. Never leave it in for more than that or you will lose a percentage of the flavor and bouquet. If you want to speed up the chilling process, just place the champagne up to its neck in a bucket of ice water for about twenty minutes. Only use a stopper made specifically for a champagne bottle.

MY WINE HAS GREAT LEGS

When you place a small amount of wine in a glass to taste and evaluate it, swirl the wine, allowing some of it to cling to the sides of the glass. The small tendrils of wine that roll down the glass are called legs or tears. Wines that are higher in sugar such as chardonnay will have good legs. This is really not indicative of the quality of the wine, but it does impress your girlfriend.

THE WINE DUNGEON

Wine will improve with aging, especially if the conditions are ideal. Wine will react to its environment, which will determine whether it will age slowly or quickly. The best temperature for wine storage is between 50 and 55°F. Frequent fluctuations in temperature of more than 10°F will alter the quality of the wine. If you feel that this has occurred, check the cork to see if it is leaking residue.

The humidity must also be controlled to keep the cork resilient. Humidity should be between 50 and 80 percent; 70 percent is the norm. Excess humidity will harm the label and may cause it to deteriorate. A dark location is preferred, as light will affect the aging process. The cellar should not experience any vibrations from traffic or even loud music, since this will upset the sediments. Smells can also affect the wine and can be picked up through the cork.

TO STAND OR NOT TO STAND

Table wine is normally stored horizontally to keep the wine in contact with the cork. The cork must be kept moist to prevent air from entering and causing oxidation. All fortified wines with the exception of port can be stored upright.

LABELS UP

When storing wine horizontally, the labels should always be up, which makes it easier to see the sediment deposit when it comes time to open the wine.

GLASS CRYSTALS?

Occasionally, when removing a cork, you may see what appear to be glass crystals on the bottom of the cork. These crystals usually result from tartaric acid residues, which form into harmless potassium bitartrate (cream of tartar).

TEMPERATURE IS IMPORTANT

The higher the storage temperature of wine, the faster it will age. White wines are more susceptible to damage from extremes of temperature than red wines.

WINE TASTING TIPS

It is best to taste only 1 ounce of each wine; otherwise you may get somewhat intoxicated if you attempt to taste too many. Always serve a dry wine before a sweet wine and a white wine before a red wine.

The proper glass for a particular wine is very important. The following are guidelines to choosing just the right glass.

CHAMPAGNE GLASS

Also called a flute, this glass should be as narrow as you can purchase. Never buy a short, bowl-shaped glass. Flutes provide less surface area for the carbonation bubbles to come into contact with and escape. Flutes also allow the bouquet to be released more slowly.

CHARDONNAY GLASS

This is a shallow glass in the style of a typical wine glass, with the exception of a somewhat narrow top.

RED WINE GLASS

Usually larger than a white wine glass, this has a slight inward taper to concentrate the fragrance so that your nose will enjoy the wine as well.

THE SEVEN STEPS TO WINE TASTING

1. Examine the color; it should be strong.
2. Swirl the wine around in the glass to release the aroma. Wine may contain more than four hundred different organic molecules, two hundred of which have an aroma. Smell the aroma and make a mental note of the different scents you recognize.

3. A small amount of wine should then be tasted and the initial taste evaluated. Remember what the wine was like after you slowly swallowed it.

4. Read the label for any information regarding the winery, type of grapes, flavors, or type of fermentation.

5. Drink a small amount of noncarbonated water between tastings.

6. Always use a clean glass to taste each wine.

7. Discuss your opinion of the wine with others to evaluate their feedback.

CHEFS' WINE SECRETS

COUNT ME IN

When cooking with wine, it should be part of the total liquid suggested in that recipe. As a rule of thumb for almost all sauces and soup recipes, use 1 tablespoon of wine per cup of sauce or soup. When wine is heated, it will reduce from 1 cup to ¼ cup in about eight to ten minutes. It's best to add wine close to the end of the cooking period.

THIS AIR IS KILLING ME

Cooking wine should be stored in small bottles. The less space between the wine and the top, the longer the wine will retain its flavor and aroma.

THIS WILL FORTIFY YOU

The more common fortified wines, such as sherry, port, and Madeira, when added to soups should be added just before serving. You want the flavor of these wines to stand out just enough to be noticed. Wine should be added five to seven minutes before the completion of the dish for the maximum flavor and aroma to be enjoyed. Never overpower a recipe. Remember that 2 tablespoons of fortified wine is equal to " cup of table wine.

CURDLING UP WITH WINE

Wine has a tendency to cause curdling in recipes that contain dairy products. Since many recipes that have dairy products in them do call for wine to be included, it is best to add the wine and blend it in before you add the dairy product; this will prevent curdling. Another key to a successful dish is to keep it warm until you serve it. If it cools too much it may curdle. Another method is to reduce the wine slightly before adding it to the dairy products.

WE JUST DON'T GET ALONG WELL

When serving different wines at a dinner party, there are a few rules that will enhance the enjoyment of the wines: always serve a young wine before an older one; a white wine before a red wine; a light-bodied wine before a hearty, robust wine; and a dry wine before a sweet dessert wine.

SOME FOODS DON'T GET ALONG WITH WINE

Foods that have a high acid content do not go well with wine. These include salad dressings with a vinegar base and citrus fruits. Some sulfur-containing foods such as egg yolks will also affect the flavor of wine. Other foods that may have a negative effect on aroma and flavor are asparagus, onions, tomatoes, pineapples, and artichokes.

BEST TO BE TRANSPARENT

Onions do not blend well with wine when combined during cooking. A good rule of thumb is to cook or sauté the onions first until they are somewhat transparent before adding the wine.

The following are a few suggestions when cooking with different wines.

♀ SHERRY

Sherry is recommended for stews, soups, and sauces. Poultry and seafood recipes seem to bring out the flavor of sherry the best. When adding sherry to cream soups, add 1 tablespoon just before serving and always use a dry white sherry. If you add sherry to a meat or vegetable soup, it would be best to use a medium sherry or even a red wine.

Dry or medium sherry can be added to cream sauces if it is added with the liquid ingredients. Use 1 tablespoon of wine per cup of liquid.

♀ ZINFANDEL AND CHABLIS

Chefs normally recommend these wines with most poultry and seafood dishes. However, it is really your individual taste that counts. If you do use a white wine, it should be a dry white wine or vermouth added to a baked or poached seafood dish when you begin baking. The wine should be accompanied by equal amounts of butter or oil. Lamb or veal will have an excellent flavor if a small amount of white wine is added after the meat is browned.

Dry white wine or sherry can be used for gravies that accompany meat or poultry dishes at a ratio of 2 tablespoons of wine to every cup of liquid. The wine should be added with the liquid and boiled.

♀ RED WINE

Richer body and stronger flavor make red wine the best choice to enjoy with chicken, beef, lamb, or pork dishes. When cooking with red wine, it will have a better flavor if used in marinades, meat sauces, stews, and hearty meat-based gravies. Try basting chicken about every ten minutes with red wine or vermouth. Game birds have an excellent flavor when basted with red wine. Dry red wine can be used on meat and lamb after they are braised.

Dry red wine can be added to brown sauces or a tomato sauce if it is added with the liquid ingredients. Use 2 tablespoons of wine per cup of liquid.

♀ DESSERT WINES

These sweeter wines are normally used in dessert dishes such as compotes, fancy fruit desserts, and sweet sauces. Try basting a ham at the beginning of the glazing period with port, sherry, or muscatel.

♀ BRANDY

Brandy will complement most meat and poultry dishes, and it is frequently used in compotes and puddings. Brandy is often used to flambé a dish. If you have a problem igniting the brandy, warm it just slightly before adding it to the food, then ignite. Another method is to lightly dampen a few sugar cubes with a lemon or orange extract, place them on the dish, and ignite.

PLAYING WITH FIRE

When you flambé a dish, always allow the flame to go out by itself. It is necessary to burn the alcohol for a few seconds to allow any raw alcohol taste to be removed. Another method of flambéing is to place the alcohol in a metal ladle and either just warm it before adding it to the dish or actually ignite it and pour it over the dish.

THIS WILL GET THE PARTY STARTED

If you would like a great dessert treat, try placing dried apricots, prunes, pears, or figs in a jar of quality brandy and allow them to remain until they have absorbed some of the brandy and have plumped up. Use these fruits on dessert dishes or as a topping for ice cream.

BRING IN THE SUB

To replace 1 cup of wine in a recipe, use 1 cup of chicken stock plus 1/8 cup of lemon juice or apple cider vinegar, or 1 cup of fruit juice plus 1/8 cup of apple cider vinegar.

Champagne Punch

1   cup triple sec
1   cup quality brandy
2   cups unsweetened pineapple juice
1   quart chilled ginger ale
3   750ml bottles quality dry champagne, chilled

In a large container, combine the triple sec, brandy, and pineapple juice. Cover and chill for at least 6 hours. When ready to serve, place the mixture in a large punch bowl. Add the ginger ale, champagne, and a block of ice, then stir gently for a few minutes.

SPECIALTY WINE DRINKS

SANGRIA

A wine, usually a white or rosé, that is mixed with a variety of natural fruit juices, orange slices, and ice. Sangria is especially great with hot Mexican dishes, Indian dishes, or spicy chili. Wines produced after 1995 tend to work best. My choice is Robert Mondavi Woodbridge White Zinfandel.

GRAPE SPRITZER

Mix 6½ ounces of chilled Perrier with 1 cup of white wine.

MIMOSA

Mix 6 ounces of champagne with 3 ounces of chilled orange juice.

DECIPHERING WINE LABELS

SECRETS OF A CHAMPAGNE LABEL

The name of the champagne will tell you whether it is sweet or dry. Brut is the driest; extra-dry is not as dry as brut; sec is sweet; and demi sec is the sweetest.

NEW LABEL ADDITION

New health information can now be added to wine bottle labels. The Bureau of Alcohol, Tobacco & Firearms has approved the following statement: "The proud people who made this wine encourage you to consult your family doctor about the health effects of wine consumption." The first wine with this statement on the label was the 1993 cabernet sauvignon from Laurel Glen Vineyard in Sonoma County, California.

NUTRITIONAL INFORMATION

RED WINE VS. HEART DISEASE

The truth is that for the most part it is not just red wine but any wine or beer. It is the lower alcohol content of these beverages that, in moderation, is capable of raising the HDL level and also has the ability to reduce the "stickiness" of blood cells, thus reducing the possibility of a clot forming. However, the skin of red grapes does contain two antioxidants, flavonoids and phenols, that have some ability to lower the risk of bad cholesterol (LDLs) from forming plaque in the blood vessels.

WINE AND MACULAR DEGENERATION

Studies reported in the *Journal of the American Geriatric Society* have shown that the risk of the eye disease macular degeneration, which is the leading cause of blindness in those over sixty-five, can be reduced by almost 20 percent by drinking a moderate amount of wine daily.

GETTING HIGHER FASTER

Carbonation will speed the absorption of champagne and sparkling wine into the bloodstream and cause intoxication in a shorter period of time than do noncarbonated alcoholic beverages.

WOMEN AND HEART DISEASE

The *Journal of the American Medical Association* reported that women who drink a moderate amount of wine (or orange juice) daily may be able to reduce their risk of cardiovascular disease by as much as 50 percent.

ZINC ALERT

The mineral zinc is very important to a male's prostate health. Excessive use of alcoholic beverages may increase the excretion of zinc. Magnesium is another mineral that may be excreted as well.

CALORIES IN AMERICAN WINES

WINE	CALORIES PER OUNCE
liqueur	110
port	43
Madeira	32
sherry	37
champagne (extra dry)	29
champagne (brut)	22
white table wine	20
red table wine	19

WINE FACTS

COOKING WINE—NOT A GOOD CHOICE

Supermarket cooking wines are never used by chefs. These are usually inferior products that contain preservatives and additives and have poor flavor compared to the "real" thing. Cooking wines must be made undrinkable by the manufacturers with the addition of other ingredients that may include excess salt or even MSG.

WHY IS WINE RED OR WHITE?

The skin of the grape is responsible for the color of the wine. If the skins are removed before the grapes are crushed, the wine will be white or pink. The length of time the skins are allowed to remain in the processing will determine the final color of the wine.

HOW TO POUR ONE THOUSAND GLASSES OF CHAMPAGNE FROM ONE BOTTLE

The largest bottle of champagne was produced by Korbel, the premium champagne producer in the United States. It was created in honor of the millennium by European glass blowers. It weighs 350 pounds, stands 5 feet tall, and holds one thousand glasses of quality champagne. It will be opened and poured at Times Square in New York City on New Year's Eve 1999.

CERTAIN LIQUIDS DON'T MIX

Wine should never be consumed with any other liquid at a meal, especially soups. Even a vinegar-based salad dressing may spoil your taste of a good wine.

PROPER UNCORKING PROCEDURE

1. Cut the aluminum foil around the top of the bottle.
2. Keep your thumb on top of the cork at all times.
3. Loosen and remove the wire cork holder.
4. Wrap a small towel around the bottle.
5. Twist the cork out in one direction; never allow it to pop and shoot out since you do not want to lose any carbonation.

DOM DE DOM DOM

One of the most expensive champagnes, Dom Perignon was invented by a seventeenth-century French monk. Never allow Dom Perignon to remain in the refrigerator or stay cold for more than 1 hour to obtain the best taste.

THE DARK SEDIMENT SECRET

When wine matures, sediment is released from the wine. When a bottle is stored on its side, the sediment will form on the side of the bottle. If you stand the bottle upright for one to two days, being sure to handle it carefully, the sediment will fall to the bottom. Then if you are careful opening the bottle and pouring the wine, the sediment will not be in your wine glass. If the sediment rises, try to allow it to settle. A wine cradle works very well. Most of the sediment is tannic acid.

SET THE THERMOMETER, WE'RE DRINKING WINE

Wine should be consumed at the following temperatures, which are considered ideal by the experts for obtaining maximum aroma and flavor:

- better red wines: 59 to 61°F
- lesser-quality red wines and complex white wines: 50 to 54°F
- less complex white wines: 46 to 50°F
- sweet white wines and champagne: 43 to 46°F

SNIFF, SNIFF

If you think that a person is sniffing a wine cork before pouring just to show off, there is more to it. By sniffing the cork, you can determine if there has been any contamination and if the wine has acquired an "off" taste.

SIZE MATTERS WHEN IT COMES TO BUBBLES

Next time you open champagne and want to appear like you really know your stuff, just inspect the bubbles after you open the wine. If the bubbles are very tiny, it is a good-quality champagne. If the bubbles are large, the champagne is of a lower quality.

ARE YOU DRINKING CHAMPAGNE OR SPARKLING WINE?

Real champagne is only produced in the north of France through a process called *methode champenoise*. All other champagnes are really sparkling wines.

HIC, HIC, HOORAY

In 1998 more than 30 million gallons of champagne and sparkling wine were sold in the United States. Americans drink 1.97 gallons of wine per person annually. This compares to soft drinks at 46.7 gallons and coffee at 28.6 gallons.

FLAMBÉD AWAY

When you flambé, use an alcoholic beverage with a high alcohol content so that it will completely burn away and not leave a residue of alcohol to affect the taste of the dish.

WINE VS. CHOCOLATE

Surprisingly enough there are now wine- and chocolate-tasting parties. Chocolate seems to complement certain wines. The wines that are the most popular with chocolate are cabernet, merlot, zinfandel, and white port.

THE FRIENDLY LADYBUG

Many grape farmers use ladybugs to reduce certain insect infestations, such as leafhoppers and red spiders. These are a treat for the ladybugs. One gallon of ladybugs can contain more than seventy thousand bugs.

ONE CHILLY DUCK, PLEASE

The term "cold duck" refers to a wine that is usually a mixture of champagne and a wine, usually burgundy. The term supposedly originated from waiters in France who removed leftover wines from the table, mixed them, and drank them with their own meals. However, it may have originated in Germany when champagne and moselle wine was made into a cold punch. The punch bowl was said to have a design that resembled a duck's head.

RINSE THAT GLASS REALLY WELL

The slightest hint of soap film on a champagne glass will ruin the effervescence.

WINE STATISTICS

THE TOP TEN WINE-PRODUCING COUNTRIES

All figures are production and consumption figures for 1997.

COUNTRY	MILLIONS OF GALLONS	CONSUMPTION (GALLONS)
Italy	1,500	942,000
France	1,485	919,320
Spain	522	392,433
United States	450	512,120
Argentina	440	360,023
Germany	298	496,231
Russia	220	332,112
South Africa	201	108,002
Portugal	192	154,931
Romania	181	192,335

CALIFORNIA—THE WINE STATE

In 1998 California shipped more than 410 gallons of wine, which accounts for more than 90 percent of all wine shipped in the United States. The estimated retail value was $11.6 billion. There are about 740 wineries in California.

SHALL WE TOAST, HAVE TOAST, OR BOTH

I'm sure we can all remember a host at a dinner party standing up and saying, "Let's have a toast." The saying originated in seventeenth-century England when pieces of spiced toast were placed in a carafe of wine or individual glass to improve the taste. When the host rose to say a few choice words, the toast was eaten so as not to offend the host.

GRAPPA DABBA DOO

Grappa is a type of wine that is produced from the skins, seeds, and pulp left over from wine making. The wine is colorless and very potent, with an alcohol proof of 120. It is aged in wooden barrels and has the flavor of juniper or oak taken from the barrels. It is usually consumed in a shot glass and at room temperature.

PRAYING FOR A MANTIS

The praying mantis is utilized by organic wine growers to consume lacewings, insects that enjoy feasting on tender young grape leaves.

BOTTLES, PREPARE FOR INSPECTION

Before you open a champagne bottle, inspect it for deep scratches, imperfections, or grooves in the glass. Occasionally, a bad bottle gets by the inspectors and may explode prematurely when you attempt to open it. Remember that if the champagne has been chilled below 45°F, it may still explode when opened and release the cork at a high speed.

WINE GLOSSARY

ACACIA

A chemical used to stabilize and clear the wine. Also called gum arabic.

ACETALDEHYDE

Can impart a sherrylike aroma to some wines. It is naturally present in wines, especially sherry.

ACETIFICATION

The aroma of wine as it ages. Also called acquired bouquet.

ACTIVATED CARBON

A carbon active in the process of precipitation of impurities during fermentation that helps clarify and purify the wine. It reduces the intensity of the color in red and black grape varieties.

ALCOHOL CONTENT

If the alcohol content is less than 14 percent, the wine may be labeled table wine. The accuracy is allowed within 1.5 percent either way. If the alcohol content is more than 14 percent, the percentage must appear on the label.

AMMONIUM CARBONATE

A yeast nutrient used to speed up the process of fermentation.

AMMONIUM PHOSPHATE

A yeast nutrient is used in the production of sparkling wines to initiate the secondary fermentation process.

ANCIENT METHOD

Utilizes the entire grape cluster instead of crushed grapes during the fermentation process. Wines made by this method usually have a very intense berry taste. Also called the whole berry fermentation.

APPELLATION

A word that appears under the word *champagne* to indicate that the champagne is actually grown in France.

ASTRINGENCY

A drying or puckering sensation in the mouth, which is usually caused by tannins.

AUTOLYSIS

A breakdown of the yeast cells inside sparkling wine bottles after the secondary fermentation takes place.

BENTONITE

A Wyoming clay substance that is safe to add to wine to remove the grape proteins, which will cause cloudiness in wine. The proteins contain a positive charge and the bentonite a negative charge, which attracts the protein. The protein-bentonite compound rises to the top for easy removal.

BOTTLE SICKNESS

Newly bottled wines or wines that have been handled roughly in shipping may develop unpleasant odors. Allowing a newly acquired quality wine to relax for a few days or weeks before you open it will usually alleviate this problem.

BREATHING

The process of allowing air to mix with wine so that unpleasant odors can escape. This may be done by leaving the cork out of the bottle or by decanting.

BRUT

The driest champagne sold. Should have no sign of sweet taste.

CALCIUM CARBONATE

Used to reduce acidity in cold stabilization of the wine.

CALCIUM SULFATE

Used to reduce the alkalinity in wines by lowering the pH.

CITRIC ACID

Used to increase the acidity of the wine.

COLLOIDAL SILICON DIOXIDE

Used to clarify wines.

COOPER

A person who makes wine barrels.

COPPER SULFATE

May be used to eliminate hydrogen sulfide, which has a rotten egg smell, from wine.

CUVEE

A specific blend of wines used to manufacture champagne.

DEACIDIFICATION

A process by which higher acid levels are neutralized to give the wine a rounder mouthfeel.

DECANTING

Removing the sediment before pouring. Pour the wine through a piece of cheese-cloth until you start seeing the sediment. Unfiltered wine may need decanting. Decanting a red wine will allow undesirable chemicals to be released into the air. Decanting may also be done by pouring the wine carefully from the bottle into a carafe.

DEFATTED SOY FLOUR

Food for yeast that increases fermentation.

DEGREE DAYS

Total heat days during the summer that is measured by the actual accumulation of heat, which determines the speed of growth of the grain and is figured on the average daily temperature within each twenty-four-hour period.

DEXTRIN

A sugar produced by the reaction of starch and malt.

ERYTHORBIC ACID

Used to reduce oxidation and preserve the color and flavor of wine.

ESTERS

Organic compounds that form by combining acids and alcohol. They are the essence of the flavor and aroma derived from fruits and flowers.

ETHYL MALTOL

Added to provide a more smooth wine.

EXTRACT

The salts, sugars, and acids, that remain when wine is evaporated.

FAT

Describes a wine that contains a large amount of natural glycerin and has a weak body. An example of a fat wine is bordeaux.

FERMENTOR

A vessel used to produce primary fermentation.

FERROCYANIDE COMPOUNDS

A chemical group that can be used to remove unacceptable levels of minerals or sulfides from wines.

FERROUS SULFATE

A chemical that is used to clear wine and stabilize the color.

FLOWERY

A taste found only in young wines.

FORTIFIED WINES

Wines with an alcohol content that has been raised to 17 to 24 percent by adding brandy or a neutral alcohol. These are usually dry sherry and cream sherry.

FUMARIC ACID

An acid that may be used to stabilize wines or increase the level of acidity.

GENERIC WINE

An examples is red table wine.

GLYCERIN

A type of alcohol formed from sugar during fermentation. If too much is produced the wine may lack body.

GLYCEROL

A sweet alcohol formed during the fermentation process.

GOUT

Not a disease, but the French word for "taste."

HOGSHEAD

A container used to ship wine in large quantities that usually has a capacity of 60 gallons.

HYDROGEN PEROXIDE

Assists in the production of sparkling wines at the start of fermentation. In other types of wine, it may be used to eliminate unwanted colors.

HYDROMETER

An instrument used to measure the dissolved solids such as sugar of a solution.

ICE WINE

A relatively rare wine that can be produced only in certain years when the grapes have been frozen on the vine. The level of sugar at harvest must be at least 35°F Brix with a residual sugar content of at least 18 percent.

INSPISSATED WINE

Unfermented grape juice that may be used to provide flavor or color.

LACTIC ACID

Used to correct acid deficiencies.

LEAF PULLING

Removing some of the leaves to allow better air circulation and sun exposure for the grapes. Makes it easier to control mildew and allows easier access when picking the fruit.

MALIC ACID

An acid found naturally in most wines. Common in unripe grapes, it is converted by yeast during fermentation into carbon dioxide and lactic acid. Occasionally added to wine to correct low acid levels.

MANZANILLA

A somewhat dry, salty-tasting sherry that is called the driest wine in the world.

METHUSELAH

Refers to champagne bottles only. These bottles hold 6 liters (24 cups) of champagne.

MOUSSE

The froth that may develop on the surface of a champagne glass.

MUST

The crushed grape mixture that contains the juice and additives before the yeast is added.

NEUTRON PROBE

A device used to measure the moisture of the soil.

NONVINTAGE WINE

The best value wine, usually produced from a controlled blend from different harvests.

ORGANIC WINE

Produced from grapes that were grown where there were no fertilizers or pesticides used. The vineyard must be free of contaminants for at least one year before a harvest. The wine that is produced must also be free of any additives, especially sulfites.

OXIDATION

A prolonged exposure to oxygen that results in negative changes to wine. If a wine cannot be finished, it should be infused with an inert gas.

POTASSIUM BENZOATE

Used as a preservative in wine.

POTASSIUM BICARBONATE

Used to reduce the acidity in wine.

POTASSIUM BITARTRATE

Crystals that form if the wine has not been cold-stabilized. Used to stabilize wine.

POTASSIUM CARBONATE

A base used to reduce overacidity.

POTASSIUM METASULFITE

Used to sterilize and act as a wine preservative.

PROPRIETARY WINE

The name of a wine that can be used only by a specific producer.

RACKING

Siphoning off the clear juice from the sediments.

ROSÉ WINE

To be classified as a rosé wine, the label must say rosé. If it doesn't, then the wine is white. The rosé coloring comes from the skin of pinot grapes.

SEMIGENERIC WINE

A wine named for and produced in the unique style of a European geographic area.

SORBITAN MONOSTERATE

A compound used to control foaming.

TANNIN

A substance found in the seeds and stems of grapes that has astringent properties and is important in the aging process of wine. As wine ages the level of astringency will diminish, and the wine will develop more of its own characteristics.

ULLAGE

The bottle fill level.

VARIETAL WINE

A wine named for a particular grape. For a wine to be varietal, it must contain at least 75 percent of a specific variety. When two or more varieties are used, both names must appear on the label.

VINTAGE DATE

The year the grapes were harvested, not grown.

VINTAGE WINE

A wine that came from an excellent harvest and will be more expensive. Vintage wines that are labeled "prestige" are the highest-quality wines.

WINE INFORMATION WEB SITES

- www.wine.com
- www.epicurious.com
- www.mayohealth.org
- www.brewery.org
- www.bevnetmarketprice.com

Chapter 5
All About Liquor

BITTERS

Basically, bitters are just flavored spirits. They may be flavored with herbs, a variety of spices, barks, roots, and fruit. The methods of extraction of the essences from these botanicals are considered trade secrets. Originally, bitters were produced as medicines. They were then used as mixers for a variety of drinks. Some bitters will have an alcohol content of 35 to 45 percent. The most common bitter is Angostura, which was named after a Venezuelan town. It has a base of rum with a unique combination of flavorings from vegetable spices and gentian. The alcohol content is almost 45 percent, and it is used as a flavoring agent in numerous cocktails and mixed drinks. It is not unusual to find Angostura being used in soups and stews in South America.

BRANDY

The Dutch coined the word *brandy* from the word *brandewijn*, which means "burnt wine." The reference was used since brandy was produced from heat distillation of wine. Its origins date back to about 1540 when a Dutch sea captain distilled wine to save space on his ship.

COGNAC

The most popular brandy is cognac, which has been produced in the Cognac region of France for almost four hundred years. Cognac is produced from the combination of three white grapes, the ugni blanc being the main ingredient, with only a small amount of the colombard and the folle blanche included. Brandy should be aged in oak casks for the best results. There are a number of reasons why cognac is the world's finest brandy: the soil in which the grapes are grown, which has a high limestone content; cooperative weather in this region; the farming methods and care of the vines; special distilling methods; location of the storage facilities; the unique blending process; and the special Limousin oak casks in which the grapes are aged.

The following is a list of special cognac label terminology.

FINE CHAMPAGNE

An excellent cognac produced from grapes grown in the Grande Champagne and Petit Champagne regions. This cognac must use a minimum of 50 percent Grande Champagne grapes.

FINE MAISON

A cognac that is matured at a faster rate and usually sold to restaurants or individuals that wish to have a private label. It is usually a smooth brandy and a good value.

GRANDE FINE CHAMPAGNE

A cognac produced only from grapes that are grown in the Grande Champagne region. One of the finest brandies produced.

VS (THREE-STAR)

A very special cognac aged at least three years.

VSOP

Very superior old pale cognac. It is not too sweet and has been aged seven to seventenn years in a special oak cask.

XO

Extra old Cognac that has aged for more than twenty years and will be some of the finest brandies produced. They may also be labeled grande reserve, extra vielle, and hors d'age.

ARMAGNAC

This is probably the first brandy ever produced. Because of the location of the production site it was difficult to transport the brandy to market, thus giving cognac most of the market share by the time it had arranged for adequate transportation means. Armagnac is still produced in the original region in stills that resemble the nineteenth-century ones. It is an excellent, high-quality brandy.

Brandy Alexander
1 shot brandy
1 shot creme de cocao
1 shot cream
 Ice

Blend all ingredients well, then strain into a flute. Sprinkle a small amount of fresh nutmeg on top.

CALVADOS

The most popular fruit brandy is Calvados. It is produced from apples, which are crushed into a pulp and cultured with yeast to produce fermentation and eventually cider. The cider is then double-distilled to an alcohol content of 55 to 60 percent. It is then aged in Limousin oak casks. Better-quality Calvados may be aged for five to ten years. Calavados is normally consumed from a brandy glass after a meal and has been referred to as a digestive aid in France.

Adam's Apple
1½ shots Calvados
¾ shot quality gin
¾ shot vermouth
2 dashes yellow chartreuse
¹⁄₁₀ teaspoon lemon zest
3 ounces ice cubes, chopped
2 cherries
 Small slice of curled lemon peel

Place Calvados, gin, vermouth, yellow chartreuse, and lemon zest into a bar mixer. Add the ice and shake. Mix well with a spoon before straining into a cocktail glass. Add cherries and curled lemon peel.

APPLEJACK

An American apple brandy first produced in New England, Applejack originally was a very spicy, strong beverage. Sailors would bar-call it "a slug of blue fish hook." In New Jersey it was called "Jersey lightening." This distilled cider drink has now been toned down and produced from granny smith or golden delicious apples. It is double-distilled and allowed to age in oak casks. One of the best brands is Laird's.

GIN

There are two basic categories of gin: dry and Dutch. Dry gin is produced in the United States and England from grain or molasses. The flavor will vary depending on the type of juniper berries and other extracts used. Other extracts may add to the flavor such as cardamom, angelica, orange, lemon, cassia bark, orris root, anise, cinnamon, and coriander. The style of the gin will determine which botanical extracts are used. Dutch gin is made from mash, malted barley, maize, or rye. The malt gives the gin a malty taste and aroma. It is this reason that Dutch gin should not be used in mixed drinks.

Dry gin is usually served over ice, with tonic water or a fruit juice. Gin with lime was the favorite drink of the British navy to keep the sailors from getting scurvy (vitamin C deficiency disease).

SLOE GIN

Sloe gin is produced by distilling grain spirits (usually barley or corn) with small purple plums from the blackthorn shrub, which are steeped in the gin for several months to give it a deep rose color and somewhat bittersweet taste. Dry gin is produced by the same method, but juniper berries take the place of the plums.

BRRR

Gin should be stored in the freezer. The alcohol content is high enough to keep the gin from freezing and the bottle from breaking. This will also help retain the flavor. Keep the tonic water in refrigerator, not the freezer.

Gin and Tonic
2   shots quality gin
    Tonic water, chilled
2   to 4 ice cubes

Combine all ingredients in a tall narrow glass. The ice cubes will not dilute the drink since everything is cold and they will not melt before you finish. Tonic water will last only one day after it is opened, so you should buy small bottles.

Martini
1½ shots Beefeater gin
¾   shot Martini & Rossi vermouth
    Ice
    Very small amount lemon peel

Place the gin, vermouth, and ice into a chilled standard bar mixer. Stir vigorously (do not shake) for no more than 15 seconds, then strain into a chilled martini glass. Squeeze a small amount of zest from the lemon peel on the top of the drink to create a thin glaze. The balance of the lemon may be added to the drink or discarded. Prolonged stirring tends to make a martini watery as the ice melts and dilutes the drink.

A dry martini is made with less vermouth. There are two popular methods to making a dry martini: use either 12 or 20 parts gin to 1 part vermouth.

LIQUEUR

This is a popular spirit that is flavored and sweetened. It is called a cordial in the United States and was first produced in Europe as medicine for colds and to reduce fevers. Normally, liqueurs are consumed after a meal and are considered an aid for digestion. Most liqueurs are produced from fruits that are mashed and mixed with brandy and placed in casks for six to nine months to age. The flavored brandy is then extracted and placed in a vat to mature for another year.

BAILEY'S IRISH CREAM

The most popular and best-selling liqueur worldwide, Bailey's was invented in 1974 in Dublin, Ireland, and contains Irish whiskey and Irish cream combined with vanilla and cocoa bean extracts. To eliminate the problem of the cream separating, it was necessary to homogenize the liqueur. The whiskey used must be at least 3 years old and aged in special casks produced from oak in the United States.

ANISETTE

Another popular liqueur is anisette, which was originally produced as a medicine.

BENEDICTINE

Bendictine was originally produced in 1510 and made to treat arthritis symptoms. It is produced from cognac and as many as seventy different herbs and botanicals. It is double-distilled and allowed to age for four years before being bottled. It is a somewhat sweet liqueur.

CURACAO

This liqueur is produced from bitter oranges that were originally grown only on the island of Curacao. Curacao was formerly named triple sec and is sold in numerous colors, including orange, blue, green, and brown.

GRAND MARNIER

After this orange-flavored liqueur produced from bitter oranges and cognac is distilled, it is blended with a sugar syrup. One of the most popular liqueurs, it is used to prepare a number of dishes such as crepes suzette and a special Grand Marnier soufflé.

KAHLUA

Produced by combining cane spirits, coffee, and vanilla, kahlua is one of the best-selling liqueurs in the world. Originally produced only in Mexico, it is also now produced in Denmark.

Other popular liqueurs are Midori, a melon-flavored liqueur, and cherry herring, a cherry-flavored liqueur.

Grasshopper

½ **shot creame de menthe**

½ **shot white creme de cacao**

½ **shot cream**

   Ice

Place all ingredients into a bar shaker and shake vigorously, then strain into a champagne flute.

OKOLEHAO

This is one of the most popular alcoholic beverages produced in Hawaii. Produced from the roots of the ti plant, which contains a high level of fructose and ferments easily, it is distilled and bottled without aging. Coke and oke is a Hawaiian favorite.

RUM

Rum is made from sugar cane and originated in the Caribbean. It is produced from molasses syrup, a by-product of sugar production. Since molasses syrup easily fermented in the hot, humid climate, it was distilled into a drinkable spirit. Originally, it was exported to England and the East Coast of America. Rum has very few congeners and may have an alcohol content of 160 proof (80 percent by volume). The better dark rums are aged in oak casks for at least three years. The lighter rums are aged a little or not at all and are less expensive. Run is often mixed with a carbonated beverage such as Coca-Cola.

The largest manufacturer of rum is Bacardi in Puerto Rico, which owns the largest distillery in the country. The two most popular rums worldwide are Bacardi and Ronrico, which are produced from blackstrap molasses, a special strain of yeast, and the purest water possible.

Daiquiri

2 shots quality rum
1 shot lime juice
½ teaspoon caster sugar
   Ice

Place all ingredients in a bar shaker and mix, then strain the contents into a cocktail glass. These drinks are sometimes decorated with a piece of orange peel.

Pina Colada

2 shots white rum
4 ounces pineapple juice
2 teaspoons coconut liquor
3 dashes Angostura bitters
1 Pinch salt
   Ice

Place all ingredients in a bar shaker and shake well. Strain contents into a highball glass, then decorate with pineapple, cherry, and orange slices on a toothpick.

SCHNAPPS

Schnapps may also be called aquavit (water of life) and is produced from potatoes or grains. It is double-distilled, then filtered through layers of vegetable charcoal to obtain a high level of purity. It is usually flavored with cardamom, caraway, dill, fennel seed, citrus zest, and cumin. The final product is stored in glass-lined containers and allowed to settle before bottling. The word *schnapps* means "gasp," which is the reaction most people have after the first swallow. Schnapps is best stored in the freezer and served in chilled glasses straight from the freezer. Usually, it is drunk in Germany after a few beers or at least a beer chaser. The best brand is Linie.

TEQUILA

This alcoholic beverage is the numero uno alcoholic beverage in Mexico. It is produced from the agave plant, also known as the century plant or mezcal plant. The blue agave plant is grown in the state of Jalisco and the distillation near the town of Tequila. Each agave plant takes eight to twelve years to mature. The heart of the plant, the pina, is harvested and will yield about 6 gallons of a sweet sap called *aguamiel*, which is Spanish for "honey water." The pina is cut into chunks and steam-cooked for forty-eight hours, converting the starch into a sugar that is more easily fermented. After fermentation the wine that is produced is called pulque and is double-distilled to produce a pure white spirit with an alcohol strength of about 50 percent.

The best tequila is Anejo, which is aged for one to three years and is the most expensive. Next best is Jose Cuervo Gold, aged for less than six months; next is Reposado, aged for six months; and last is Silver Tequila, which is not aged at all.

There are two methods of drinking tequila:

SHOOTING

A shooter ritual entails placing a pinch of salt on the back of your hand between the thumb and forefinger while holding a slice of lime in the same two fingers. The other hand holds a shot of tequila. Lick the salt, down the shot, then bite and squeeze the lime to get most of the juice. After three or four shooters, you won't care what country originated the shooter.

SLAMMING

A slammer is a combination of tequila and lemonade or sparkling wine. The mixture is placed into a glass with a solid bottom, covered with a napkin or your hand, then slammed down hard on the top of the table. The drink will begin foaming, which is when you down the entire concoction in one gulp.

Margarita

Margaritas are commonly prepared in a blender, but always be sure to tell the bartender to blend it well or you will have small chunks of ice in your drink. If the drink is too frozen and not easily drinkable, much of the flavor will be lost.

1 shot tequila
1 shot curacao
2 teaspoons lime juice
   Ice
   Small piece lime
   Very fine salt

In a bar shaker, pour the tequila, curacao, lime juice, and ice and shake well. Rub the rim of the cocktail glass with the piece of lime, then dip the rim in a saucer containing the salt. Strain the mixture into the glass.

Tequila Sunrise
   Ice
2 shots tequila
   Orange juice
1 teaspoon grenadine

In a highball glass, place the ice, tequila, and sufficient orange juice to reach just below the top of the glass. Add the grenadine and a small slice of orange or a cherry if desired, and drink with a straw.

WAITER, THERE'S A WORM IN MY DRINK

The worm in the bottle of tequila has little to do with the tequila. It was placed there by the manufacturers of Mezcal tequila to denote the difference in that particular liquor from the standard tequila. The worm is actually a fat grub that resides in the maguey plant, which is the plant used to produce Mezcal tequila. The worm contains only a small amount of alcohol and is harmless when consumed. Tequila lollypops (Hotlix) are also being sold with the worm inside. Bottles of Mezcal tequila may also have a small bag attached that contains special "worm salt" composed of dried and ground-up worm, some chili powder, and salt to be taken as a chaser.

VODKA

Vodka has always been associated with Russia and means "little water" in Russian. Called vodka because it is colorless, tasteless, and odorless, it was originally produced as a medicine in the twelfth century. One of the original drinks in the United States was invented in California, the Moscow mule, was made with vodka, ginger beer, and lime juice. Vodka can be produced from molasses, grains, or potatoes, whichever is most plentiful. The raw materials are fermented into a "wash," which is distilled and processed in a still. Vodka, which is as close to a pure spirit as is possible, is then filtered to remove all traces of color, flavor, and residues.

Vodka should be stored in the freezer and should be consumed directly from the freezer in a small chilled glass. When vodka is ordered in better restaurants, it will be served in a bottle that is in an ice bucket similar to champagne. Two common methods of drinking vodka are to serve it over ice mixed with either orange juice for a screwdriver or tomato juice for a Bloody Mary.

Sex on the Beach

1 shot vodka
½ ounce melon Midori
½ ounce raspberry liquor
1½ ounce pineapple juice
1½ ounce cranberry juice cocktail
   Ice

In a bar shaker, combine all ingredients and shake vigorously. Pour into a chilled highball glass.

Fuzzy Navel

½ shot peach schnapps
½ shot vodka
   Orange juice

Place the schnapps and vodka in a highball glass, fill with orange juice, and stir well.

WHISKEY

MALT WHISKEY

The initial stages of whiskey production are almost identical to that of beer. Barley grain is used and goes through a malting process, then germination, kilning, grinding, mashing, and finally fermentation. It is then distilled, allowed to mature, and placed in casks.

GRAIN WHISKEY

The only difference between malt whiskey and grain whiskey is that other grains such as maize or wheat are used as well as barley. The maize or wheat is ground as fine as flour before being mixed with the barley.

BLENDED WHISKEY

Blended whiskey is a combination of malt and grain whiskies. The more malt whiskey that is used, the more expensive the whiskey. The percentage of malt may be anywhere from 20 to 50 percent of the total volume.

Whiskey is produced in several countries, all making their own special blends and utilizing a variety of production methods. The following are only some of the different types and methods of the major producers:

⚗ AMERICAN WHISKEY

The most popular grains used are maize (corn), rye, millet, and barley. There are two yeasting processes that are commonly used in the United States: sweet mash and sour mash. One of the most popular whiskies is bourbon, which was originally produced in Bourbon County, Kentucky. The number one–selling bourbon is Jim Beam, whose main grain is corn. It must be matured in new, charred oak casks for at least two years. The following are styles of American whiskies:

Straight Whiskey

Produced from one type of grain, usually maize or rye. The main grain must be at least 51 percent of the total volume. A full-bodied whiskey that must age for two years in oak casks.

Blended Whiskey

Contains a minimum of 20 percent straight whiskey. This whiskey will be of a lesser quality than a straight whiskey. A percentage of the whiskey flavor will be lost.

Light Whiskey

Just as the name implies. Does not have the character or flavor of the better whiskies.

Rye Whiskey

Produced from mash that is 51 percent rye, of an excellent quality, and full-bodied. Has an excellent flavor and aroma. Mixes well with citrus, bitters, and liqueurs.

Corn Whiskey
Produced from mash, which must contain 80 percent maize. Not aged for a long period and has somewhat of a harsh, strong flavor.

🥃 CANADIAN WHISKEY

The Canadian government will allow the production of whiskey only if it is produced from a number of grains and utilizes the continuous method of still distillation. The whiskey must also be aged for a minimum of three years in casks. The grains normally used are corn, barley, wheat, and rye. Canadian whiskey is usually a relatively light-bodied, delicate-tasting, somewhat sweet whiskey. The finest-quality Canadian whiskey is Crown Royal.

🥃 IRISH WHISKEY

Irish whiskey was the first whiskey ever produced. The Irish made a harsher grain whiskey that was not readily accepted and lost their lead in the industry to the Scots, who produced a more pleasing whiskey blend. Now Irish whiskey is triple-distilled to produce a smoother product that is more acceptable to Western taste.

🥃 JAPANESE WHISKEY

The first whiskey to be sold by Japan was schochu in 1929. The Japanese method of production utilizes a pot and continuous still for distillation and use American oak barrels charred for the maturing.

🥃 SCOTCH WHISKEY

Scotch whiskey was first produced by the farmers in the Highlands of Scotland who were unhappy with the government for placing high taxes on whiskey. Thousands of farmers had illegal stills until the law was changed and a reasonable tax was levied. The whiskey is a blend of light-grain whiskies and the heavier whiskey and produces a light, smooth-flavored product. Contributing to this high-quality, excellent-tasting whiskey is the purity of the water, the nonpolluted air, and the special oak casks used to mature the whiskey. Chivas Regal is an excellent example of a fine Scotch whiskey.

Scotch connoisseurs are very fussy regarding the purity and flavor of scotch.

If you wish to enjoy scotch at its best, be sure to use a very clean glass with not even a hint of soap residue. The water used should be purified and the ice cubes made from boiled water and washed before being used.

Manhattan

3 shots rye whiskey
1 shot sweet vermouth
1 dash Angostura bitters
   Ice

Blend all ingredients, then strain into a cocktail glass. Add a small slice of lemon peel and a cherry, if desired.

Whiskey Sour

2 shots whiskey
1 shot lemon juice
½ shot gomme syrup (sugar water)
   Dash egg white
   Ice

Combine all ingredients, shake vigorously, and strain into a goblet.

Old-Fashioned

1 teaspoon Casters sugar
1 teaspoon water
1 dashes Angostura bitters
2 shot quality bourbon
   ice cubes

Combine the sugar, water, and bitters. After mixing well, add the whiskey and ice cubes, then stir gently and pour into a glass. Decorate as desired.

Hot Whiskey Toddy

1 sugar cube
2 shots quality blended whiskey
   Boiling water
1 slice lemon
   Pinch nutmeg

Place a sugar cube in a mug and add a small amount of water to dissolve the cube. Add the whiskey and fill with boiling water. Stir and garnish with the lemon and nutmeg.

ALCOHOL MANUFACTURING INFORMATION

FUSEL OIL

This is a common name for alcohol by-products that are formed during the processing and does not mean that the liquor is bad, just that it will have an "off" taste. Poor purification is usually the cause of an increase in fusel oil.

POISONING

This is rarely if ever a problem even if the alcohol produced has an "off" taste. Even if the alcohol has impurities in it, it can usually still be consumed. There is alcohol that is poisonous, such as rubbing alcohol (methyl alcohol).

ACTIVATED CHARCOAL

This type of charcoal is used to purify the alcoholic beverage and looks like it contains hundreds of small sponges, which tend to absorb the impurities and sediments. Activated charcoal is electrically charged and literally acts like a magnet to the impurities. Sufficient carbon must be used since there is a saturation level that can be reached.

PURIFYING METHOD

The best purifying method is to pour the alcohol down a very long glass tube filled with activated charcoal. The base of the tube should have a double-filter paper stopper held on with a stainless steel jubilee clip. This is the method preferred by distillers worldwide.

ESSENCES

Liquors may be flavored with essences. These are produced from raw materials and are in the form of oils or solutions of the original substance. Essences are derived from coffee oil, herb oils, oil of aniseed, orange oil, and a variety of spices. Many are distilled to create a stronger extract. Essences are added to create a better aroma and, in some instances, to mask unwanted aromas and flavors.

ALWAYS STAND UPRIGHT

Spirits should always be stored in an upright position. If the bottle has a cork stopper, the cork may rot away if it is in continuous contact with the alcohol. Spirits should also be stored in a cool, dark location and never allowed to be in direct sunlight for any amount of time.

THE PROPER GLASS IS A MUST

There are fifteen different glasses used at most bars:

Snifter: . . . . . .4 ounces **Sherry:** . . . . . .2 ounces **Martini:** . . . . . .4 ounces

Collins: . . . . . .12 ounces **Brandy:** . . . . . .3 ounces **Highball:** . . . .8 ounces

Cocktail: . . . . .3½ ounces **Whiskey sour:** 5 ounces **Pilsner:** . . . . . .10 ounces

Old-fashioned: 8 ounces **Parfait:** . . . . . .12 ounces **Champagne:** . .8 ounces

Shot: . . . . .1½ ounces **Beer:** . . . . .12 ounces **Wine:** . . . . . . .4 ounces

MIXERS

The following are the most common mixers used with alcoholic beverages.

LIGHT BEVERAGE CARBONATED MIXERS

Any standard cola, diet cola, 7 UP, or tonic water. These are best when mixed with the lighter alcoholic beverages such as rum, vodka, and gin.

DARK BEVERAGE CARBONATED MIXERS

Club soda, seltzer water, ginger ale, Perrier, and 7 UP. These are best when mixed with the darker alcoholic beverages such as scotch and bourbon.

JUICE MIXERS

Orange juice, tomato juice, and grapefruit juice. These are normally used for Bloody Marys and screwdrivers.

CHEFS' SECRETS

BRANDY

Brandy is one of the most versatile spirits and can be used in many different dishes. It is especially complementary to soups, shellfish, beef, lamb, peaches, pears, and a number of puddings.

CALVADOS

Calvados is excellent with all dishes made with apples, especially when used on baked or stewed apples. Small amounts tend to complement recipes that have chicken, veal, or pork in them.

GIN

Gin may have too overpowering a flavor for most dishes. It is best used on game dishes to mask the gamy flavor. An age-old favorite is to use a small amount of gin in tomato soups or a tomato sauce. It will also complement the flavor of sauerkraut.

LIQUEURS

Since liqueurs are sweet, they tend to go well over desserts and especially fruit salads. Ice creams are excellent with a small amount of a flavored liqueur. Grand Marnier goes well with any dish that has oranges included. Benedictine is an age-old favorite on sponge cake.

RUM

Rum is very effective in flavoring sweet dishes, especially desserts. It is commonly used on rum cakes, fruitcakes, and bananas Foster.

VODKA

Since vodka has no flavor it is rarely used in cooking, with the exception of marinades.

WHISKEY

Small amounts of quality whiskey will aide in bringing out the flavor in many foods and specialty dishes. It is typically used to replace brandy in many recipes. It is especially good when used in shellfish recipes but will complement almost any type of meat or poultry dish. Whiskey is commonly used on chocolate mousse, coffee sorbet, and fruitcakes.

Hard Cider

4 gallons quality sweet cider (not pasteurized)
3 pounds natural honey
2 packages champagne yeast
3 pounds brown sugar

Strain ½ gallon of the sweet cider and all of the honey into a pot and heat slowly until the mixture is fully dissolved. Strain the rest of the sweet cider into a 5-gallon pot and do not heat. Pour the cider and honey mixture into the unheated pot, add the yeast, and seal with an airtight a seal as possible. When the fermentation activity stops, add the sugar, which will produce carbonation. Allow to stand for about three weeks.

COOKING WITH ALCOHOL

The boiling point of alcohol is 175°F, which is lower than the boiling point of water, 212°F. When alcohol is added to a recipe it will lower the boiling point until it evaporates. For example, if you decide to change your recipe by adding some wine to replace some of the water, you will need to increase your cooking time by about 10 percent.

CLOSE THE WINDOWS, WE'RE LOSING THE ALCOHOL

The following will provide information regarding cooking with alcohol and how much alcohol is left after a dish is cooked. Some alcohol will dissipate, but not as much as most people may think.

METHOD OF PREPARATION	ALCOHOL REMAINING
Alcohol not added to boiling food until after the food was removed from heat	86 percent
Alcohol added to a flambé and ignited	75 percent
Alcohol used in a marinade and not heated	70 percent
Alcohol stirred into a baked dish and simmered for:	
15 minutes	40 percent
30 minutes	35 percent
1 hour	25 percent
2 hours	10 percent
3 hours	0 percent

WHOOOSH

If you want to flame a mixed drink safely, put a small amount of the preferred liquor into a teaspoon and hold a match under the spoon for a few seconds until some of the fumes burn off. Then ignite the liquor in the spoon and pour it over the mixed drink. Never place your face too close to the drink you are flaming, just in case there are more fumes rising. Rum flames up better than most alcoholic beverages.

NUTRITIONAL INFORMATION

UP, UP, AND REALLY AWAY

If you wonder why you feel the effects of alcohol more when you are flying, it is due to the increased cabin pressure. When the pressure increases it forces the alcohol into the bloodstream at a faster rate, also causing you to become thirsty more frequently.

NO DIGESTION NEEDED?

Alcohol needs no digestion and is immediately absorbed into the bloodstream. It tends to concentrate more in the blood and brain, and a small amount is exhaled. Almost 90 percent of the alcohol must be metabolized by the liver, which can really be placed under pressure if you consume a large quantity of alcohol.

HOOK UP A HOSE TO THE COFFEEPOT

Drinking large quantities of black coffee has little effect on relieving the effects of overindulgence. What you end up with is a wide awake drunk; it's best to just sleep it off. In fact, most people who try to reduce the effects of the alcohol with coffee, which is very acidic, usually end up with a stomachache as well. The body

will only metabolize " ounce of alcohol an hour, so you have no choice but to wait for relief.

PASS THE WATER

Your body requires about 8 ounces of water to metabolize 1 ounce of alcohol. To reduce the aftereffects of a hangover, drink a sufficient quantity of water in relation to the amount of alcohol you drank.

CALORIES IN POPULAR COCKTAILS

COCKTAIL	CALORIES
Daiquiri (5 ounces)	275
Gin and tonic (8 ounces)	200
Martini (3 ounces)	185
Screwdriver (7 ounces)	170
Tom Collins (8 ounces)	145
Bloody Mary (5 ounces)	110

LIQUOR FACTS AND SECRETS

BODY HEAT IS A MUST

The proper glass to drink brandy out of is called a "brandy snifter" It should be a very thin-walled glass to allow the body heat from your hands to penetrate the glass and stimulate the release of the aroma. Never artificially warm a brandy snifter.

STOP, YOU'RE KILLING ME

Only stir a drink if necessary and for the shortest time possible since the more you stir, the faster the ice melts and dilutes the drink.

CHEAPSKATE!

When you are preparing a mixed drink, always place the least expensive ingredients in first. If you make a mistake, you won't ruin the whole mixture.

IT'S NICE AND WARM IN HERE

Never drink from a bar glass that is stored upside down over the bartender's head. Glasses that are stored in this manner tend to contain residues of cigarette smoke, germs from people coughing, and anything else that is floating around.

THERE'S A CUKE IN MY DRINK

One method of reducing an overalcoholic taste in punch or almost any drink is to float a few slices or strips of cucumber in the drink. A chemical in the cucumber tends to neutralize some of the "off" taste of certain alcoholic beverages.

GASP, GIVE ME AIR

When pouring brandy into a snifter, allow at least 80 percent of the glass space for air, which allows the aroma to be released and contained above the brandy. Only 20 percent of the snifter should contain brandy.

WHOSE TWO FINGERS—HERS OR MINE?

A "real" bartender almost never uses a jigger to measure a shot; he just wraps his two fingers around the bottom of the glass and pours up to the top of the fingers. This saves time and is fairly accurate. Using a jigger may also tell your guests that you are cheap and need to measure the liquor.

LIQUOR GLOSSARY

ABV

Stands for alcohol by volume.

AGING

Maturing of spirits in barrels or casks made of oak. Different spirits are aged for different periods of time, which is an important factor in the final quality of the beverage.

ALCOHOL

This is the amount of ethyl alcohol in a beverage obtained by the process of fermentation and subsequent distillation.

ALEMBIC

A special type of still used exclusively to produce cognac.

BITTERS

Spirits flavored with fruits or botanicals. They all tend to have a somewhat bitter taste.

BOB

Stands for buyer's own brand. A number of manufacturers will provide their whiskey for private labeling.

BOTANICALS

Flavorings derived from fruits or flowers that are used in neutral spirits when producing gin or a liqueur.

BOTTLED IN BOND WHISKEY

The only whiskey that is bottled in bond is straight whiskey. It is a 100 proof whiskey (50 percent alcohol) that is allowed to be produced and stored in government warehouses for a maximum of four years or until the producer removes the whiskey and pays the taxes. A green stamp is then placed over the stopper to prove that the tax was paid.

CASK

A barrel made of oak. Usually smaller than a normal barrel, it is used for maturing alcoholic beverages.

COBBLER

An iced drink prepared from wine or liqueur with added sugar and fruit juice.

CONDENSER

The part of a still that is responsible for liquefying the alcohol vapors.

CONGENERS

The flavorings and aromas that are the result of the organic compounds being broken down by the fermentation and distillation processes. The more a beverage is distilled, the fewer congeners it will contain and the purer the beverage.

DAISY

A gin or whiskey drink that includes a sugary syrup and a liqueur.

DISTILLING

The process of releasing and capturing vapors from a liquid. The vapors are then put through a condenser, which reliquefies the vapors into a more potent alcoholic beverage.

DRAM

A degree of measure used mostly for Scottish whiskeys.

ESTERS

Produced from the combination of acids and alcohol to form a more volatile substance, providing alcoholic beverages with their unique aroma.

FIREWATER

The American Indian name for alcoholic beverages, which burn as they go down the throat.

FLIP

A drink that contains liquor, spices, sugar, and egg.

FRAPPE

A liqueur served over crushed ice.

GROG

A drink made from rum and diluted with water.

HARD LIQUOR

A beverage with a high alcohol content, usually measured in "proof."

INFUSION

The process of putting a flavor into an alcoholic beverage so that it will remain a permanent part of the beverage.

LEES

The residues of yeast, fruit skins, or other extraneous matter left after fermentation. These leftovers are sometimes used to produce pomace brandy.

LIMOUSIN

A type of oak that originates in a forest near Limousin, France. This is considered the best wood for producing oak barrels and casks to mature cognac and other spirits.

MOONSHINE

The illegally produced alcoholic beverages during Prohibition in the United States.

MUDDLE

To mash up certain ingredients such as mint leaves in order to make a paste that can be used in a drink.

MULL

To heat a drink and add spices.

NEAT

An alcoholic beverage that is consumed undiluted. Vodka is commonly referred to as a neat drink.

NELSON'S BLOOD

A term used by the British navy for rum.

POMACE

Debris left after the juice is extracted from grapes.

PROOF

The actual strength of an alcoholic beverage. Pure alcohol would be 100 percent alcohol or 200 proof. If the label reads 70 percent alcohol, the beverage is 140 proof.

RECTIFICATION

Purification of alcoholic spirits utilizing the process of double distillation.

RICKEY

This term refers to any drink that uses club soda and lime. Other ingredients may be added, such as sugar.

SOUR MASH

The debris left over from fermentation process, which can be included in the processing of some bourbon whiskies.

TODDY

A hot drink that usually consists of rum, sugar, water, and spices, usually cinnamon.

TRONCAIS

A source of oak in France that is used to produce maturing casks or barrels.

WASH

Liquid left over from the fermentation process and intended for distillation.

Chapter 6
Fruit and Veggie Juices

The information contained in this chapter suggesting health improvement and uses of juices for other than general health purposes is meant to be taken in a historical perspective and not meant to be used to treat or imply that the juice will help any medical condition. Your family physician is still your first line of medical care and treatment.

COMMON TYPES OF FRUIT AND BERRY JUICES

APPLE JUICE

Almost 50 percent of all apples grown in the United States are processed into apple products or juice. The average American consumes about 30 pounds of apples annually in the form of juice, applesauce, and pie filling.

♡ JUICING UP YOUR BABY

Most pediatricians tend to recommend apple juice as a baby's first juice. Apple juice is a mild laxative and has a very acceptable sweet taste. It is also commonly fortified with vitamin C; this will allow the baby to absorb more iron, which is very important for growth.

♡ NUMERO UNO APPLE JUICE PRODUCT

If you enjoy apples, then Martinelli's products are worth a try. Martinelli's has produced quality products since 1868 and its sparkling cider can't be beat. All products are 100 percent pure juice and have no flavorings, concentrates, or preservatives. They are only lightly carbonated. The company started out producing cider and carbonated soft drinks in California's first commercial orchard.

♡ THE SAUCE FROM APPLES

Whether your applesauce is smooth or chunky usually depends on when you add the sugar to the recipe. If you would prefer chunky applesauce, you should add the sugar before cooking the apples. If you prefer a smooth applesauce, then add the sugar after the apples have been cooked and mashed. Commercially prepared sweetened applesauce can contain as much as 77 percent more calories than unsweetened varieties.

♡ GET THE SMELLING SALTS, THE APPLE HAS COLLAPSED

When you bake an apple, the peel will hold the apple together and help it maintain its shape. The peel contains an insoluble fiber called ligan, which reinforces the peel. However, the pectin in the cell walls is easily dissolved by hot water and allows the apple to turn into applesauce. Bakers add calcium to apples when they use them for baking to hold them together and keep them firm. If you slit the skin in a few places when baking an apple, the skin will not wrinkle.

♡ BUTTER ME AN APPLE, PLEASE

Apple butter when made properly does not contain any fat. It should be prepared with mashed apples, cinnamon, and allspice.

♡ APPLE JUICE TO THE RESCUE

When apples lose their moisture, just slice them, pour apple juice over them, and refrigerate for about thirty minutes.

APRICOT JUICE

Apricot juice is very high in vitamin A and contains a good amount of sulfur. The juice has been used to reduce the effects of aging, such as premature wrinkling of the skin. The combination of vitamins, minerals, oils, amino acids, and enzymes may even be related to slowing the aging process. The juice is also being studied in relation to slowing the growth of cancerous tumors.

☀ THE APRICOT ASTRONAUT

One of the favorite fruits taken on an Apollo moon mission was apricots. One ounce of the juice can contain 20 percent of your RDA of vitamin A in the form of beta-carotene. Apricots also contain a high level of iron.

BANANA JUICE

Banana juice has been known to ease the suffering of people that have colitis and heartburn. It is an excellent source of potassium and vitamin A.

☀ BERRY, BERRY INTERESTING, BUT NOT FUNNY

Bananas contain less water content than most other fruits. They are actually a "berry" from a plant classified as an herb tree, which is capable of reaching heights of 30 feet. The banana tree is the largest plant in the world with a woody stem.

BERRY JUICES

In cultures that have to survive by adding a significant amount of berries and nuts to their diet, there is little if any incidence of cancer. Most berries and a number of nuts contain ellagic acid, which researchers are investigating to see if it has an effect on cancer cells. In tests on mice that were fed ellagic acid, they had 45 percent fewer tumors than mice not fed ellagic acid. Berry juice is also an important source of iron.

※ BERRY BAKING—THE SINKING SOLUTION

When you make a dish with berries, be sure the batter is thick enough so that the berries can easily be held in suspension. If the batter is too thin, they will just sink to the bottom.

※ BERRY STAIN REMOVAL

Berry juice stains can easily be removed from your hands by using a small amount of lemon juice.

Raspberry Shrub

This was a favorite about seventy years ago.

3 pints fresh or frozen raspberries, hulled and cleaned
2 cups water
1½ cups granulated sugar
1 cup lemon juice
2 quarts pure water

In a medium saucepan, mix together the raspberries, 2 cups water, and sugar. Strain the mixture through a very fine sieve. Cool and then stir in the lemon juice and pure water.

CITRUS JUICE

The first citrus juice dates back to 500 B.C. and was prepared from the citron, which resembles a knobby lemon and is somewhat tart.

All citrus fruit must ripen on the tree, since it will not continue to ripen once picked. Before the fruit is picked, representative samples are taken and evaluated as to their Brix and acid content. As soon as the percentages are correct the fruit is harvested. Almost 98 percent of all citrus fruit is still harvested by hand.

⊛ THE CASE OF THE GREEN ORANGE

It is not uncommon to see oranges with either a hint of green or quite a bit of green. The green color is caused by temperature changes. For an orange to be a nice orange color, it needs warm days and cool nights. If the nights remain too warm, the orange cannot turn as orange as we are used to. The fruit will continue to ripen normally, but the green coloration will remain. The fruit will be just as good even if it has a green tint. Another factor may be that the tree had an extra shot of chlorophyll in the spring, but again the quality and the sweetness of the fruit are unaffected. When making juice it doesn't matter whether the oranges are orange or somewhat greenish.

Storing Juice Oranges

Never store oranges in sealed plastic bags. If they are stored in too airtight a container, small drops of moisture will form and cause mold to grow. The best temperature to store any citrus is around 45°F. Refrigerators are the recommended location.

The Juiciest of the Juicy

The best oranges for juicing are hamlin and valencia. Both will be found to have thin skins and either no seeds or very few seeds and will produce the most juice.

The Tropicana Story

Tropicana purchases almost 25 percent of Florida's oranges directly from the growers, which amounts to more than five hundred truckloads per day that must be processed. The company is capable of processing more than 50 million oranges per day. The juice extractors are capable of extracting juice from seven hundred oranges per minute and produce 1 million gallons of juice per day.

Lemon and Lime Juice

Lemon juice is an excellent flavoring for many dishes and can replace salt in most of them. The high acid content tends to mask the need for the salty taste. Both lemon and lime have the ability to blend well with a number of foods such as potatoes, rice, all types of salads, and most cooked vegetables. When the juice is processed it does tend to lose a good percentage of its flavor, so try to use freshly squeezed juice for the best results and taste. A real treat is to use key lime juice, which may be found only in health food stores. They also are great in salads to replace vinegar.

Old-Fashioned Lemonade

For limeade, replace the lemon rind with lime zest and the lemon juice with the juice of 8 limes.

1 cup water
1 cup granulated sugar
rind from 2 lemons, chopped
4 cups pure water
juice from 6 fresh lemons (not reconstituted lemon juice)

In a medium saucepan on low heat, combine the 1 cup water, sugar, and rind. Stir until the sugar has melted, then boil for about 6 minutes. Remove from heat and allow to cool, then add the pure water and lemon juice. Serve over crushed ice.

Cooking Fish With Lime Juice And No Heat

Acids have a tenderizing effect on the meat of fish, and when placed in lime or lemon juice for about ten hours, the meat will turn white instead of translucent. There is no heat generated, but the meat will look as if it were cooked. Two foods that utilize acidic cooking are pickled herring and seviche.

Natural Tenderizer

Both lemon and lime juice are natural tenderizers for any type of fowl dish.

⊛ GRAPEFRUIT JUICE AT ITS BEST

The best grapefruit for juicing is white seedless. It has a thin yellow peel with almost white flesh and is almost seedless. Another good one is the flame grapefruit, which contains more soluble fiber in one grapefruit than 2 cups of popcorn.

⊛ THE BEST OF THE BEST

If you are going to make orange juice in a blender, always use the white membrane just under the skin. The membrane, called the albedo, contains a higher percentage of vitamin C than the pulp or juice. Albedo is also being studied for its cholesterol-lowering qualities.

⊛ DON'T YOU DARE PUCKER UP

Markets are starting to sell a sweet lemon grown in California called the millsweet. It resembles a cross between a lemon and a lime. Now you can make lemonade without adding sugar.

CRANBERRY JUICE

Cranberries are too tart to be used for juice without the addition of a sweetener. That is why it is rarely sold as 100 percent cranberry juice; instead it is usually mixed with other juices.

⊛ BLADDER BE HEALTHY

There have been numerous studies regarding cranberry juice and its relationship to bladder infections. Studies have shown that cranberry juice does not abnormally raise the acid levels in the bladder, which was originally thought to lower the incidence of bladder infections. However, the latest studies now show that there exists an antioxidant compound that protects the walls of the bladder from bacteria adhering to it. Studies are still being conducted regarding both cranberries and wild blueberries in relation to bladder health.

FIG JUICE

Fig juice is normally not a drink but used as a meat tenderizer. Fresh figs contain the chemical ficin, a proteolytic enzyme capable of breaking down proteins with a similar action as that of papain from papaya or bromelain from pineapples. Ficin is effective in heat of 140 to 160°F, which is the most common temperature range when simmering stews. If you add a few fresh figs to a stew, the figs will tenderize the meat and impart an excellent flavor. If the temperature rises above 160°F the ficin will become inactive.

GRAPE JUICE

Grape juice has more calories than any other fruit juice due to its high sugar content. It contains no vitamin C once processed. Make sure the label reads "pure grape juice" or 100 percent, since grape juice is frequently blended with other juices that do not contain a high level of sugar. If you do purchase 100 percent grape juice, it can be diluted with water or seltzer for a great drink.

⊛ THE SECRET IS OUT

Researchers are isolating biologically active flavonoids (anthocyanins), which may lower the risk of heart disease and strokes. It was thought that drinking red wine was the reason the French had a lower incidence of heart disease, but it is actually the flavonoids in the red grape. The active flavonoids can be found in the skin, the seeds, and even the stem of the red grape plant. Drinking 8 to 10 ounces of red grape juice daily may reduce your risk without drinking the wine or taking aspirin. The American Heart Association does not recommend drinking red grape juice for any health benefit; however, the University of Wisconsin found that 10 ounces per day reduced the clotting of blood platelets better than red wine and aspirin together. In fact, there are ongoing studies by the University of Illinois that are relating the phytochemical compound reservertrol found in red grape skin, which ends up in the juice, as a potent cancer fighter.

GRAPEFRUIT JUICE

The heavier the grapefruit, the more juice it will hold. However, grapefruits grown in the western United States have a thicker skin and a lower juice content.

⊛ MEDICAL ALERT

A researcher at the University of Western Ontario found that grapefruit juice caused a threefold increase in the absorption rate of a blood pressure medication. Some of the medications that may interact and increase absorption are calcium-channel blockers, such as Procardia and Cylosporine; antihistamines, such as Seldane; hormones, such as the estrogen Estinyl; sedatives; antiviral agents; and immunosuppressants. Researchers are trying to isolate the guilty ingredient.

PAPAYA JUICE

The most effective papaya juice is derived from the green papaya, the stage before it ripens to an orange-yellow color and turns sweet. At the green stage the papaya contains a higher level of the chemicals papain and fibrin. Green papaya juice has been used to heal ulcers. In the South Pacific, papaya leaves have been used to speed the healing of serious lacerations with phenomenal success.

PINEAPPLE JUICE

A nutritious drink that contains a number of minerals including potassium, iron, phosphorus, and calcium, pineapple juice also contains good levels of vitamins A and C. Pineapples also contain the enzyme bromelain, which has been effective in treating an intestinal blockage condition called a phytobezoar and as an anti-inflammatory. Bromelain is used as an effective meat tenderizer in marinades.

⊛ KONA HAWAII ISLAND JUICE

Yes, it's spelled right! This is a 100 percent juice with a pineapple base. The non-pasteurized drink is one of the finest and most flavorful juice beverages on the market.

WATERMELON JUICE

Historically, watermelon juice was used to cure a number of ailments. The juice was squeezed out, made into a syrup, and given for arthritis, gout, colic in babies, and fevers. Indians used it to soothe their stomachs. Skin problems, especially those related to an overacidic condition, were treated with watermelon juice.

STORAGE OF JUICES

Once thawed and reconstituted, frozen juices should be stored in well-sealed containers. The vitamin C content will last for only a few days at a decent concentration. Fresh squeezed orange juice will keep for only twenty-four hours before it loses a percentage of vitamin C. All juices should be kept cold to reduce their nutrient losses.

Juice purchased in paper cartons or glass or plastic containers from the supermarket should retain 90 percent of their vitamin C content for at least one week and up to 70 percent after two weeks. However, opening and closing the container too often will change these percentages significantly.

ADDITIVES/PRESERVATIVES

When purchasing any type of juice it is always wise to check the label and read the list of ingredients. Many products including lemon juice add a number of preservatives. While most of the preservatives and coloring and flavoring agents are harmless, it would be best to limit the use of products that contain these added chemicals. If possible it is always best to use the raw, natural food.

Even if the label reads 100 percent juice, it may still contain an additive. 100 percent pineapple juice still has an antifoaming agent included; if it didn't, it would be difficult to pour.

☺ WELL, FIZZLE MY FIZZ

Fill a tall glass with orange juice or lemonade and add ¼ teaspoon of baking soda. Stir well and it will go crazy fizzing. This makes a fun drink and reduces the acidity in the juice.

NUTRITIONAL INFORMATION

THE MUSICAL JUICE DRINK

We are all too familiar with the fact that beans cause intestinal gas, but there are a number of fruit juices that will precipitate a real good attack of gas. This occurs when fructose, the natural sugar in the fruit, combines with the chemical sorbitol. If you want to avoid gas from fruit juices, stay away from apple, pear, cherry, plum, prune, and peach juices. Since these are healthy juices, my recommendation is to reduce the serving size, which may eliminate the problem. Also, sorbitol is a very common sweetener used in diabetic products, and if you consume one of those products and drink almost any fruit juice, you are combining fructose and sorbitol.

E. COLI IS AT IT AGAIN

Be sure that when you purchase apple juice it is pasteurized and not just "raw." *E. coli* bacteria really get around, and anywhere a cow goes the bacteria may follow. If a cow walks through an apple orchard and leaves manure, it may get on the apples that fall off the trees, which are the ones more likely to be used in apple juice and cider since they don't look good enough for the market. If the product is not made under strict sanitary conditions, the *E. coli* will contaminate the batch. Also, it is never wise to eat any fruit off the ground without washing it with an organic cleaner.

ONE OF THE HEALTHIEST JUICES

An 8-ounce serving of orange juice contains at least 60 milligrams of vitamin C, 20 percent of the RDA of folic acid, 15 percent of the RDA of fiber, and 12 percent of the RDA of potassium. The National Institute of Health, however, recommends 200 milligrams of vitamin C daily, which would be a little more realistic with our stressed-out lifestyles.

PUTTING A LABEL ON IT

The only three beverages that contain the required amount of nutrients and vitamins to be called a "healthy" drink are orange juice, grapefruit juice, and skim milk, according to the FDA. For a food to be considered "healthy," it must be low-fat, must contain no more than 60 milligrams of cholesterol or 480 milligrams of sodium, and must have at least 10 percent of the RDA of vitamin A, vitamin C, protein, or fiber.

A SAFE SQUEEZE

Before oranges are squeezed they are inspected for damage and contamination. The oranges are then kept chilled to help retain the vitamin C content. All fruit is then washed with a neutral detergent, sanitized, and rinsed with pure water. The orange is then squeezed from the outside to eliminate the bitter taste from the peel. As soon as it is squeezed it is chilled to below 0°F and placed in cold storage.

DON'T GIVE YOUR BONES A BREAK

Orange juice is an excellent source of calcium. One 8-ounce glass of Tropicana Pure Premium Calcium Juice contains 350 milligrams of calcium. The calcium is of a type that is easily absorbed and usable. Orange juice is also an excellent source of folate, a B vitamin that studies show is very effective in reducing the risk of heart disease and certain birth defects.

ANOTHER LIME DISEASE?

If your child likes limes and gets the oil found in the skin on his or her skin, it may cause a rash that looks like a bad burn. In fact, bergamot oil, if allowed to remain on the skin and exposed to sunlight, will actually cause the skin to burn. There are a number of other foods that contain the oil and will cause this photo-toxic reaction, such as carrots, celery, figs, parsley, parsnips, coriander, caraway seeds, fennel, and anise.

AN APPLE A DAY

A new study conducted at the National Public Health Institute in Helsinki, Finland, found that an antioxidant flavonoid compound in apples called quercetin reduced the risk of lung cancer by 46 percent. Fruit juices are one of the best sources of flavonoids.

WHERE'S MY VITAMIN C?

When apples are processed into juice or cider, virtually all the vitamin C is lost. Many apple products fortify their products with vitamin C.

APRICOT NECTAR: A HEALTHY DRINK?

Apricot nectar is high in beta-carotene, which is instrumental in producing vitamin A in the body. Apricot nectar has only slightly more calories than does orange juice and is a good source of potassium.

PEACH NECTAR

Most cans contain 100 percent of the RDA of vitamin C and some minerals. Peach nectar is high in carbohydrates, and most products contain 35 to 40 percent juice with a lot of sugar added.

PAPAYA NECTAR

Most contain only 25 to 30 percent juice. The vitamin C content is 100 percent of the RDA, and the majority of the drink is sugar and water.

STRAWBERRY NECTAR

Most contain only 20 to 25 percent juice. The vitamin C content is 100 percent of the RDA, and the majority of the drink is sugar and water.

MANGO NECTAR

Most contain 25 to 30 percent juice. The content of vitamins A and C is higher than most nectars, with the balance of the drink high in sugar and water.

ORANGE JUICE AND ANTACIDS—NOT VERY FRIENDLY

Antacids that contain aluminum should not be taken within three hours of drinking orange juice or even eating an orange. A 4-ounce serving of orange juice will increase the absorption of aluminum tenfold. High levels of aluminum can be a health risk.

JUICY FACTS

CHRISTOPHER COLUMBUS—THE ORANGE KING

Orange trees were brought to the Americas by Christopher Columbus in 1493, but were not introduced to Florida until about 1540 by Ponce de Leon. Grapefruit didn't arrive until the French brought a tree to Florida in 1806. The Chinese were actually the first to grow a citrus tree in 2200 B.C.

FLORIDA: ONLY NUMBER TWO

The largest producer of oranges in the world is Brazil. Together the United States and Brazil produce 42 percent of the world's crop. Florida produced a record 254 million boxes in the 1997–1998 season and will produce 1.5 billion gallons of orange juice and 150 million gallons of grapefruit juice. Nine out of every ten Florida oranges are used for juice.

BEST TO BE THIN-SKINNED...

...at least when it refers to an orange! Florida oranges are thin-skinned, which means that they have more juice than all other oranges. The climatic changes in other growing states cause the oranges to develop a thicker, more protective skin and less juice.

THIS WILL TAKE CARE OF A REALLLY BIG COLD

The Florida Department of Citrus unveiled the largest glass of orange juice in the world. It stands 8 feet tall, holds 730 gallons of juice, and contains more than 700,000 milligrams of vitamin C.

BRRR

For citrus fruit to be "seriously damaged" by freezing, the freezing temperatures must cause the fruit to appear dry more than ½ inch from the stem end. If the dryness extends only ¼ inch, then the fruit is considered only "damaged."

SUNNY DELIGHT

Sunny Delight is a tangy citrus beverage that contains orange and tangerine juice. It has a pleasant taste and is enriched with vitamins A, C, and B1. Additional flavors are sold that combine a number of fruit flavors. Refrigeration is recommended by the manufacturer after purchase in order to retain the taste and preserve the drink. Sunny Delight's flavor will last for only about ten days without refrigeration.

NEW YORK, NEW YORK

New York City is the biggest consumer of orange juice—a record 64 million gallons per year. New York may want to consider changing its nickname from The Big Apple to The Big Orange.

CLEAR THE AISLES, GET OUT OF MY WAY

Prune juice is an excellent source of vitamins and minerals, especially iron and potassium. Prunes also contain the chemical diphenylisatin, which is a relative of biscodyl, one of the active ingredients in laxatives. Prunes should have the same laxative effect in most individuals.

A SPARKLING, SPARKLING JUICE

Renee is one of the finest sparkling nonalcoholic beverages produced that is made from pineapple and peaches. It is sulfite-free, looks like champagne, and is worth a try.

WATERED-DOWN JUICE AND PUNCH TASTE TERRIBLE

Chefs have a great trick to keep punch and fruit juice cold without placing ice cubes in them, which waters them down. All you have to do is place one or two plastic sealed bags that contain ice cubes in the drink.

PEPSI FRUIT DOESN'T GROW ON TREES

Pepsi has unveiled a new fruit drink to be in the competition for the fruit drink market. FruitWorks®, the new noncarbonated Pepsi fruit product, contains 5 percent real fruit juice and sugar and is fortified with vitamins. Five percent is just a start in the right direction.

BUYER BEWARE

As of 1993, labels on juice drinks must contain the percentage of actual "real" juice that the product contains. It is wise to read the label and look for the actual percentage of juice in that beverage if you are interested in purchasing a drink with a high nutrient content. 100 percent means just that—the drink contains 100 percent of that particular juice. If the label reads 10 percent, the product contains only 10 percent of that juice and is not a particularly high-nutrient product, unless it has been fortified.

THE NAME GAME

Companies want you to think that their products have a higher nutritional content than they really contain. A drink that is low in nutrients may include " juicy" or "juice drink" in the name to fool the consumer. It is important to read the label to know what you are really buying.

UP IN THE SKY—LOOK! IT'S SUPER NECTAR

Super Nectars are now being sold in health food stores. These drinks provide a 100 percent fruit blend drink with different herbs and may contain up to 100 per-

cent of the RDA of at least 8 different vitamins. These juices may contain chi'i
green tea, high levels of vitamin C, red
guarana, ginkgo biloba, or high protein
levels. All are healthy drinks and are a
good alternative to soda pop.

COMMON TYPES OF GRAIN AND VEGGIE JUICES

ALFALFA JUICE

Alfalfa juice is very rich in chlorophyll and is traditionally used to increase resistance to infections. It is very strong and is best when mixed with a compatible
juice such as carrot and/or celery juice. In fact, the combination of all three has
been used to strengthen the roots of hair. Alfalfa juice also contains saponin, a
compound found in a number of herbs and grasses that may have a cleansing ability on the plaque deposits on the walls of the arteries.

ASPARAGUS JUICE

This juice contains an alkaloid known as asparagine, without which a plant cannot grow or even remain alive. Cooking or canning asparagus kills the alkaloid
but when juiced, the alkaloid remains active. Asparagus juice has been used historically as a diuretic and is usually recommended in combination with other
juices, since it is fairly harsh on the system. It is a milder and more potent diuretic if combined with carrot juice.

AVOCADO JUICE

This juice was used by the Mayans to keep their joints moving freely and to eliminate diseases related to the joints such as rheumatism and arthritis. These diseases were unheard of in their culture as long as they consumed avocados. The
juice may also lower total cholesterol while raising HDL. Hardening of the arteries was also not a problem for the Mayans and many South Americans who are
lucky enough to have avocado trees on their property.

BEET JUICE

In small quantities this juice was used traditionally as a blood cleanser. Both the
roots and tops may be used; however, a first-time user should mix the juice with
carrot juice and use more carrot juice than beet juice. The combination of the beet

juice with carrot juice and coconut juice will provide a drink that has been used as a kidney and gallbladder cleanser. Cucumber juice may be substituted for coconut juice.

BARLEY GRASS/WHEAT GRASS JUICES

Wheat grass is used only when it is in a young growth stage, while barley grass should mature to a point when it develops stems. It is at this point that the grasses have their highest level of available nutrients and are high in calcium, phosphorus, potassium, and magnesium salts. The juice from these grains has been used to treat liver disorders, cleanse organs of drugs, increase energy levels, and improve the efficiency of the immune system.

BRUSSELS SPROUTS JUICE

Historically, brussels sprouts juice was consumed to help the pancreas regenerate cells that produce insulin. Before insulin injections, this juice was one of the only treatments available. When combined with carrot, string bean, and lettuce juice, it tends to be more effective.

CABBAGE JUICE

Cabbage juice has been implicated in intestinal gas production, causing many people to shy away from drinking it. However, the gas formation may be due to excess putrefied matter on the walls of the intestines that became loosened by the juice. Cabbage juice has a high sulfur and chlorine content plus a good level of iodine, all of which provide a cleansing effect on the stomach walls and may possibly be effective in duodenal ulcers. Sauerkraut juice, because of its high lactic acid content, has a soothing effect on the intestinal tract.

CARROT JUICE

Just a 6-ounce serving of carrot juice contains more than 400 percent of the RDA for vitamin A and is a good source of vitamin B6. Carrot juice would make an excellent alcohol chaser since vitamin B6 is destroyed by alcohol. Carrot juice has been used as a body tonic for many years and was especially used by nursing mothers to improve the quality of their milk. It has even been used to reduce the incidence of cancer.

The carotene that gives carrot juice its orange color is one of the leading antioxidants in today's studies regarding cancer. Through the use of the latest electron microscopes, it has become evident that there is a relationship between the human blood molecule and the carrot molecule, which may account for the juice's beneficial effects on a number of human ailments.

CELERY JUICE

Celery juice contains a high percentage of organic sodium (the good salt) that is needed to assist calcium in more efficient utilization. It may even have a protective effect from a number of other chemicals, such as oxalic acid, that tend to cause calcium to be excreted prematurely. Table salt is composed of inorganic, insoluble elements, which are not beneficial to the body. Celery juice has been used as a nerve tonic and may have a beneficial effect on the nervous system. Celery juice has also been suggested to relieve attention deficit disorder in children.

CUCUMBER JUICE

This juice is one of the best-known diuretics in the vegetable family. It was used long before diuretics to promote natural urine flow. Its high silicon and sulfur contents have been related to hair growth, which is enhanced by adding carrot juice to the cucumber juice. Cucumber juice has also been used effectively on poison ivy and poison oak rashes to alleviate the symptoms. Sunburns can also be relieved to a degree with an application of cucumber juice.

DANDELION JUICE

This juice is high in magnesium and iron and was used to prevent a number of bone disorders, especially osteoporosis. The juice has also been known to improve lung function.

ENDIVE JUICE

Endive is a relative of lettuce and dandelion and may be called chicory or escarole. The juice is normally used as an additive to other juices, such as carrot or celery, and to improve the function of the muscular and nervous systems. It also may have a significant beneficial effect on the health of the eye and the optic nerve in particular.

FENNEL JUICE

The only variety of fennel that is suitable to be juiced is the florence or finocchio fennel. The sweet garden-variety fennel is not suited for juicing. The florence fennel is a member of the celery family and has been used as a blood builder, especially during menstrual periods.

GARLIC JUICE

Garlic juice is high in mustard oils and has been used as a blood cleanser for hundreds of years. It has also been used effectively to rid the body of parasites. Garlic juice should not be made in a juicer since it will take days to get rid of the aroma.

LETTUCE JUICE

Iceberg lettuce can be used for juicing because even though it has a high water content, it still contains a number of minerals, such as iron and magnesium. The juice assures the liver and spleen of an ample supply to produce new red blood cells. In World War II lactucarium, an extract from lettuce, was used to relieve pain and also as a cough suppressant.

PARSLEY JUICE

Parsley, considered an herb, makes for one of the most potent juices and should always be mixed with other juices for the most beneficial results. Carrot, celery, or lettuce juices are the most common mixers. Parsley juice is related to thyroid and adrenal function and healthy arteries. Drinking too much pure juice may adversely affect the nervous system.

PEA JUICE

This juice, when prepared similar to soup, has been known to relieve the painful symptoms of irritable bowel syndrome. Common garden peas need to be juiced and warmed with a pinch of powdered cardamom and ginger root for added flavor.

POTATO JUICE

The juice of raw potatoes has been used to clear up a number of skin disorders and blemishes. Never use a potato that has a green tint since it may have a high solanine content, which is a chemical that humans should never consume. In fact, even consuming a greenish potato may affect the nerves that control the sexual organs. A sweet potato has more beneficial qualities than a standard Idaho or Irish potato.

SPINACH JUICE

An excellent cleansing juice for the intestinal tract, spinach juice has the ability to relieve constipation almost as well as prune juice and has a positive effect on the teeth and gums. Spinach is best raw and should not be consumed cooked if at all possible. Cooked spinach releases a level of oxalic acid crystals that may not be beneficial to the body and can affect proper utilization of calcium. The oxalic acid crystals become inorganic when heated and may form the crystals in the kidneys.

TOMATO JUICE

A 6-ounce glass will provide you with a good supply of vitamins A and C and folate. It's best to purchase the low-sodium variety. If you have an allergy to aspirin, you may have to avoid tomato juice since it also contains salicylate. It is an excellent tonic to keep your metabolism working at a healthy level. When tomatoes are cooked a number of the beneficial elements change to the inorganic form and are not healthy. Kidney and bladder stones may be the result of consuming a diet high in cooked tomato products.

STRING BEAN JUICE

This juice may assist the pancreas in the production of insulin by keeping the cells healthy. This is an excellent vegetable to mix with other juices to enhance the overall benefits.

TURNIP JUICE

The leaves as well as the root should be used since turnips contain a high level of calcium. The potassium content of the leaves is also high, and the juice has been used for growing children and people who may be at risk of osteoporosis. Turnip juice in combination with spinach, carrot, and watercress juice has been reported to alleviate hemorrhoids.

WATERCRESS JUICE

This is a high sulfur drink that includes a number of minerals and salts, which make the drink an effective intestinal cleanser. Because it is so powerful it should never be consumed without the addition of other juices, such as carrot, spinach, and lettuce juice.

NUTRITIONAL INFORMATION

THE CABBAGE SOUP DIET

This is a diet program that took guts for someone to even print and sell. The diet consists of consuming nothing but soup made from cabbage, onions, peppers, tomatoes, and celery. This is basically all you eat for a week. Anybody will lose weight; however, this will be a result of mostly water loss. After a few days you may experience gas, nausea, and even lightheadedness.

THE MINIMUM IS A LOT

If you consumed just 16 ounces of fresh vegetable juice each day, you would receive the same level of vitamins, minerals, and enzymes found in two very large vegetable salads. The enzymes in the vegetable juices will assist the body in metabolizing and absorbing the nutrients in almost all foods consumed.

JUICING

This is one of the most efficient methods of adding vitamins and mineral to your diet. While it is possible to eat only a limited quantity of fruits and vegetables without overfilling yourself, juice, which contains a large percentage of the nutrients, is more easily consumed and allows the nutrients to be more easily absorbed.

By assisting your body in breaking down the cell walls in fruits and vegetables you allow more of the nutrients to be utilized. Fruits and vegetables are now being studied more than ever before to unlock the secrets of the phytochemicals they contain. There are more than 100,000 of these phytochemicals (also called phytonutrients) that may be instrumental in reducing the risk of many diseases, including cancer. Juicing provides you with more of these special nutrients than any other source.

HELP! I'M LOSING MY FIBER

We all worry about not getting the fiber from the fruits and vegetables when we juice. However, juice contains a good percentage of fiber, though you will still need to eat foods rich in fiber if you are drinking healthy juices. Juices are one of the best sources of fresh, natural nutrients in a quantity that most people never get.

HOW MUCH IS ENOUGH?

Most nutritionists recommend drinking two to three glasses of a combination natural juice drink every day to maximize your nutrient intake. It is recommended that the majority of the juice be from vegetables, which will contain less sugar.

JUICING TIPS FOR THE BEGINNER

• If possible, use organically grown produce. There is always the possibility of fertilizer or pesticide contamination.
• Wash all produce—even organically grown produce—with a good organic cleaner and remove any damaged areas.
• Many fruits and vegetable skins and greens are not good candidates for juicing.
• Remove all pits and seeds.
• Some stems and leaves are acceptable, especially those from red grapes.
• Cut all produce into workable pieces to make it easier on your juicer.
• Mix produce with a smaller liquid content for a more drinkable juice cocktail.

KNOW YOUR FRUITS AND VEGETABLES

Some people think that you can just throw any fruit or vegetable into the juicer and come out with a healthy drink. Not true! If you are going to juice, I suggest you buy a book that tells you how to juice before starting. It is not healthy to eat too much of the skins of oranges and grapefruits. Apple and apricot seeds contain a small amount of cyanide. Rhubarb and carrot greens may also be toxic. Celery leaves are just too bitter...I think you get the idea.

JUICE GLOSSARY

100 PERCENT PURE/100 PERCENT JUICE

If the label has either one of these percentage terms, the product must contain 100 percent of that juice. There can be no sweeteners or water added—just the juice from the fruit.

ACEROLA

A red berry found in the West Indies known to be one of the richest sources of vitamin C.

ENZYMES

Complex substances found in fresh fruits and vegetables that assist the body in breaking down and utilizing nutrients.

CANNED JUICE

Common juices such as orange and grapefruit juices that are pasteurized and sealed in cans. This gives the product a shelf life of at least a year. Once opened, these juices should be refrigerated and have a life of only about one week.

CHILLED, READY TO SERVE

Normally found in the dairy section of the supermarket and prepared from frozen concentrate.

FRESHLY SQUEEZED JUICE

A fresh product that has not been pasteurized and is kept cold until purchased.

FROZEN CONCENTRATE

Fresh juice that has most of the water removed and has been frozen. When reconstituted, the water is added back in.

GINKGO

The ginkgo biloba tree can live as long as one thousand years and reach heights of more than 100 feet. The Chinese have used its extracts for medicinal purposes for hundreds of years. Historically, it has been used to improve oxygen flow in the body.

N.F.

Stands for natural flavors.

NFC

Stands for not from concentrate.

SHELF JUICE

Juice that is found on the shelf in paper or bottle containers and not under refrigeration. It has been pasteurized and may be made from concentrate. The containers are sterilized and the juice has an excellent shelf life.

W.O.J.C.

Stands for with other juice concentrates.

Chapter 7
Liquid Nutritional Products

DIET DRINKS

The liquid and powder diet drinks on the market are for the most part formulated with a milk, soy, or grain derivative as the main ingredient. Many companies now use glucomannan, an appetite suppressant, in their products, herbs, tea extracts, enzymes, vitamins, minerals, and free amino acids. Some of the more popular products will be mentioned along with some of their claims. While most of these are high-quality products that contain good ingredients, after practicing weight control for twenty-three years, I have not found any product that was effective for any length of time without a good structured program of exercise, nutrition education, stress management, and behavior modification.

BE TRIM TOO

This is a concentrated product in liquid form. Just a few drops are placed in a glass of water or juice. The ingredients are herbs, vitamins, minerals, and enzymes. This company also sells a product that claims to assist the body in metabolizing stored body fat while you sleep and contains L-carnitine, amino acids, green tea, atractylodes extract, B vitamins, choline, and chromium picolinate.

CRAVE CURE

This drink is being sold as a diet drink and a general nutrition drink since it contains numerous vitamins, minerals, grain derivatives, and amino acids as well as an appetite suppressant. Also referred to as an energy drink, it is recommended for breakfast or lunch. It is a nutritionally sound drink, and if it were a component of a structured weight program, it would get my nod.

FORM YOU 3

This is a meal replacement drink that is sold in a variety of flavors and contains soy protein isolate, folic acid, and twenty-five additional vitamins and minerals. Low-fat and lactose-free, it is sold in packets and can be mixed with water or juice.

MAXIMUM FAT BURNER LIQUID ENERGY

This is a highly concentrated liquid fat burner product that contains L-carnitine, choline, inositol, vitamin B6, 10 grams of carbohydrates, and chromium picolinate.

PERFECT SUPER RIPPED

This is one of a number of beverages sold using the Perfect brand name. The company claims that there are many "fake fat burning drinks" on the market and is quick to display their own formulation as the best and one of the "real" ones. The drink contains 3 milligrams of ephedra from Ma Huang (a low-potency stimulant), 2 milligrams of chitosan (a fat absorber), 1 milligram of white willow bark, 250 milligrams of L-carnitine, and 100 milligrams of caffeine. Chitosan is usually derived from the exoskeleton of shellfish, and there is not one double-blind study that I am aware of that relates the compound to increasing fat metabolism in humans.

SLIM-SLIM

One of this company's weight management products is called Total Toddy, which contains seven major minerals, up to sixty-five trace minerals in liquid bioelectrical organic form from plants, sixteen vitamins, nineteen amino acids, and phytonutrients from vegetables and fruits. The company claims that the product is 98 percent absorbable. Other products include Ultra Body Toddy and Slim-Slim Metabolic Fuel.

LIQUID L-CARNITINE 1000

Sold as a "high-potency fast-absorbing" source of L-carnitine, it is composed of L-carnitine, filtered water, vegetable glycerine, and B vitamins to assist in the absorption of the L-carnitine.

COLLOIDAL MINERALS

A colloid is a substance that is able to retain its identity when placed into a liquid and stay in suspension without falling to the bottom of the bottle. Collidos are extremely small particles that are easily absorbed into the cells. Quality colloidal products are produced from special ancient soils called humic shale. The minerals are extracted and processed, then separated into the minerals that are the most beneficial to human health—minerals for the most part that we are deficient in.

Colloidal minerals can be 98 percent absorbed, and claims are made that they will eliminate "nutritional fatigue" in most individuals. They also tend to be easily transported to the cells for utilization. Claims are also being made that colloidal minerals provide natural cleansing and detoxifying for the body.

HI HO SILVER—COLLOIDAL THAT IS

Silver is now being sold in liquid form since studies show that we may be deficient due to lack of this trace mineral in the soil. A number of farmers are now adding silver to the fertilizers. While it is present in the body only in small amounts, silver may be beneficial to a number of body functions. Products should be sold only with concentrations of 10 parts per million or less to be on the safe side.

LIQUID VITAMINS

One of the most common questions asked of nutritionists is whether it is best to obtain your vitamins from solid foods or liquids. The answer is that as long as your digestive system is functioning normally, it really doesn't make any difference. Vitamins are vitamins, and the body will metabolize both food and liquid in the same manner. Many companies claim that liquid vitamins are more easily absorbed; while this is true, there is also more risk of the liquid vitamins being destroyed by stomach enzymes and acids.

SQUIRT YOUR VITAMINS

The latest method of taking your daily dose of vitamins is a spray mist, which is sprayed under the tongue and has a higher absorption rate than many tablet vitamin products. The companies selling the product claims that the absorption rate is as high as 90 percent, while tablets may only provide a 10 percent absorption rate.

TODDIES

Most toddy products sold contain vitamins in liquid form and a number of herbs that are related to blood cleansing and are frequently associated with claims of recuperative benefits. Some toddy products incorporate food-grade hydrogen peroxide into their drinks as well as colloidal minerals. The number of different toddy products sold is increasing every day, since the public seems to prefer a flavored drink to a tablet.

HAVE A SHOT OF COD LIVER OIL

Cod liver oil is a good source of omega-3 fatty acids and a lot less expensive than the omega-3 nutritional supplements being sold. However, you may want to flavor it and thin it out somewhat. On second thought, keep taking the ampoules.

NUTRITIONAL INFORMATION

SARSAPARILLA ROOT EXTRACT

This extract is now being sold as a quickly absorbed herb that has the ability to increase the body's production of testosterone. It claims to enhance athletic performance.

NEW ANTI-IMPOTENCE LIQUID

A new dietary supplement called ArginMax has been released that can be taken in liquid form for the enhancement of male sexual performance. The product has been studied by the University of Hawaii and Albany Medical College and found to be 89 percent effective. ArginMax is supposed to increase the product ion of nitric oxide, which is a critical factor in the enhancement of male sexual intercourse.

CALCIUM CHECK

If you are curious whether your calcium supplement is of a good quality, try placing a tablet in vinegar. If the tablet dissolves completely within eight minutes, it is a good quality product. The government allows fifteen to thirty minutes for vitamins.

THE GREEN LIQUID

Chlorophyll is not available in liquid form as a nutritional supplement. Companies that market the product state that the product can be taken as a blood cleanser and will increase the production of hemoglobin, strengthen cells, improve immune system response, and act as an overall body deodorizer.

CAN YOU POWER UP WITH LIQUID CREATINE?

The products that are sold are actually creatine monohydrate and are being marketed as the "most effective sports supplement ever sold." Creatine is reported to allow the body to work harder and longer without tiring and is used by body builders worldwide and many sports teams. It is not a steroid, and from all indications to date, the chemical is safe. The liquid form tends to be effective in a shorter period of time and is recommended for those in a hurry for the effects to kick in.

HOW STABLE ARE VITAMINS IN BEVERAGES?

○ VITAMIN A

May be damaged by oxygen, heat, metal ions, and ultraviolet light. Health drinks that add vitamin A should have a warning regarding these factors. The bottles should be a dark color.

○ VITAMIN B1

Can be damaged at a pH of 6 or over, which means that the more basic the liquid, the more damage will be done. Exposure to heat and oxygen will also take their toll.

○ VITAMIN B2

Can easily be damaged by light in liquids but not in dry products. Bases will also damage B2 since they prefer a somewhat acid environment.

○ NIACIN

A very stable vitamin that is almost impossible to destroy.

○ VITAMIN B6

Usually very stable in most beverages.

○ **VITAMIN B12**

Can be destroyed by sunlight and prefers a pH of 4 to 5.

○ **PANTOTHENIC ACID**

May be destroyed in an acidic environment.

○ **VITAMIN E**

Usually stable, unless the beverage is basic in nature.

○ **VITAMIN C**

Easily destroyed by oxidation. The potency is reduced if it comes into contact with iron or copper. Heat will also adversely affect vitamin C.

○ **VITAMIN D**

Can be damaged by light, heat, and oxygen.

SUPER FOODS

A number of drinks are now calling themselves "super foods." These drinks are led by the Naked brand of beverages and contain a variety of fruit juices mixed with everything from royal jelly to spirulina to spinach to broccoli. If you don't want pure juice, this is one of the better substitutes.

SPORTS DRINKS

Current literature regarding sports drinks all come to the same conclusion that unless you are performing a strenuous sports activity or exercising for more than one hour, there is no need for a special drink other than water. Sports drinks may be beneficial under certain conditions. You can make your own by mixing 1 quart of orange juice with 1 quart of water, then adding 1½ teaspoons of salt.

Most of these drinks are sold to body builders and athletes, the target market. The majority of the drinks are healthy, but it is questionable how effective these drinks really are, since there are few if any good double-blind studies to support the claims. The drinks are harmless and do supply a number of nutrients that may replace ones that are depleted through strenuous exercise or sports activities.

ALOE VERA DRINK

This is a natural health/sports drink that is composed of aloe vera (no aloin), vitamins, minerals, and amino acids.

POWERADE®

This drink is supposed to have more electrolytes and carbohydrate content than Gatorade. It is manufactured by Coca-Cola, and I am sure the company will take its name off this product if it is still on the market when this book is printed. The drink looks like green water and is supposed to be a lemon-lime drink, but it has almost no flavor at all.

PRO COMPLEX ® "THE DRINK"

This is produced for athletes and contains 40 grams of whey protein isolate and 2 grams of carbohydrates. Claims are made that you will get a faster recovery and "pack on lean muscle" with this drink.

PRO-LIFE®

This is a combination of lemon, lime, and orange juice with a large number of micronutrients. It also includes 5 grams of soluble fiber. The taste is excellent.

GATORADE®

Gatorade is now owned by the Quaker Oats Company. The University of Florida developed Gatorade in 1965 for the Florida Gators football team. The formula is supposed to help prevent dehydration, replace electrolytes (especially sodium), and supply carbohydrates. Supplying these needed nutrients during strenuous exercise periods has proved to be only somewhat beneficial. Gatorade is one of the better-quality, good-tasting drinks in this category.

In 1998 Gatorade sold $200 million of its new Frost line of drinks, which included Whitewater, Splash, and Alpine Snow.

ULTIMATE ORANGE®

This has been sold as a sports drink since 1982. Ultimate Orange is recommended to be consumed before and after training to increase and renew energy supplies, respectively. It is mixed with water and contains Ma Huang, guarana seed, green tea, ginseng, bioflavenoids, omega-3 fatty acids, xylitol, natural flavors, lecithin, cellulose gum, and food coloring. It's one of the better sports drinks.

RATINGS OF SPORTS DRINKS

The following sports drinks were rated on the number of calories, carbohydrate content, level of sodium and potassium, cost per container, and cost per 8-ounce serving.

1. 10-K
2. All Sport
3. All Sport Lite
4. Exceed (liquid and powder)
5. Gatorade (liquid and powder)
6. Gatorade Lite
7. Hydra Fuel (liquid and powder)
8. Nautilus Plus
9. Powerade
10. Snapple Snap-Up

Source: Consumer Reports

ENERGY DRINKS AND GELS

Since it is possible to review only a limited number of energy drinks, I have chosen some of the more popular ones on the market. Many of these beverages use guarana and caffeine in combination to produce temporary mood elevation and a state of being wide awake. People tend to confuse the state of not being tired with increased energy levels, which is really not the case. High caffeine levels in these drinks will cause an addiction similar to coffee addiction in many susceptible individuals if they consume enough of the product on a regular basis.

BATTERY ENERGY DRINK®

This is yet another guarana and caffeine (136 milligrams per can) powered drink. It has a somewhat bitter taste, probably due to the high caffeine content and citrus base. Drink one can thirty minutes with 8 ounces of water.

Consuming high-carbohydrate foods just before a strenuous exercise period may accomplish the same as the gel. Gels are recommended for athletes who work out or perform a sport for more than 2 hours. The gels are not recommended for postexercise recovery; a combination of protein and carbohydrates will resupply the lost glycogen faster.

GUTS®

This is a relatively new product that utilizes guarana fruit extract as the main flavoring. The extract used is 100 percent organic, and the product has no chemical substances from the extraction processing. Guts was the first energizing carbonated soft drink in North America.

DYNAMITE ENERGY DRINK®

Sold in 8.4-ounce cans, the drink contains vitamins, minerals, and a small amount of caffeine and taurine. It has a somewhat sweet, berrylike taste and is a good thirst quencher.

GINSENG ENHANCED WATER

A number of companies are now selling ginseng water as an energy enhancing drink. Normally sold in capsule form, ginseng has been used to increase energy levels for hundreds of years. Ginseng that has been diluted with water may not have adequate potency and should be studied further before any claims are made.

PERFECT TNTEA®

This is a 0-calorie tea that claims to increase energy levels. The ingredients include guarana, bee pollen, gotu kola, Citrimax®, and cayenne. It is sweetened with aspartame.

POWER UP®

This is an energy drink composed of skim milk, water, sugar, skim milk powder, corn oil, gum arabic, sodium caseinate, maltodextrin, emulsifier, flavorings, vitamins, minerals, carotene for color, and stabilizers. It is sold only as an energy drink.

SOBE ENERGY®

This is basically a sugar-water drink with a few herbs, such as guarana and yohimbe, added for energy.

REBEL ACTIVE®

This is another guarana beverage with a high caffeine content. The drink is made from orange, pineapple, lime, and passion fruit. It does contain a number of vitamins and minerals but is a somewhat overpowering drink.

THE BLUE PIG®

This energy drink is lightly carbonated and has a somewhat sweet flavor. This is a potent beverage containing guarana, caffeine, and a large number of vitamins and minerals. The drink also bills itself as a dietary supplement due to its high nutrient levels. The taste is only fair and it comes across as a somewhat strong drink.

XTC—GUARANA POWER DRINK®

This is a very carbonated, powerful drink that may not be recommended for young children or diabetics. It has a slightly bitter taste and a high level of caffeine. Drink one can and you should not fall asleep for some time.

LIQUID SPRAYS

A number of all-natural homeopathic sprays are now available through distributors nationwide. These sprays are formulated from a number of all-natural ingredients and homeopathic nutritional extracts. They are sprayed under the tongue and therefore can be absorbed and utilized very quickly. There are studies that show the efficacy of these products, and more studies should be surfacing in the next year or two that will relate to larger population studies and positive results in a good percentage of the population.

Liquid sprays have almost no side effects, unlike conventional pharmaceuticals, which make them an excellent alternative form of medicinal product. All products are sold in 2-ounce spray bottles (not aerosol) with an expiration date and a list of ingredients. These products would make a great natural addition to the family medicine cabinet. The ingredient names are homeopathic tongue twisters, so they will not be included here.

These products should be used only for specific medical problems after consulting with your family physician:

- Headache Relief
- PMS Relief
- Children's Cough
- Overly Active Children & Learning Formula
- Colds & Flu
- Muscle & Joint Injury
- Artery/Cholesterol/Blood Pressure

- Allergy & Hay Fever
- Menopause
- Sinus Relief
- Arthritis Symptom Reliever
- 911 Stress & Anxiety Formula

GENERAL NUTRITIONAL DRINKS

There are a number of drinks on the market, and more appear almost daily. This category includes drinks such as Ensure®, Sustain®, Boost®, and Resource®. They all contain different formulations but for the most part all contain water, sugar, oils, milk or milk derivatives, vitamins, and minerals. Some now contain herbs. Sales of Ensure in the United States in 1998 were about $325 million out of these drinks' estimated total sales of $700 million.

These drinks are not a replacement for a meal but offer a level of additional nutrition, especially to those who find it difficult to eat properly on certain days or have medical problems that affect their absorption of nutrients in whole foods.

ENSURE

In an 8-ounce serving, Ensure has 250 calories, 6.1 grams of fat (22 percent of the total calories), 40 grams of carbohydrates, and 8.8 grams of protein. It costs about $1.65 per serving and is one of the better-quality drinks.

NUTRITIONAL INFORMATION

THE CURE FOR SEA SICKNESS

Ginger has been used for hundreds of years to alleviate seasickness and does work when taking the capsules. A new beverage, Sailor's Ginger Delight, claims to have the answer to seasickness. If the claims are true, this is an easy way to cure a miserable problem. The drink is a sparkling beverage that tastes like tropical passion fruit and ginger. It contains no artificial flavors, caffeine, or sodium and gets very high marks in the taste category.

NEW TEST FOR MINERAL CONTENT

There is a new piece of equipment available to the general public that will evaluate the mineral content of solid foods and liquids. The Meridian Liquid & Food

Tester sells for $79.95; further information can be obtained by calling (313) 272-3045.

TAKING AN IRON SUPPLEMENT? DON'T TAKE IT WITH TEA

Studies show that taking an iron supplement with tea may block your body's ability to absorb the maximum amount available.

Chapter 8
Tea

A BRIEF HISTORY OF TEA

Tea was probably first consumed in China around 2737 B.C. when Chinese emperor Shen Nung was boiling his drinking water and some leaves from the *Camellia sinensis* plant accidentally dropped into his pot. The tea leaf was then commonly used to flavor water, which had a somewhat "off" taste after being boiled to purify it. The Emperor felt that the new beverage gave him added energy and called the new beverage the "vigor of the body."

Tea was introduced to Japan by the Chinese and was immediately hailed as a beverage of choice. Presently, the island of Ceylon is the world's leading grower of quality tea. The tea is still picked by hand; an experienced picker is capable of picking 35 to 40 pounds of tea leaves per day.

The most popular tea in the United States is black tea, with imports reaching about 154 million pounds in 1998. The annual consumption in the United States is now more than 47 billion servings, with the majority of the tea being imported from India.

Iced tea, an American favorite, was first introduced at the Louisiana Purchase Exposition held in St. Louis in 1904.

MAJOR VARIETIES OF TEAS

GREEN TEA

Green tea is produced mainly in China, Japan, India, and Taiwan. Green is the natural color of green tea since oxidation does not affect the chlorophyll content of the tea leaf and the tea is not fermented. The manufacturing process has only three stages. First, the tea leaf is steamed to inactivate the enzymes and prevent fermentation and oxidation. Second, the leaves are rolled and dried until they are crisp. This releases the juices, which are held by the leaf. Third, repeated controlled firings produce a stable, well-hardened tea that has retained its flavor and essential elements. The final product contains only 3 percent residual moisture and therefore is incapable of any further changes.

Chinese green teas are graded by age and style, with the finest being gunpowder produced from tiny balls that are made from very young or at least moderately aged leaves. The next best is called young hyson, and then imperial. The quality of Japanese green tea is graded as follows: extra choicest, choicest, choice, finest, fine, good medium, good common, nibs, fanning, and dust. Indian green tea is graded as follows: fine young hyson, young hyson, hyson number one, twankay, sowmee, fanning, and dust. The ***Encyclopedia of Chinese Teas*** lists 138 different varieties of green teas and 12,500 subgroups. However, only about five hundred varieties are really recognized.

CHINESE GREEN TEAS

Pouchong

Used frequently to prepare jasmine tea. The leaves are oxidized to a greater extent than most green tea leaves, which allows them to retain the flavor of jasmine better. The jasmine flower has been imported from Persia for one thousand years to flavor the tea.

Ching Cha

This variety is grown in mainland China and includes some of the more famous and best-tasting green teas, such as pi lo chun and tai ping hou gui.

Chunmee

Grown in the province of Yunnan, with a somewhat plum flavor. Care needs to be taken so as not to overbrew, which is easily done.

Dragonwell

This is one of the favorite teas of mainland China, with a sweet, fresh taste. There are eight grades of dragonwell, the highest being qing ming.

Emerald Tips

A dragonwell type of tea grown in an area that borders the Dragonwell growing area. Though not quite as good as dragonwell, this is still a good quality tea.

Gunpowder

The first tea ever exported from China to Europe and the most popular Chinese tea in Europe. If the tea "pellets" are fresh, they will resist pressure and not easily crush.

INDIAN GREEN TEAS

Assam

The most plentiful tea in India, accounting for one-third of all tea produced. The tea is grown to produce a strong aroma and flavor; only a small quantity is grown for green tea.

Darjeeling

This tea is grown on the southern slopes of the Himalayan Mountains near Nepal. This variety has been called the champagne of teas. However, very little of the tea is produced as green tea. If you are lucky enough to find "single-estate" Darjeeling green tea, you will enjoy an unusual cup of tea.

JAPANESE GREEN TEAS

Bancha

The most common tea sold in Japan. The green bancha is actually somewhat bitter and not one of the better green teas.

Fukuiju

A higher-quality green tea with a pleasant aftertaste.

Gyokuro

The highest-quality green tea produced in Japan. Very fragrant and flavorful, it is sometimes mixed with lower-grade teas to enhance their flavor and aroma.

Spiderleg

Another high-quality green tea that has an excellent aroma and flavor. Occasionally has a cherry aroma.

BLACK TEA

During the processing of tea leaves, the insides are exposed to oxygen, which causes oxidation and the darkening of the resulting tea. The actual steps involved are withering, rolling, roll breaking, fermenting, and firing. The withering process involves spreading the leaves on long tables and allowing them to remain for eighteen to twenty-four hours. In India the climate is so dry that the leaves will actually wither on the vine. Natural withering is preferred so that the leaf is never overheated. The leaf is then rolled, which breaks up the plant's cells to release the juices and enzymes, producing the flavor of the tea. However, when the leaves are rolled they may become twisted and balled up and may need to go through a roll-breaking process of vibrating the leaves. Fermentation is then introduced to the crushed leaves and the flavor process is completed. The final stage is the firing, which stops the fermentation process and further oxidation by totally destroying the enzymes and bacteria.

The most common tea sold in the United States is black tea. Black teas are sometimes called red teas since their color is more reddish than black. The Chinese rarely drink black teas. (Green teas are their first choice, with oolong coming in second.) There are more than forty varieties of black teas, with the best coming from Sri Lanka, China, and India.

OOLONG TEA

This type of tea is only partially fermented and is a blend of black and green teas. It has a greenish-brown color and is usually grown in Taiwan and sold as Formosa oolong tea. One variety of oolong teas is pouchong and is mixed with gardenia blossoms or jasmine flowers. Grades of oolong teas are really a mouthful: choice, finest to choice, finest, fine to finest, superior, on superior, good to superior, good up, fully good, good, on good, and standard.

MAJOR TEA-PRODUCING COUNTRIES

CHINA

China produces about 350 million pounds of tea annually in the form of green, black, oolong, and brick teas. The first plucking which is the finest, is called show-chun. Most Chinese tea is a high- quality tea.

INDIA

India produces about 1 billion pounds of tea annually on 900,000 acres. Since each Indian consumes about 1 pound of tea annually, India exports only about 50 percent of its tea. The United Kingdom purchases about 150 million pounds, while the United States buys only about 17 million pounds. Almost all the tea grown in India is manufactured as black tea.

JAPAN

The third largest tea producer, Japan manufactures about 200 million pounds annually. Almost all of the tea is green tea, and very little is exported since the Japanese are big tea drinkers. The finest Japanese teas are grown in the district of Yamashiro.

INDONESIA

The fourth largest tea producer, Indonesia manufactures about 170 million pounds of tea annually. More than 75 percent of the tea is grown in Java and the balance in Sumatra. Most Indonesian teas are used for blends and are black teas.

SRI LANKA

Black tea is the most common tea produced in Sri Lanka, where more than 500 million pounds is produced annually from 500,000 acres. Sri Lanka exports more than 400 million pounds, with about 400,000 pounds going to the United States. If the tea is imported from Ceylon it will usually have a stamp stating that it was grown there. The color of most Celanese teas is a reddish-brown and most are of excellent quality.

TAIWAN

Taiwan produces about 65 million pounds of green, black, and oolong teas annually, with 85 percent of their crop being exported. Formosa oolong tea is a popular, excellent-quality tea sold in the United States. The tea is grown only on the northern tip of the island and is processed with great care.

BOTTLED AND CANNED TEAS

In supermarkets and health food stores, tea is sold in bottles and cans with the addition of a number of herbs. These drinks are being sold as energy and sports drinks or supplement drinks using the various types of teas as their base. Many are high in sugar and contain preservatives and artificial coloring agents similar to soda water; it would be best to choose the all-natural beverages. Since there are hundreds of different teas presently on the market, we will only discuss a few.

MAD RIVER TEAS

One of this company's popular teas blends ginseng and ginkgo biloba, two energy-providing herbs that have also been related to providing people with a sharper mental alertness. Other teas sold by this company include green tea with lemon, oolong tea with honey, and red tea with guarana. All utilize pure cane sugar to enhance the taste and are infused with significant amounts of *Echinacea purpurea* to improve natural resistance to disease. No preservatives or artificial ingredients are used in the teas, which are some of the premium teas on the market.

BREWING METHODS

HOT, HOT, HOT

According to tea experts on two continents, green teas should be brewed between 180 and 200°F; oolong teas should be brewed between 185 and 205°F; and black teas should be brewed between 190 and 210°F.

The better-quality teas should be brewed at a lower temperature since they will release their flavor more readily.

BREWING LIKE YOU KNOW WHAT YOU'RE DOING

The following steps will lead you through the process of making the perfect cup of tea.

1. Use the best grade of tea that you enjoy.
2. Use pure, quality cold water and bring it to a top boil. Only use the water when it is bubbling rapidly. Never use water from a hot-water under-the-sink unit.
3. Rinse the teapot with the hottest water possible or use boiling water. The teapot should be warm before you add the tea.
4. When pouring the boiling water into the teapot, take the kettle to the teapot to assure that the water will be as hot as possible.
5. Brew the tea for three to five minutes depending on your taste and the type of tea. Most teas should never be brewed for more than five minutes.
6. Make sure that the tea is kept as hot as possible as it is brewing.
7. Always have a tea leaf strainer that is easily removable to eliminate the tea leaf residues. Always stir the tea after removing the infusion.
8. If the tea cools after you pour it, it would be best to brew another batch and not try to reheat it.

HOW TO MAKE A STRONG TEA

The problem most people have when trying to make a strong tea is that it usually turns out bitter. Never increase the steeping period; always add more tea leaves. The longer the leaves remain in the hot water, the more polyphenols are released, thus producing a bitter tea.

I'm A Strong Tea Leaf

TEAPOTS AND SUCH

One of the original teapots was more of a solo pot called a yixing (e-ching). These small pots can be found in all different shapes. They may be in the shape of a vegetable or flower and were made from red clay that was only found in the Yunnan province of mainland China. The Chinese used a pot for only one tea variety, which protected the pot from absorbing different flavors.

The red clay tended to hold the heat, keeping the flavor in and the tea hot for a long time. Since the clay did not conduct the heat well to the exterior of the pot, the outside was cooler and could be handled easily.

There are also small individual cups that are available in many different sizes and shapes. One of the more popular is the Chinese-style guywan cup, which has a lid to keep the tea hot while the infusion process is taking place.

A quality teapot is crucial to enjoying the full flavor of the tea. Someone who really enjoys tea will never place a tea bag in a cup of water and heat it in the microwave.

THE STEAMING LEAVES

The reason why you would keep a cover on a cup or pot of steeping tea may seem simply that it keeps the heat in. However, another very important reason is that it traps the steam and dampens any tea leaves that are floating on the top, thus extracting their flavor.

MINE ENEMIES ARE LIGHT AND HUMIDITY

Loose tea should always be stored in a cool, dry location. Humidity and heat will reduce the quality of the tea significantly. A sealed container works well, since it allows little oxygen to come into contact with the loose tea. Containers should be just large enough to hold the tea and opaque, since the light can have a negative effect as well. A large container will retain too much oxygen and may cause undue oxidation to take place. Tea bags should be kept in their original container.

CAFFEINE CONTENT

One pound of tea contains 205 milligrams of caffeine. The primary effects from the caffeine in tea last from fifteen to forty-five minutes depending on the individual's sensitivity to caffeine.

TEA (8 OUNCES)	AMOUNT OF CAFFEINE (MILLIGRAMS)
Green tea (five-minute brew)	35
Black tea (one-minute brew)	24
Black tea (three-minute brew)	41

TEA (8 OUNCES)	AMOUNT OF CAFFEINE (MILLIGRAMS)
Black tea (five-minute brew) 50	
Iced tea 34	
Instant tea 28	
Decaffeinated tea 10	

GROWING METHODS

The tea plant prefers a jungle climate with a continual level of heat and humidity at an elevation of 5,000 feet above sea level. The cool nights cause the plants to grow more slowly, making them richer in flavor. The evergreen tree variety can grow as high as 30 feet; however, the quality of the tea decreases with the size of the tree. Ideally the rainfall where the trees are grown should amount to about 100 inches per year.

Tea is presently grown on small green bushes that stand about 3 to 4 feet high, which take about two years to mature. Tea grows rapidly and can produce about thirty-five hundred bushels per acre. They are normally clipped flat on top, which gives them the appearance of a hedge. The new leaves and buds are cut from the top of the hedge and are then brought to the manufacturing plant to be withered, cured, dried, and packaged. Processing is performed at the site for the better-quality teas; the freshness is significantly higher than that of the blends sold in supermarkets.

Chef's Secret Green Tea Ice Cream

This is a favorite dessert in most Japanese restaurants in Japan as well as the United States. When preparing the ice cream, never use a metal spoon; only use a wooden one. Metal spoons should never be used since they tend to impart a poor taste to a number of foods.

1¼   teaspoons good-quality green tea leaves
1   cup pure water
5   fresh egg yolks
¾   cup granulated sugar
1   cup half-and-half or light cream
2   cups heavy cream
1½   teaspoons pure vanilla extract
½   teaspoon lemon zest, freshly grated
     Dash nutmeg, freshly ground

Brew the green tea leaves in the water for thirty minutes to extract the flavor. Remove the tea leaves and refrigerate in a covered dish.

In a medium saucepan, whisk the egg yolks until creamy. Add the sugar a small amount at a time while whisking slowly, then set aside.

In a small saucepan, mix the half-and-half with 1 cup of the heavy cream and stir with a wooden spoon. Cook the mixture over low heat until you see tiny bubbles forming around the edges of the saucepan. Reduce the heat and stir for 10 minutes.

Pour the hot cream mixture into the egg mixture very slowly to avoid curdling, and continue cooking over low heat. Stir the mixture continually until the mixture coats the back of the spoon. Slowly stir in the vanilla and allow the mixture to cool slightly, then pour it into a large glass bowl. Cover the bowl with plastic wrap and refrigerate for 4 hours.

Remove the bowl from the refrigerator and stir in the chilled tea liquor, zest, and nutmeg. Beat the remaining cup of heavy cream into stiff peaks, then stir into the chilled mixture. Place the mixture in an electric ice cream machine and freeze using the manufacturer's directions. Store the ice cream in a bowl with a piece of plastic wrap on top.

NUTRITIONAL INFORMATION

WHERE OH WHERE HAVE MY FLUIDS GONE

Tea has a diuretic effect on the body and should never be relied upon as a source of liquid.

TEA AND CHOCOLATE ARE NOT GOOD FOR FIDO

Tea contains theophylline and theobromine, two alkaloids that relax the smooth muscles, while caffeine stimulates the heart and respiratory systems. Theobromine is also found in chocolate in amounts that are high enough to kill a dog if it should ingest too much. If your dog got into a candy dish and shows symptoms of excessive thirst, nervousness, urinary incontinence, spasms, seizures, or diarrhea, take it to the vet immediately. Small amounts of chocolate are not dangerous, but it would be wise to never give a dog any. In humans, high dosages of theobromine tend to have a diuretic effect and stimulate the heart to beat faster.

HEALTH BENEFITS OF GREEN TEA

There are numerous studies and articles that have been written regarding the health benefits of drinking green tea. Green tea has been used as a medicine in China for more than four thousand years and was written about by the father of medicinal herbs, Shen-Nung. Recent literature has related green tea to lowering cholesterol, especially LDL, while increasing HDL. It has also been related to lowering blood pressure, acting as a blood thinner, lowering the risk of stroke, reducing the risk of cancer, prolonging life, improving the function of the immune system, and even preventing cavities.

The active ingredients in green tea are catechins, a powerful antioxidant family. This family includes epigallocatechin gallate, epigallocatechin, epicatechin gallate, epicatechin, and catechin. All are considered powerful antioxidants and free radical scavengers. The connection between these antioxidants and cancer is being investigated by a number of major universities. The effective amounts may be about ten cups per day, which is more than most of us will ever drink.

The M.D. Anderson Cancer Center in Houston and the Memorial Sloan-Kettering Cancer Center in New York are presently studying green tea extract for possible use in treatments.

HEALTH BENEFITS OF BLACK TEA

While a number of studies did not show any significant relationship between drinking black tea and disease prevention or cure, one study did show a positive correlation in the reduction of cholesterol levels and reduced risk of urinary and digestive disorders. Drinking 2.7 cups of black tea per day may also reduce the risk of stroke, compared with men who drank less. Black tea does contain antioxidants.

WHOOPS, THERE GOES SOME MORE IRON

There has never been a study that shows any risk factors in drinking tea. Tea does contain tannins, though, which have been known to interfere with the absorption of iron and certain B vitamins.

SPRUNG A LEAK?

A popular tea in Asia that is used as a diuretic is corn silk tea. It is one of the best diuretics that can be prepared from any herb. Corn silk tea has been proven to lower blood pressure. If your doctor ever recommends that you take a diuretic, you might ask your doctor if he would approve your trying corn silk tea first. He may get a surprise.

DANGER: TOXIC TEAS

There are a number of teas that do fall into the toxic category and should be avoided unless used in a prescribed manner by your physician or herbalist.

TEA	POSSIBLE PROBLEM
Buckthorn	Diarrhea
Burdock	Blockage of nerve impulses to organs
Comfrey	Liver problems
Foxglove	Heart arrythmias
Groundsel	Liver problems
Hops	Destruction of red blood cells
Jimsonweed	Blurred vision and hallucinations
Kava-kava	Deafness and loss of balance
Lobelia	Liver problems
Mandrake	Blockage of nerve impulses to organs
Meliot	Hemorrhage
Nutmeg	Hallucinations
Oleander	An cause heart stoppage
Pokeweed	Breathing difficulties
Sassafras	Liver cancer
Senna	Diarrhea
Thorn apple	Blockage of nerve impulses
Tonka bean	Hemorrhage
Woodruff	Hemorrhage

One tea that you should stay away from is made from the germander plant (Teucrrium chamaedrys) and may still be used in some weight control products. Researchers in France have found that the tea will cause liver damage. A number of cases of hepatitis were reported in people consuming the tea for three to eighteen weeks. Dosages ranged from 600 to 1,620 milligrams per day when taken in capsule form. Teas will contribute enough germander to be considered dangerous as well. Herb shops are still able to sell the tea.

CAUTION REGARDING TEA SOLD AS MEDICINAL TEA

Teas that are sold relating to cures or specific disease processes are not regulated by the FDA. These manufacturers do not have to prove their claims, and you are on your own when it comes to safety and effectiveness.

ALL-NATURAL IS BEST

There is a substance in tea that has been isolated and is being studied in relation to cancer prevention. Polyphenol is found in sufficient quantities only in tea that has not been processed. The high sugar content of canned or bottled teas reduces the effectiveness significantly.

DECAFFEINATION PROCESS

Tea is decaffeinated using the same chemical used to produce decaffeinated coffee. Ethyl acetate is used to bind the caffeine, which is removed by forced water-filtration methods.

BOTTLED COMMERCIAL TEA VS. "REAL" HOME-BREWED TEA

The major antioxidants found in green or black tea are for the most part absent from commercial tea drinks. It is best to brew your own tea. It doesn't matter whether it is hot or cold—you will still obtain the highest level of antioxidants. Commercial tea also has a higher sugar content.

VITAMINS, NUTRIENTS AND CHEMICAL COMPOUNDS IN TEA

SUBSTANCE	CONCENTRATION IN ABOUT 1 OUNCE OF TEA LEAVES
Antioxidants (polyphenols)	10 to 25 percent
Caffeine	25 to 30 milligrams
Carotene	14 to 30 milligrams
Flavenoids	0.6 to 0.7 percent
Fluoride	90 to 350 ppm
Glycosides	0.6 percent
Magnesium	400 to 2,000 ppm
Polysaccharides	0.6 percent
Saponins	0.1 percent
Selenium	1 to 1.8 ppm
Theanine (amino acid)	trace
Vitamin B2	trace
Vitamin C	150 to 200 milligrams (green tea only)
Vitamin E	25 to 70 milligrams
Zinc	30 to 75 ppm

Absorption of these nutrients when consumed in green tea is excellent compared to other forms of supplements. The only other tea that is comparable to "real" green tea is maté tea.

TEA FACTS

CUBE IN, FLAVOR OUT

When preparing iced tea or coffee, always have an ice cube tray ready with cubes made from tea or coffee. When you dilute these beverages, you lose up to 40 percent of their flavors.

THE NUMBER ONE ORGANIC TEA

This tea comes from the oldest gardens in Darjeeling, the Makaibari Tea Estates. They grow the finest certified pure organic teas in the world. One of their most popular teas is makaibari green, which has a taste of darjeeling, though it is still a green tea.

CLEARING UP THE PROBLEM

If cloudiness is a problem with your iced tea, allow the tea to cool to room temperature before refrigerating it. If the tea is still cloudy, try adding a small amount of boiling water until it clears up. Minerals that are released during the brewing process cause the cloudiness.

THIS WILL KEEP YOU AWAKE

A tea with one of the highest caffeine contents is Bigelow English Teatime, with about 60 milligrams of caffeine per cup.

POUND FOR POUND, DOES TEA OR COFFEE HAVE MORE CAFFEINE?

A pound of tea has almost twice the caffeine content than a pound of coffee. Tea goes farther, making about 180 to 200 cups, compared to a pound of coffee, which only yields about 40 cups. The taste of tea that is made with the equivalent measure of a coffee scoop would be too powerful to drink.

QUALITY MAKES A DIFFERENCE

The better the quality of the tea, the less you have to use per cup. Poor-quality tea may take up to 1 teaspoon per cup to give the desired taste, while the higher-quality green teas may take only half that much. Your typical supermarket teas may be a blend of sixty different teas, and most people will never know what a good cup of tea really tastes like.

TEA OVERBOARD

Never drink hot tea from a Styrofoam cup with lemon added. The citric and tannic acids will react with the heat and eat a hole through the cup, leaving a puddle on your desk and adding a number of carcinogens to the tea from the Styrofoam. If you don't believe it, try it for yourself. It works only with hot tea and lemon.

TEA IS SECOND ONLY TO WATER

Tea is the second most consumed beverage in the world.

BOY, AM I FRESH

If you want to test the freshness of tea, just close your fist very tightly around a small amount of tea or a tea bag and breathe in as you release your fingers. The aroma should be sweet and somewhat grassy. If you do not smell a strong aroma, the tea is probably old and should be thrown out.

TEA GROWN IN AMERICA

There is only one tea grown in the United States, which is black tea grown near Charleston, South Carolina, on the island of Wadmalaw. Tea plantations were established in 1799 by a French botanist. American classic tea, the official tea of the White House since 1987, is one of the finest black teas available. The first flush is harvested every May, with harvesting continuing every fifteen to eighteen days until October. The plantation prides itself on using no pesticides or fungicides, thus producing a high-quality product. For more information regarding the only American tea, call (800) 443-5987.

HAVE A BRICK OF TEA

The leftovers from tea manufacturing are made into bricks of tea. The bricks are usually produced in China and shipped to Russia and Tibet, where small pieces are shaved off and used for tea. The bricks may contain twigs, leaves, and even the stems of the bush.

THIS WILL FILL A FOOTBALL STADIUM

Total tea production is about 2.13 billion pounds annually, mostly from India and Sri Lanka. This will easily fill a football stadium.

DON'T BE A DUNKER

There is nothing wrong with purchasing a quality tea in a tea bag. They come in an odorless, tasteless filter paper that is very convenient and not as messy as loose tea. The mistakes most people make is not using very hot, almost boiling water or allowing the bag to remain in the water until the desired flavor is achieved. To dunk the tea bag a number of times defeats the purpose of the bag and does not result in a quality cup of tea. The water needs time to absorb the flavor, and the cup should have a cover on it while it is steeping.

GREAT FOR HALLOWEEN

If you would like to firm up the skin on your face with a mask that really works, just mix 1 cup of mayonnaise with 1 heaping teaspoon of Matcha tea. You'll find this in any health food store. Mix well and apply evenly on your face, avoiding your eyes. Relax for about twenty minutes, then rinse the mixture off with warm water. Pat your face dry using a soft towel and apply a moisturizer.

COLOR ME TEA GREEN

The color of tea can tell you a lot about the tea even before you drink it. Black tea should not have any greenish tint to it; this is indicative of an underwithered, overfermented tea. Green teas should have a green-gold color. If the color of green tea is a somewhat brownish yellow, the tea is old or was produced from low-grade leaves. A good rule of thumb: the lighter the color, the higher the probability that it is a quality green tea.

GET OUT THE SPYGLASS

Since most tea is imported into the United States it must pass stringent regulations established by the FDA and is inspected by special "FDA tea examiners."

WHO INVENTED THE TEA BAG?

The tea bag was accidentally invented in 1904 by Thomas Sullivan in New York when he was shipping tea samples to a customer. Samples were normally sent in small tins but he felt it would be less expensive to send them in small bags. He ordered hundreds of hand-sewn silk bags, placed tea in them, and shipped them out. The response was overwhelming when his customers found that by just pouring hot water over the bags they made their tea with no mess or fuss. Presently, tea bags are used to prepare about 55 percent of all tea in the United States.

NO MORE MOSQUITOES

Next time you have a barbecue, place a fireproof bowl on the patio with some crushed dried green tea leaves and a charcoal briquette and light it. The smoke will chase any mosquitoes or flies away.

CAN'T LIVE WITHOUT TEA

The British drink more tea than any group of people in any country in the world. The average Brit drinks at least four cups of tea per day. Most of the tea is still made by infusion, but tea bags are coming on strong. The British consume about 8 pounds of tea per person annually.

WHY THE ENGLISH STARTING ADDING MILK TO TEA

The tea that was originally imported by England tended to be a bit astringent, so the English tried adding a small amount of milk, which reduced the astringency caused by the higher tannic acid content. The milk protein would bind with the tannic acid. By reducing the tannins, the tea became less constipating. Problems did arise, however, when the tea with the added milk had less aroma and flavor than they were used to. But the habit stuck and a large number of the English still prefer their tea with milk.

LOOK INTO MY TEA

In many societies, reading tea leaves is serious business. The Chinese read the patterns of the leaf residues left in the bottom of the cup to foretell future events in a person's life. In Scotland the tea leaf reader, called a spae-wife, reads her tea leaves every morning to find out how the day will progress. To have sufficient tea leaves to read, the tea must be prepared without an infuser.

The reading is always done from the left of the handle and progresses around the cup. If the leaves look like anchors, stars, a leaf, a tree, a flower, a crown, a cow, an egg, a heart, dogs, or a bridge, it means that you will have good luck. If the leaves look snakes, crosses, a coffin, rats, a church steeple, a weapon of any kind, ravens, monkeys, cats, or a monkey, it means you will have bad luck.

WHEN USING YOUR GOOD CHINA, SPOON IT

When pouring hot tea into a good china cup, it would be a wise move to place the spoon in first. The spoon tends to absorb the heat, so you will not risk cracking the cup. Many of the cracks are microcracks that cannot be seen for many years. If they do appear, just boil a small amount of milk and pour it into the cup. Allow it to stand for about twenty minutes and the milk protein will seal the microcracks. Another method is to rinse the cup under very hot tap water before adding the tea or coffee.

MARBLING EGGS WITH TEA BAGS

A unique way to serve hard-boiled eggs is to marble them. The easiest method is to boil the eggs for two minutes, remove the eggs one at a time, and just tap the shell to crack them. Continue cooking the eggs for two minutes more in the same water that has had 6 tea bags added. Remove the eggs and allow them to cool before removing the shells. The eggs will be marbled.

THE ALL-AROUND TEA INFUSER

Almost any herb can be put in a tea infuser and placed in your soup or stew to add the flavor of the spice without allowing the spice to fall apart and be more difficult to retrieve. The infuser can even be used to stir your dish while the flavor of the spice is being released.

TANNINS, BE GONE FROM MY TEAPOT

To remove stains left by tannins, place ½ cup of borax into a teapot full of boiling water, remove from the heat, and allow to stand overnight. Clean thoroughly before using.

CHINA TEAPOTS NEED CAREFUL CLEANING

To clean the inside of a china teapot, just place a small amount of baking soda on a damp cloth and rub firmly.

GETTING FOGGY IN HERE

If your tea is cloudy, just add a pinch of baking soda to the teapot.

TEAISTICS

The tea sales in the United States are increasing at an unbelievable rate. In 1991 tea sales were $1.9 billion; in 1998 they grew to $4.2 billion.

ODORS A PROBLEM? GREEN TEA TO THE RESCUE

✄ LITTER BOXES

Green tea leaves should be crushed and sprinkled in a litter box to keep the odors as well as any fleas away.

✄ KITCHEN ODORS

If you want to get the smell of garlic or onions off your hands, try rubbing your hands with wet green tea leaves. The leaves can also deodorize your pan or bowl.

✄ PET BED

Sprinkle some green tea leaves in your pet's bed.

✄ REFRIGERATOR

Keep a bowl with used green tea leaf bags in the refrigerator to eliminate odors. It works as well as baking soda.

Chapter 9
Herbal Tea

THE FIRST TEAS

Herbs have been with us since the beginning of vegetation on earth. Early man probably placed the different plants or leaves in liquids or just ate them. Herbs have been used for medicinal purposes for thousands of years. There are only three ways to acquire herbs: grow them, forage for them, or go to your local health food store or herbalist and buy them, this last being the easiest method. Herbs may be powdered and placed in capsules, made into tablets, liquefied, or made into a tea. Tea will be discussed since it is one of the more common methods of obtaining herbs and their benefits. Every single herb has a story and historically has been used to cure some disease.

The following herbs are some of the more common herbs used for teas. The medicinal uses for these herbs will be given for informational and historical purposes only and not for use as a medicine to cure any specific illness. The author does not recommend any of these herbs as a cure for any disease process.

AGRIMONY

This herb may go by a number of different names including cocklebur or sticklwort. It may be found in fields or along the road in North America and Europe, but is easily cultivated almost anywhere and can grow to a height of 3 feet. Both the leaves and flowers are used to make a tea that has a flavor similar to apricots. The tea is used to strengthen the liver, improve the skin, and cure colds and sore throats.

ALFALFA

Also called lucerne, alfalfa can be grown almost anywhere and can be found in the wilderness around streams and damp meadowlands. The plant grows to a height of 1 to 2 feet and was thought to be a vegetable by the Chinese. The tea is somewhat bland and grassy and is made from the leaves and flower heads. It is high in vitamins, minerals, and digestive enzymes and contains more protein than wheat and corn. The tea is used to cleanse the kidneys, cure ulcers and arthritis, and improve muscle tone.

ANGELICA

Aso called wild parsnip or archangel, the plant has bright green leaves that are 2 to 3 feet long and bears yellow flowers. It was originally found only in Europe but is now being grown in North America. The herb has had a history of being linked to angels in many languages and was said to help cure plague. It was used as a remedy to fight witchcraft, rid the body of poisons, and cure gout and lung diseases. Angelica was also known as the "root of the Holy Ghost." The flavor of the tea is similar to juniper berries.

ANISE

This herb may also be called cumin or anise seed. Anise is somewhat sweet and tastes like licorice. The Bible mentions anise as a protector against evil, especially the "evil eye." The tea has been used to cure gas, coughs, and a number of digestive problems.

BALM

This is a very fragrant plant that is found in southern Europe and grows to a height of 1 to 2 feet. It is easily grown in the United States and sometimes found wild in the woods of the Northeast. Balm may also be called lemon balm or bee balm and has been known as the "elixir of life." Legend has it that it is the fountain of youth and has been used to assist in the healing of open wounds. It is very attractive to bees and is therefore rubbed on beehives to keep the bees close to home. The tea is made from the flowering tops and the leaves. Other medicinal uses are for reducing fevers, improving nervous disorders, and prolonging life.

BASIL

Basil was originally found in India and was known as the "herb of hatred." It is now grown in a number of warm regions of the globe and was a sacred herb of the Hindu religion. History tells us that basil was buried with Hindus and used as their passport to paradise. The tea has a taste similar to anise and has been used to treat nausea.

BAY

Known as the "herb of prophecy," bay can grow to a height of 50 to 60 feet, but is usually controlled and grown as a bush. It is more common in the Mediterranean. The herb was sacred to the Greek god Apollo and was made into wreaths and placed around the neck of victorious warriors and athletes. The tea has a pleasant aroma but is slightly bitter, and is used to cure stomach upsets, ease the pain of childbirth, cure coughs, and get rid of the cobwebs in the brain.

BERGAMOT

Bergamot may also be called horse mint or Oswego tea and can grow to a height of 3 to 4 feet. This member of the mint family can easily be grown in your garden. The tea was commonly used by the Winnebago Indians to cure skin conditions and especially acne and is also used to cure a variety of stomach disorders, bronchial problems, and headaches.

BIRCH

Harvested from a tree that may be found in Europe, Iceland, northern Asia, and North America, its nickname is "lady of the woods." The inner bark was powdered and consumed with caviar by the Russians. The powder was also baked in bread and pastries by the Swedes and even made into a paste, rolled, dried, and then smoked by Alaskan Eskimos. The tea has a somewhat wintergreen flavor.

BORAGE

Also called miner's candle, talewort, and cool tankard, borage has been known as the symbol of courage and brought increased energy levels to the Crusaders. The plant has beautiful blue star-shaped flowers and can be grown in most climates. In many locations it grows wild and is regarded as a weed. The tea was used to relieve depression and tastes like fresh cucumber. The tea has also been used for bronchial problems, to increase the flow of mother's milk, and as a diuretic.

BURNET

The tales of this herb date back to medieval times when a Hungarian king was said to have cured the wounds of thousands of his soldiers that were injured in battle with the juice of burnet. The tea has been used to stop bleeding from open wounds and relieve diarrhea.

CHAMOMILE

This herb has also been called manzanilla or sweet chamomile and has had a reputation for its curative powers for thousands of years. It has an applelike aroma but is somewhat bitter. The tea was used as a relaxant and to relieve stress. The herb has been used to soothe the effects of withdrawal from alcohol and drug addictions.

CARAWAY

Also called kummel, caraway is one of the oldest condiments, having been found in archeological digs that were more than five thousand years old. The secret to ensuring that lovers remain faithful is for them to eat caraway seeds (it's that easy). The tea has a somewhat bitter flavor and tastes like parsley. It has been used to relieve a toothache and as a breath freshener.

CATNIP

This herb is a member of the mint family and is commonly found growing wild along the sides of the road. The tea has been used to flavor meats and is commonly used in salads. In England it was one of the favorite teas long before tea was imported from China as well as a favorite of the American colonists. The tea is normally prepared from the young leaves and flowering tops of the plant and has a slightly bitter, mintlike taste. It has been used to relieve abdominal discomfort and to regulate menstruation.

CINNAMON

This herb is harvested from the evergreen tree that is a member of the laurel family. The inner bark of the tree is dried. The most famous incident involving cinnamon was when the emperor Nero burned a year's supply of cinnamon after his wife died to accentuate the level of his grief. The tea was used to relieve stomach problems and also as a stimulant.

CLOVER

This herb may also be called red clover and has the motto "Think of me." It was originally grown as a fodder plant and is one of the earliest cultivated herbs. A four-leaf clover is guaranteed to bring you good luck, especially in Las Vegas. The tea became popularized by the American Indians who ate the leaves and flowers raw. It is a soothing tea that has been used to treat ulcers, skin conditions, and even cancer.

CLOVE

Cloves are from clove trees that are for the most part grown in Southeast Asia. They are the dried seeds of the clove tree flowers that are harvested before they develop and their seeds removed. The trees will provide cloves for about one hundred years. The Chinese called cloves the "chicken tongue spice" because of their shape. In Java they are smoked and in India they are chewed. They produce a strong, pungent tea that has also been used as an antiseptic.

COLTSFOOT

This herb grows wild in many areas of the United States and has been called coughwort and ass's foot. It has an asparaguslike stem and can grow to heights of

1 to 2 feet. Each blossom resemble a dandelion blossom, which is outlined by green leaves, making it look like a horse's hoofprint. The herb is commonly used in British tobacco products and was once thought of as the most powerful herbal medicine. The tea has been used for bronchial problems and coughs.

COMFREY

Actually a weed that grows wild, comfrey was used for thousands of years to cure battle wounds and even broken bones. The herb contains the chemical allantoin, which speeds up cell duplication and assists injured cells in healing faster. The tea has a mild flavor and is normally made from the leaves and ground root. It has been used to heal ulcers and stop diarrhea.

DANDELION

The name originated because the yellow jagged leaves resemble a lion's teeth. Dandelions can be found almost everywhere, especially where you don't want them. The tea has been used in India for liver ailments and the flowers are made into dandelion wine. The leaves are one of the more nourishing greens that can be found in the entire herb kingdom; they are high in vitamin A, calcium, and potassium. The tea is somewhat bitter and has also been used to improve kidney and liver function.

ELDER

Sometimes referred to as elderberry, this herb grows wild in Europe. Legends surrounding the herb include the fact that the wood used in Pan's pipes and the cross of Calvary were made from the elder tree. Another legend is that Judas was hung from an elder tree. The berries are used to make elderberry wine and the tea has been used to cure the flu.

FENNEL

Fennel, a member of the parsley family, originated in southern Europe and Asia, for the most part growing wild. Fennel is used on cow's udders to prevent the milk from becoming bewitched. The tea has a flavor similar to anise or licorice and has been used to improve memory, as an appetite suppressant, and to stop a cough.

FENUGREEK

Also called bird's foot, fenugreek grows wild in the eastern Mediterranean. The Egyptians used fenugreek as a food source and placed it in their "holy smoke." The sprouts were a popular favorite in salads and the powdered seeds were used to increase hair growth on bald men. The tea was used to lower fevers, soothe stomach disorders, and help regulate blood sugar levels.

FLAX

This is one of the most well known herbs in the world and is easily found in the wild. The Egyptians wrapped mummies in flax, and it was used in the tabernacle in Exodus and the white sails in Homer's *Odyssey*. The tea has been used as a cough suppressant and a remedy for colds and flu.

GINGER

The herb can be found in the wild throughout North America in cool, wooded areas and has been used in recipes for hundreds of years. The tea has been used to relieve motion sickness and is effective for a number of stomach and digestive problems.

GINSENG

This herb has been known as the fabulous cure-all herb and has been written about in all literature that mentions healing and herbs for thousands of years. The root tends to resemble the human form; the more it looks like that, the more pow-

erful it is said to be. Longevity and sexual prowess have always been associated with ginseng. Daniel Boone hunted and sold ginseng root to China when the country's supplies ran low. The Chinese made more money selling the root than they did from their fur trade. The Russian astronauts took ginseng with them into space to prevent infections. The tea is prepared from the ground-up root, has a taste similar to licorice, and is supposed to strengthen the cardiovascular system, cure diarrhea, and even act as a pain suppressant.

GOLDENROD

Also known as blue mountain tea, it grows wild in the northeastern United States. Because of the excellent quality of the tea, it was exported to China, where it was a delicacy of the upper classes. The tea has been used to reduce fever, aid in digestion, control nausea, and even dissolve kidney stones.

HAWTHORN

Commonly called whitethorn or mayblossom, hawthorn is related to the apple tree and can grow to heights of 30 feet. The tree was considered a sacred tree since Christ's crown of thorns was made from hawthorn. If a hawthorn branch was brought into a home in medieval times, it was thought to have foretold death. The tea is made from the berries and has been used to treat cardiac disease, kidney problems, and sore throats.

HOLLYHOCK

Originally grown in China but found to grow wild in North America, hollyhock has leaves that were commonly used in Egyptian cooking. The tea was used for bronchial problems and to assist with digestion.

HOPS

A vine that has a tough, flexible stem, hops has male flower in loose bunches and female flowers that appear as small greenish cones. The female cones are used to brew beer and the pulp is sometimes used to produce paper products and even linen. The tea has a somewhat bitter flavor and is used to induce sleep and improve a person's appetite.

HOREHOUND

Also called bull's blood and eye of the star by ancient Egyptian high priests, this member of the mint family was used in ancient times as an antidote for poisonings. It is one of the bitter herbs eaten on Passover. Both the leaves and flowers are used to make tea, which has been used to relieve coughs and help bronchial conditions and congestion.

HYSSOP

An easy-to-grow garden herb that was used by the Hebrews to cleanse the lepers, hyssop was also supposedly offered to Jesus at the time of his crucifixion to act as a relaxant. The tea has been used to regulate blood pressure and treat upper respiratory infections.

LAVENDER

Lavender grows wild in many regions of the world and may have originated as a tea in India. It was used by the ancient Romans as a perfume for their baths and potpourri bowls. The tea has a strong aroma and has been used as a mild sedative and to eliminate bad breath.

LEMON VERBENA

This herb is mainly found in Central and South America and was a favorite tea in England in the eighteenth century. It is now grown in India and has a lemon flavor and aroma. The tea has been used to relieve indigestion and as a relaxant.

LINDEN

Linden may also be called lime or basswood and grows in Europe and North America. The inner bark of the tree has been used as an antiseptic. Linden tree blossoms produce one of the finest honeys in the world. The tea has been used as a relaxant and to relieve the cramps of menstruation.

LICORICE

Sometimes known as Spanish juice or sweet root, licorice was a very desired herb by the Egyptian Pharoahs. In fact, when Tutankhamen's tomb was opened a large quantity of licorice was found. Licorice is very sweet and tends to quench a person's thirst. It has been chewed as a treat for two thousand years. The tea has been used for bronchial conditions and to help people to stop smoking.

MALLOW

Also called marshmallow and commonly found in swampy coastal areas, mallow has the reputation of being one of the oldest herbs used as a food it is mentioned in the Old Testament as a substitute for meat. It is also the ingredient used in marshmallows. The tea has been used to reduce mucus in the body and to alleviate the symptoms of colds and sore throats.

MARIGOLD

This is one of the easiest flowers to grow in your garden. The plant is actually considered sacred in India and is used to decorate temples and shrines. Gypsies claim that if you drink marigold tea you will have the ability to see fairies. However, if you are in Mexico or Germany, it is the "insignia of death." The tea has been used to improve the complexion and to treat ulcers.

MARJORAM

Also known as oregano, marjoram is considered a sacred plant to some religions of India. The herb was planted on the graves of Romans to ensure peaceful rest. It is one of the popular herbs used by European chefs and was called the herb of grace by William Shakespeare. The tea has been used as a relaxant, a headache reliever, and a digestive aid.

MATÉ

Also known as yerba maté, this herb is brewed from the dried leaves and stemlets of the perennial tree *Ilex paraguarensis*. The name was derived from the gourd from which the Indians drank the tea. The plant grows only between the tenth and thirtieth parallels in the Parana and Paraguay River basins. The plant requires twenty-five years to mature. The tea has a somewhat bittersweet flavor similar to alfalfa and is said to be a natural stimulant with no side effects. The Guarani Indians use the drink to boost immune system response, detoxify the blood, restore hair color, slow the aging process, fight fatigue, keep the mind sharp, suppress the appetite, reduce stress, and eliminate insomnia. The tea also contains a number of vitamins. Call (800) 717-6001 for additional information.

MEADOWSWEET

Meadowsweet flowers were always scattered on the floor of the apartment of Queen Elizabeth I because they were her favorite. The herb can be grown worldwide in most temperate zones. The tea has been used to combat rheumatism and to relieve an upset stomach.

MINT

One of the popular herbs for tea can be found in hundreds of varieties worldwide. In ancient times mint leaves were rubbed on a table before guests arrived as a gesture of friendliness. Mint leaves were considered a source of power and virility to the Greeks. The tea has been used to relieve the symptoms of arthritis, increase appetite, and cure nausea and stomach problems.

MUGWART

Mugwart is the symbol of forgetfulness and was thought to ward off the devil and lightning. It was also believed that if you placed a small amount of mugwart in your shoes in the morning, you would be able walk 40 miles before noon without tiring (wish I'd known that when I was in the army). The tea has been used to eliminate gallstones, cure serious skin rashes, and regulate the menstrual cycle.

MULLEIN

Also called beggar's blanket or witch's candle, mullein can grow to heights of 8 feet. The "herb of love," it was thought to protect against black magic and sorcery in India. The tea is somewhat sweet and must be strained, since it may contain some of the small, fine hairs that cover the plant. It has been used to control asthma, to relieve coughs, to suppress the effects of hay fever, and as a relaxant.

NETTLE

This is an unusual herb in that it contains small stinging hairs that contain formic acid. An irritant in the wild, it is high in iron, protein, and vitamins A and C. In Scotland nettles were made into the finest linen, and in England they were used as important medicine. The tea has been used to relieve bronchitis and as an appetite suppressant.

NEW JERSEY TEA

This is one of the more popular American herbs and is also known as snowball or red root. It grows over most of the East Coast and was a popular beverage of the colonists, especially when it was difficult to get English tea during the great tea boycott. The taste is similar to that of black tea.

NUTMEG

A relative of the evergreen family, the nutmeg tree can grow to 60 feet and produces a yellowish fruit that resembles an apricot. Inside, the seed is an oily dark brown color. The nutmeg is considered to be a potent aphrodisiac by the Arabs. The tea has a somewhat sweet, spicy flavor and has been used to cure bad breath, headaches, fevers, and kidney problems.

PENNYROYAL

Called squaw mint in America, this herb has a potent aroma and is a beautiful garden herb. It acts as a flea repellent and is popular with hunters. Early American colonists found the tea to be the most flavorful of the wild herb teas. It has been used to treat whooping cough, asthma, indigestion, and headaches.

PURSLANE

Each purslane plant may have as many as fifty thousand seeds. Also known as pigweed, the herb was grown in India and Iran more than two thousand years ago, when it was thought you could ward off the devil by lining your bedding with purslane. It is commonly used in salads and was made into a popular tea by the American Indians. The tea has been used to lower fevers, stop coughs, and cure insomnia.

RASPBERRY

There are hundreds of varieties of raspberries grown worldwide. Many varieties of this berry grow wild, and raspberry tea is one of the most popular teas. The tea has been used for hundreds of years to cure the discomfort of menstrual cycles, frigidity, and labor pains.

ROSE

Roses are one of the oldest known cultivated herbs, with more than ten thousand varieties worldwide. Their history can be traced back to Persia, where it was called the mother of all nutritious fruits. Roses have been consumed as food for centuries in a variety of dishes and jellies. The end of the flower just under the stem is the rose hip, which is exceptionally high in nutrient content, especially vitamin C. The tea has been used to strengthen the heart, cure colds and coughs, and help memory.

ROSEMARY

This is an evergreen shrub that grows in most areas of the world, but is native to the Mediterranean region. It was highly regarded as a cure-all by the Romans. The color of the rosemary flower two thousand years ago was said to have been white and changed to blue when Mary, who was escaping from King Herod with the Christ child, washed her blue robe and hung it to dry on a rosemary bush; thus the name "the rose of Mary." The tea has been used for digestive problems, as a liver tonic, to strengthen the heart, and as a relaxant.

SAGE

Sage is a member of the mint family with more than seven hundred varieties. The Romans placed sage in their baths to ease the pain of sore feet. The shoots are commonly added to salads in the Middle East. The tea, which is somewhat bitter, has been used to cure colds, relieve headaches, strengthen muscles and nerves, and cure delirium tremors.

SARSAPARILLA

Originally grown in Central and South America and exported to Europe from Mexico in the 1500s, this was the favorite drink of pirates, who thought that it would cure syphilis. American Indians used the herb to cure arthritis and skin disorders. The tea tastes somewhat like bitter licorice and was used as a pain reliever, especially for the cervical vertebrae.

This herb has been used as a natural aphrodisiac for centuries. The plant contains chemical compounds that are similar in their action to testosterone and progesterone. Historically, the root was boiled in a pint of water for thirty to forty-five minutes and 4 ounces were consumed daily.

SASSAFRAS

Also called cinnamon wood or smelling stick, this a member of the laurel family was one of the original exports from the Americas to Europe in the 1500s. The Spanish used sassafras for medicinal purposes. The tea has been used as a blood cleanser, to relieve the pain of rheumatism, and to cure gout and diarrhea.

SAVORY

This pepper-flavored herb, which originated in southern Europe and the Mediterranean, was used by the Romans in meat and fish dishes. The use of savory declined as pepper became more readily available. In the Middle Ages, drops of savory oil were considered a cure for earaches. The tea is not very appealing since it has the flavor of pepper, but it was used to reduce fever, cure colds, and soothe intestinal disorders.

THYME

There are more than fifty varieties of thyme, with the most famous grown in Greece and used to produce some of the world's finest honey. The Romans thought that by consuming thyme it would increase their bravery in battle. Thyme was also mentioned in the Bible to be in the straw in the manger of the Virgin Mary and the Christ child. The tea was used to cure headaches and as an antiseptic for wounds.

WINTERGREEN

Also called mountain tea or woodsman's tea, wintergreen grows wild in North America. The oil contains the same chemical found in aspirin. The tea was used to relieve pain, cure colds, fight the flu, and ease coughs.

YARROW

This herb has also been called a bunch of daisies or soldier's woundwort, since it was used on soldiers' wounds during the Trojan War. If brides carry a bouquet of yarrow when they get married, they are guaranteed seven years of happiness. American Indians used the herb for stomach upsets and toothaches. The tea has been used as an intestinal cleanser and to speed the healing of wounds.

PREPARATION OF HERBAL TEAS

If the herb is in the form of a flower or leaf, an infusion ball may be used to make the tea. Place ¼ to ½ teaspoon of the crushed herb into the infusion ball and pour boiling water into the cup or pot, allowing it to steep for ten to fifteen minutes depending on the desired level of potency. If you are using one of the milder herbs, use ½ to 1 teaspoon for best results. If you make tea from the bark, seeds, or root of the herb, it would be best to use the decoction method. To prepare 1 pint of tea, just place 1 ounce of the herb in 1½ pints of pure water and boil for thirty minutes. Whenever possible, use a tea bag.

STORAGE

If you are purchasing dried herbs, they should be stored in a cool, dry location and in as airtight a container as possible. A well-sealed plastic container is usually the container of choice. If you plan on storing the herbs for a long period and not removing small amounts on a regular basis, then you should purchase an automatic heat sealer and plastic bags.

POISONOUS PLANTS

The following is a partial listing of some of the more popular plants whose parts are considered to be dangerous and could cause serious harm if consumed in any form.

PLANT/HERB	POISONOUS PART(S)
Azalea	Bulbs
Buttercup	All parts
Cherry tree	Branches, leaves
Daffodil	Bulbs
Elderberry	Shoots, leaves, bark
Foxglove	Leaves
Hyacinth	Bulbs
Iris	Roots
Jimson weed	All parts
Larkspur	Young plants, seeds
Lily-of-the-valley	Leaves, flowers
Mistletoe	Berries
Narcissus	Bulbs

PLANT/HERB	POISONOUS PART(S)
Oak trees	Leaves, acorns
Oleander	Leaves, bark, branches
Poinsettia	Leaves
Poison hemlock	All parts
Poison ivy	All parts
Potato	Leaves
Rhubarb	Leaves, blades
Water hemlock	All parts
Wisteria	Seeds, pods

NUTRITIONAL FACTS

THE MYSTERY OF HERBS

Herbs were found to cure many diseases in ancient days and were hailed as magical potions. However, a study of the history of certain periods now tells us that diseases such as scurvy, poor eyesight, and skin problems were for the most part due to vitamin deficiencies and were cured by consuming different herbs. The men who studied these illnesses and cured them had a very poor understanding of nutrients in herbs, but were smart enough to try different herbal remedies until they found one that worked, then used it for that illness all the time.

ON THE RUN AGAIN

When decaffeinated tea and coffee was introduced, a rumor started that since the caffeine was removed these beverages would not have the same diuretic effect as caffeinated tea and coffee. Sorry—wrong again! The caffeine did have a lot to do with the frequency of urination, but there is another chemical that is still in tea and coffee—theophylline, a bladder stimulant.

VITAMIN AND MINERAL HERBAL SOURCES

The best herb source for trace minerals is kelp.

VITAMIN OR MINERAL	SOURCE(S)
Vitamin A	Alfalfa, cayenne, garlic, kelp, marshmallow, parsley, rasp berry, red clover, watercress, yellow dock
Vitamin B1	Cayenne, dandelion, kelp, parsley, raspberry
Vitamin B2	Alfalfa, dandelion, fenugreek, kelp, parsley, safflower, watercress
Vitamin B6	Alfalfa
Vitamin B12	Alfalfa, kelp
Niacin	Alfalfa, burdock, dandelion, kelp, parsley, sage
Vitamin C	Alfalfa, burdock, catnip, cayenne, dandelion, garlic, hawthorn, kelp, parsley, pokeweed, raspberry, rose hip, watercress, yellow dock
Vitamin D	Alfalfa, watercress
Vitamin E	Alfalfa, dandelion, kelp, rose hip, watercress
Vitamin K	Alfalfa, plantain
Calcium	Alfalfa, chamomile, cayenne, dandelion, kelp, nettle, pars ley, pokeweed, raspberry, rose hip, yellow dock
Iodine	Garlic, Irish moss, kelp, sarsaparilla
Iron	Alfalfa, burdock, cayenne, dandelion, kelp, mullein, nettle, parsley, pokeweed, rhubarb, rose hip, yellow dock
Magnesium	Alfalfa, cayenne, dandelion, kelp, mistletoe, mullein, pep permint, raspberry, wintergreen
Phosphorus	Alfalfa, caraway, cayenne, chickweed, dandelion, garlic, Irish moss, kelp, licorice, parsley, pokeweed, purslane, raspberry, rose hip, watercress
Potassium	Alfalfa, birch, borage, chamomile, coltsfoot, comfrey, dan delion, fennel, Irish moss, kelp, mullein, nettle, parsley, peppermint, raspberry, wintergreen, yarrow
Selenium	Kelp
Sodium	Alfalfa, dandelion, fennel, kelp, parsley, willow
Sulfur	Alfalfa, burdock root, cayenne, coltsfoot, fennel, garlic, kelp, nettle, parsley, raspberry, sage, thyme
Zinc	Kelp, marshmallow

HERB GLOSSARY

ACRID

Describes a substance that produces a hot, irritating sensation.

ALKALOID

An irritant that may produce hallucinations and may be poisonous. Some alkaloids affect the nervous system, while others may have an astringent effect.

ANALGESIC

A substance that reduces pain.

ANTISEPTIC

A substance capable of preventing the growth of or destroying bacteria.

APHRODISIAC

A substance capable of improving sexual potency and desires.

ASTRINGENT

A substance that causes tissues to dry and contract.

CATHARTIC

Having a laxative effect on the bowels.

DECOCTION

An herbal tea made from the seeds, bark, or roots of a plant. The ingredients need to be boiled for a period of time to release the herbal extracts.

DEMULCENT

A substance used to coat tissues that have been irritated.

DIURETIC

An herb or compound capable of increasing the flow of urine.

FOMENTATION

A piece of cloth that has been doused with a hot infusion or decoction, then applied to the desired area.

INFUSION

A tea prepared from the leaves or blossoms of a plant. A tea ball or tea bag may be used and the hot water poured over it.

POULTICE

A warm moist cloth or towel pack that is either soaked in freshly prepared powdered herbs or herbal paste and applied directly to the affected area.

TINCTURE

An extraction of herbs in a solution of alcohol or vinegar, preferably apple cider vinegar.

TONIC

A substance designed to stimulate a specific system or the whole body.

VOLATILE OIL

A complex chemical compound that is capable of producing the aroma and taste of herbs. Usually obtained from the fresh plant.

Chapter 10
Coffee

THE STORY OF COFFEE

The coffee tree is believed to have originated in central Africa, where the natives would grind coffee cherries into a powder and mix it with animal fat, then roll it into small balls that they took with them on long journeys or hunting trips. Raw coffee is high in protein (until it is diluted with water) and when combined with the fat provided adequate calories and a stimulant.

The first factual information relating to the actual drinking of the beverage is by Arabs in the Middle East. The Arabs protected the coffee bean seed to such a degree that they would not allow it to be exported under the threat of death. However, in 1660 some of the coffee seedlings were smuggled into Holland and then transported in 1727 to Brazil, where the climate was more favorable. The climate and soil conditions were ideal and the coffee trees thrived.

A coffee tree requires at least 70 inches of rainfall annually so that the tree can produce at least two thousand coffee cherries—which makes only 1 pound of coffee. The United States consumes about 50 percent of the world's coffee production, which amounts to about 400 million cups per day. Eight out of every ten adults drink at least 1 cup of coffee every day.

COFFEE-PRODUCING COUNTRIES

BRAZIL

For the last one hundred years Brazil has led the world in coffee production. Almost 650 million acres can be planted in coffee trees; however, only the areas least likely to be hit by frost are being planted at present. All coffee grown in Brazil is aribica; if you wish to try a Brazilian coffee, it would be best to try a Brazilian bourbon santos. While most Brazilian coffee is considered only of fair quality, santos is produced using a high-quality bean, grown in the Sao Paulo region, that derives its flavor from the rich soil.

COLOMBIA

Presently, Colombia is the second largest exporter of coffee in the world. The quality is excellent since the majority of the coffee is grown at high elevations. Colombia has more than 2 billion coffee trees. The United States purchases about 50 percent of all coffee grown in Colombia. The top grade of coffee is the supremo; if you purchase a 100 percent supremo Colombian coffee, you will really be able to tell the difference from any other coffee you have been drinking. The best Colombian coffee to try is the Colombian medellin excelso.

COSTA RICA

Costa Rican coffee is grown at high altitudes and is all aribica, one of the more popular coffees of Europe. The coffee is graded depending on the hardness of the bean. The higher the altitude, the harder the bean and the better the quality of the coffee. The best-quality been is the "good hard bean" (GHB) and is grown at altitudes above 4,000 feet.

DOMINICAN REPUBLIC

Most of the Dominican Republic crop is sold to the United States. The best grade is barahonas, though the coffee is rated only as fair.

UNITED STATES

Coffee is grown only on the slopes of the Mauna Loa volcano at elevations of 1,500 to 2,000 feet. The volcanic soil produces a coffee tree that is never bothered by disease, which is unique to the world. The average crop per acre on Hawaii is about 2,000 pounds compared to only 650 pounds in Latin American countries. The total production, however, is only about thirty thousand bags.

JAMAICA

Jamaican coffee is grown on the slopes of a mountain ridge at an elevation that reaches 7,000 feet. Jamaican coffee is rated as one of the finest in the world. If you can find Jamaican blue mountain or high mountain supreme coffee, try it.

AFRICA

Africa is now one of the largest growers of coffee in the world, with an increase in market share every year. One of the best coffees is 100 percent robusta, which is difficult to find. Angola is actually the fourth largest coffee exporter in the world.

There are a number of other countries that grow coffee, including Mexico, Puerto Rico, Indonesia, Ecuador, El Salvador, Guatemala, Haiti, Peru, Venezuela, India, and Yemen.

ROASTING THE BEANS

Raw coffee beans must be roasted to change an unappetizing seed into a beverage that is desired by 80 percent of all adult Americans. Roasting shrinks the bean about 15 percent and then increases its size by 50 percent in a process similar to corn popping. The longer a bean is roasted, the darker it becomes. Darker roasts do not necessarily produce stronger coffee.

Heat is applied to the bean in such a manner that every surface of the bean receives the same amount of heat. The heat is at the lowest temperature to perform the roasting and for the shortest period possible.

TYPES OF ROASTS

🍵 LIGHT CITY ROAST

The bean is not fully matured and has a cinnamon instead of brown color. The flavor is somewhat weak.

🍵 STANDARD CITY ROAST

This is the most popular roasted bean sold in the United States. It may be sold as American roast or just brown roast. The beverage that is brewed is somewhat dull and a little on the flat side.

FULL CITY ROAST

A popular roast on the East Coast, this is roasted for a slightly longer period than the standard roast to produce a darker cup of coffee. The coffee bean is a dark brown with no hint of oil on the surface. Most specialty coffee shops on the East Coast will carry this roast.

BRAZILIAN ROAST

This has no relation to Brazilian coffee. The bean is roasted a bit longer than the full city roast, and the coffee has a darker color and a flavor that tastes like a very dark roast.

FRENCH ROAST

The bean has an oily appearance on the surface and the color is a somewhat dark golden brown. The coffee has a smooth, rich flavor and is easily distinguished from the lighter roasts.

FRENCH/ITALIAN ROAST

This is also called Spanish or Cuban roast. The bean is roasted darker than the French roast. This coffee makes excellent espresso.

ITALIAN/ESPRESSO ROAST

This is the darkest roast possible without carbonization of the bean or roasting it to death. The bean has a shiny, oily surface and looks black.

ESPRESSO

The smaller Pavoni espresso machines first used were capable of producing only about 150 cups per hour. Since this was not sufficient to serve larger crowds, a bigger version called the La Victoria Arduino machine was invented, which was capable of producing about one thousand cups per hour. This is why many older machines are so large. These early machines, however, had the tendency to overextract and pull too much coffee out of the grounds, scalding the coffee and producing a somewhat bitter espresso.

The machines that are now in use utilize a horizontal water boiler, which allows the steam and water to mix more efficiently. The steam and hot water are forced through the coffee under high pressure, producing an excellent cup of espresso with good strength and taste.

Espresso is prepared by rapid infusion, which forces the coffee through almost boiling water. A high-quality dark, fine, gritty ground (never powdered) coffee should be used. The darkness of the coffee, how dense it is packed, and the amount of water being forced through will determine the strength of the final product. Always use the recommended amount suggested by the manufacturer of your machine. Espresso should never be served with cream.

WELL I'LL BE

A new espresso beverage has recently been introduced called Sunrise Espresso. This espresso in a bottle is a prebrewed beverage that is 100 percent natural, full-strength espresso. A problem with espresso is that it takes too long to brew, but Sunrise states that their product can be ready in ten seconds. Their product is prepared from the finest aribica beans and prepared by master coffee roasters.

CAPPUCCINO

This is prepared by combining one shot of a strong espresso with very hot steamed milk, topped with a layer of frothy milk.

CAFFE MOCHA

One shot of espresso is topped off with the froth from hot chocolate. A somewhat sweet coffee drink, it tends to taste similar to hot chocolate.

CAFFE LATTE

One shot of espresso is combined with about 4 ounces of steamed milk. Usually, extra milk rather than more cappuccino is added, the drink is topped off with a large head of foam.

MACCHIATO

This is one shot of espresso with a very small amount of foam on top.

LATTE

This is a small amount of espresso on top of a glass of steamed milk.

CAFÉ AU LAIT

Espresso is not used, but this is prepared with a very strong coffee blend and steamed milk. It will occasionally be served in a bowl.

DECAFFEINATION PROCESS

The chemical process to decaffeinate coffee was actually invented in 1900 but was not used, since there did not seem to be the need to produce decaffeinated coffee and the chemicals and cost were somewhat prohibitive. The actual process of decaffeination starts with a raw green bean, which is softened with steam and water, allowing the bean to double in size. The beans are then doused with a chemical solvent—originally chlorine, which had the ability to soak completely through the bean. The beans are vibrated for about an hour in the solvent, which loosens the caffeine and combines it with the chlorine. The solvent is drained off and the beans are heated and dried with steam until all traces (we hope) are removed.

This process must be repeated dozens of times on the same beans to produce a bean that is almost completely decaffeinated. Needless to say, all this processing takes its toll on the flavor of decaffeinated coffee, which is why some people will never drink it.

WATER IN, FLAVOR OUT

The safest method to remove the caffeine from coffee was invented by the Swiss. This process soaks the green coffee cherries in water for several hours, which removes about 97 percent of the caffeine as well as some of the flavor components. The liquid is then passed through a carbon filter that removes the caffeine and the flavor components. The water is then added back to the beans before they are dried.

A GOOD GAS

The only other safe method, which is becoming popular, is the carbon dioxide method. The green beans are dampened with water, then placed into a pot that is then filled with carbon dioxide. The carbon dioxide has the ability to draw 99 percent of the caffeine out of the bean. The beans are then dried to remove the excess moisture.

HELP! WE'RE RUNNING OUT OF MICE

In 1973 new chemicals were discovered that could more efficiently be used to remove the caffeine in coffee. Two years later the companies found out that these chemicals caused cancer in mice. In 1975 new chemicals were used, but again studies showed that these new chemicals caused cancer in mice. However, the FDA said that the residues were minimal and posed no health threat. In 1981, however, just to be on the safe side (they thought), the companies switched to ethyl acetate, a chemical found in pineapples and bananas but also used as a cleaning solvent for leather and in the manufacturing of plastics. Studies now showed that the vapors from this chemical could cause liver and heart damage in mice, though this chemical is still in use today.

COFFEE CAFFEINE SENT TO POP MAKERS

The caffeine that is extracted from coffee and tea is sent to soft drink and drug manufacturers to be used in their products.

BREWING METHODS

DOUBLE-BOILED WATER IS A NO-NO

Never use water that has been previously boiled and cooled to make coffee or tea. The water will lose a good percentage of its oxygen content and produce a somewhat flat beverage.

SAVING THE TASTE

One of the major causes of poor-tasting coffee is a dirty pot. The preferred method of cleaning is to use baking soda and hot water. Never use soap, since the slightest hint of soap scum will alter the taste of the coffee. If you are using an aluminum pot that has black stains, just boil a small amount of rhubarb juice in the pot and the stains will disappear.

CLEANING THE COFFEEMAKER

Most coffeemakers build up hard water residues and should be cleaned often. The easiest method is to run straight apple cider vinegar through a cycle, then run water through the cycle twice to clean out the vinegar.

TEMPERATURE IS IMPORTANT

When you brew coffee, it is necessary to brew at the proper temperature, which will allow the maximum extraction of the caffeol compounds, the taste and aroma enhancers. The proper temperature also protects the coffee from producing an overabundance of polyphenols (tannins), which will give the coffee a somewhat bitter taste.

Professional coffee brewers keep the brewing temperature between 185 and 205°F. If the temperature is too low, the coffee grounds will not release sufficient caffeols, and if too high the tannins take over.

THE PERFECT TEMPERATURE FOR DRIP COFFEE

Studies have proven that the ideal temperature for drip coffeemaking is 95 to 98°F. If the water is any cooler it will not extract enough caffeine and essential oils from the coffee bean. When coffee is brewed above this temperature range, the acidity level becomes too high and the coffee is ruined.

GREAT CUP OF COFFEE VS. HEALTH RISK

The *cafétiere*, or French coffee press or plunger pot, is the hottest craze to hit the coffeemaking industry in years. A number of retailers are advertising the *cafétiere* as the perfect method of brewing coffee ever invented. The unit does not use a filter; it just presses the coffee and water into a cup. However, studies are showing that if you drink five to six cups of pressed coffee per day, it could increase your cholesterol levels by as much as 10 percent and raise LDL levels by 14 percent. Using the standard filter method allows the cafestol and kahweol, two of the harmful ingredients in coffee, to be removed. Espresso is also guilty of high levels of these two compounds.

PAPER TOWEL TO THE RESCUE

If you ever run out of coffee filters, try using a piece of plain white (no design) paper towel. Cloth filters work very well; however, a new cloth filter should be washed before using it.

IF YOU GRIND IT, USE IT OR LOSE IT

When coffee beans are ground, a large percentage of their surface is exposed to the air, thus allowing the breakdown of the flavor components and their rapid destruction. The process is called oxidation and takes its toll on all surfaces of every food when you expose the delicate innards to the air. The other problem that occurs is that the longer the ground-up bean is stored, the more carbon dioxide lost, which also contributes to the aroma and flavor of the bean. If you do grind up more than you can use, store the remainder in a well-sealed container in the refrigerator and use as soon as possible.

MAKING THE PERFECT CUP

To prepare the perfect cup of coffee, always grind the beans just before you are ready to brew. Always use clean equipment, high-quality water, and fresh coffee beans.

THE RIGHT POT MAKES ALL THE DIFFERENCE

Metal coffeepots may impart a bitter or metallic taste to your coffee. A glass or porcelain pot is recommended. If you are going to use a metal pot, the only one that is acceptable is stainless steel. Copper and aluminum are not recommended at all. If you are using a percolator the brewing time should be no more than six to eight minutes, while a drip pot should take about six minutes and vacuum pots about one to four minutes.

TREAT YOUR COFFEEPOT WITH TLC

At least once each week you should clean out your coffeepot and filter holder. Bitter oils that are released will make their home on the walls of glass containers and plastic filter holders. Both should washed with soap and hot water. Rinsing will not remove the bitter oils. The taste of the coffee will be noticeably improved.

NEVER USE HOT TAP WATER

If your tap water is not filtered, it is not a good choice for coffeemaking. Hot water from the tap tends to pick up a number of metals and chemicals that will more easily be absorbed by hot water. The best water for coffee is pure water if you would like a clean, fresh taste.

HOPE YOU'RE NOT USING A PERCOLATOR ANYMORE

If you like a bitter cup of coffee, then use a percolator. This type of coffeemaker can boil coffee for seven to fifteen minutes, which is long enough to cause even the best coffees to turn bitter. The aroma of the coffee is also adversely affected, since the coffee is exposed to the air for too long a period.

FLAVOR YOUR OWN COFFEE

When grinding your coffee beans, try adding a small amount of any spice or herb that you like so that the coffee and the herb blend well before brewing. The coffee grinder can also blend a number of different spices before you add them to a stew or soup to release the flavors more efficiently. However, make sure you clean the grinder thoroughly before grinding coffee.

DON'T BUY SPECIAL FILTERS

Special water filters are being sold to remove the chlorine from the water when preparing coffee. These are really not needed, since chlorine will be released into the air as soon as the water is heated high enough to prepare the coffee. There will not be enough chlorine left to affect the taste.

BUYING AND STORAGE

BUY IT RIGHT

When you purchase coffee, it would be best to purchase it in a vacuum-sealed container. If you purchase coffee made from freshly roasted beans, be sure that it is packed in nonairtight bags to allow the carbon monoxide that is formed during the roasting process to escape. If the carbon monoxide does not escape, it will adversely affect the flavor of the coffee.

KEEP IT COOL

When storing coffee the ideal method is to place the unused coffee in a well-sealed glass jar in the refrigerator. The glass will not impart any flavor as will metal. This is recommended for fresh coffee beans; ground coffee can be stored this way but must be used as soon as possible. Coffee beans can also be frozen for no more than six months, but must be sealed really tight.

COFFEE FACTS

THE CASE OF THE FLOATING CREAM

Almost every coffee drinker at one time or another has been irritated by the presence of floating cream. A thorough investigation was conducted and the results are in. The stronger the coffee, the more acid that may be formed, and if the cream is not very fresh it will contain just enough lactic acid to cause a reaction and rise to the top. However, if the coffee is too acidic, it may cause even the freshest cream to go bad almost instantly and thus rise to the top.

AMERICA'S BEST

Hawaii is the only state that is capable of growing coffee. The island of Hawaii is the home of the fabulous kona coffee. The soil is rich in minerals from volcanos, and the rainfall is sufficient to provide the trees with just enough moisture. In fact, in taste tests, kona coffee was judged to be almost equal to the finest coffees in the world. The coffee is now being exported to the continental United States. Try to purchase the pure coffee, not a blend. If you do purchase the 100 percent pure kona, you will use less than you normally would.

TIME IS RUNNING OUT

After you brew coffee, it will retain its maximum flavor and aroma for only about thirty minutes. When coffee becomes stale from sitting too long, try placing a pinch of salt in your cup; then reheat it for a big surprise. The sodium chloride will revive the flavor and aroma for a few minutes.

IN COFFEE BEANS, SIZE DOES MAKE A DIFFERENCE

The size of the grind does make a difference, both in taste and in caffeine content. Espresso should be made with a fine ground, while Turkish coffees need an even finer ground. The majority of American coffee is ground into a "drip grind" providing the maximum surface area, which makes the coffee rich and never bitter. However, if the grinds are microfine, the water will take longer to filter through, which will result in an increase of tannins and thus a bitter taste.

ONE CUP OF COFFEE, HOLD THE ACID

If you have a problem with overacidity or are overly sensitive to acidic beverages, just add a pinch of baking soda to the drink. Baking soda is a mild base and will neutralize a small percentage of the acid.

WHERE DID "CUP OF JOE" ORIGINATE?

Alcoholic beverages used to be allowed onboard U.S. Navy vessels. However, this practice was discontinued when Admiral Josephus "Joe" Daniels became naval chief of operations. He discontinued all alcoholic beverages with the exception of special occasions. The seamen then took to drinking their second-choice beverage, coffee, and nicknamed it "a cup of Joe" as a bit of sarcasm directed at the admiral.

SUPERMARKET COFFEE

Most supermarket coffee brands usually contain too much debris. The cost of producing a fresh-quality coffee is too high for markets to produce and the price will be more than most people will pay. Most supermarket coffee is a combination of aribica and robusta beans. Coffeehouses usually sell only aribica. Robusta beans are higher in caffeine and less expensive to produce. Look for 100 percent aribica for a great-tasting coffee. Vacuum-packed coffee in a supermarket must have an expiration date, which should be checked before you purchase it.

TYPES OF ACIDITY

If the coffee you are drinking leaves a dryness on the top of your mouth or on your tongue, this is usually due to acidity levels in the coffee. This not necessarily a negative, since some people like a coffee that is somewhat dry, similar to a dry wine.

COFFEE TOO HOT? SIP IT

Your ability to drink burning hot coffee that is capable of burning you and not your mouth is easily explained. When you sip a very hot cup of coffee, you tend to suck in more cool air than you ordinarily would. This instantly lowers the temperature of the hot coffee through convection (air currents) as well as evaporation. Another factor is at work—your saliva—which tends to partially coat the inside of the mouth, insulating it against a burn.

WHERE DID "JAVA" COME FROM?

The island of Java, which is part of Indonesia, produced some of the finest coffee in the world and was well known during World War II, when coffee plantations were devastated by the war. Some companies use the name "java" to denote a good coffee, but they are restricted from using the name java robusta, which can only be used on the "real" java coffee.

FRAPPE COFFEE

Frappe coffee is more popular in Europe and Latin America than in the United States. It is prepared by shaking 1 to 2 teaspoons of instant coffee with ½ teaspoon of sugar, water, and ice cubes. It is usually served in a tall glass and sometimes a small amount of milk is added. If shaken properly it will have thick foam on top.

QUICK, SERVE THE COFFEE

The longer coffee remains on a warmer, the more the oils tend to impart a bitter taste and a percentage of the aroma is lost.

LOOK! THE ACID IS EATING MY STYROFOAM

We know that hot tea with lemon has the ability to corrode Styrofoam and place carcinogens in your tea, but now there are studies that show that if the coffee has a high enough acid content it will chew away at Styrofoam as well. Use a glass cup; it's safer and the coffee will taste better.

THE ALL-AROUND COFFEE GRINDER

A coffee grinder can be used to grind herbs and spices. To clean the grinder and rid it of the coffee aroma, just grind up a few pieces of bread before you grind your herbs or spices.

SUGAR CUBES MAKE FOR A FRESH SMELLING COFFEEPOT

To eliminate the musty smell in a coffeepot between uses, just place a few sugar cubes into the pot and store it without the lid. Sugar cubes have the ability to absorb moisture, which causes the musty odor.

HERE YE, HERE YE—LAMB LOVES COFFEE

Coffee tends to bring out the flavor in lamb. Next time you prepare lamb stew, add a cup of black coffee to the stew as it is cooking. It will enhance the flavor and give the sauce a richer color.

COFFEE CAN REPLACE ALCOHOL

If you don't want to use alcohol when preparing a chocolate dessert, try substituting the same quantity of black coffee. You will be amazed at the flavor of the dessert compared to the same dessert with alcohol.

CAFÉ COCOA BEAN

If you would like to try a different cup of coffee, try adding a small piece of plain chocolate in the coffee filter. A piece of vanilla bean works great, too.

TASTE BUDS GOING CRAZY

Coffee can elicit a number of different taste sensations depending on the brand you choose. The taste can be sweet, caused by sucrose; sour, caused by tartaric acid; salty, caused by sodium chloride; or bitter, caused by quinine.

REALLY HOT BEANS

When coffee beans are roasted to a temperature of 465°F, chemical changes occur and the beans are capable of emitting their own heat, which then causes the temperature of the roasting oven to rise. This process is called pyrolysis.

THE LATEST CRAZE

Bottled coffee drinks are the latest craze in coffee. One of the innovators was Starbucks, with Nescafe following close behind. One of Starbucks' best sellers is Frappuccino, which is sold in 9.5-ounce bottles. Starbucks' bottled coffee has more calories—190 compared to Nestle's 140, which has less sugar. The taste of Nestle's is weaker than Starbucks but more palatable. Neither could be classified as a nutritious drink by any stretch of the imagination.

CURDLING UP WITH CREAM

If you want to stop cream from curdling up in your coffee, just add a pinch of baking soda to the cream before pouring it in. The baking soda will neutralize the acid in coffee just enough so as not to alter the flavor but to eliminate the curdling.

NUTRITIONAL INFORMATION

HAVE A FEW WRINKLES WITH YOUR COFFEE

The latest studies now show that both caffeine and nicotine may cause your skin to dehydrate and cause premature wrinkling. If you drink more than two cups of coffee per day or smoke more than four cigarettes per day, be sure to drink sufficient water. Remember that coffee may have a diuretic effect on your system.

MEDICAL WARNING

One cup of coffee has enough caffeine to keep your brain alert for about four hours in the average person who does not consume large quantities. If you are going to consume coffee that has not been decaffeinated, try not to drink any after about 4 P.M. However, the more coffee you drink, the higher your tolerance will be to caffeine. Also, if you suffer from stomach ulcers, coffee has been shown to reduce healing time.

MEN: TOO MUCH CAFFEINE MAY MEAN USING THE LITTLE BLUE PILL

Studies show that excessive caffeine consumption may cause reduction in zinc absorption and lower a man's sex drive. It may also adversely affect the prostate gland and cause increased stress levels.

ARE HOT DRINKS BODY WARMERS?

Other than a psychological response, hot drinks do not actually affect the body at all. The U.S. Army Research Institute of Environmental Medicine discovered that in order to raise body temperature with liquids, a person would have to drink 1 quart of a liquid at 130°F. They also found that it would be difficult to retain that much liquid at one time. The hot beverages do cause a dilation of the surface blood vessels, which makes you feel warmer as the blood flow increases; however, this soon makes you lose warmth.

WHOOPS, THERE GOES MORE CALCIUM

Studies from the University of Washington stated that regular coffee drinking may lead to an excessive loss of calcium through the urine. This loss amounts to 7 milligrams of calcium for every cup of coffee or two cans of caffeinated soda. However, if you consume 2 tablespoons of milk for each cup of coffee you drink or 1 tablespoon for every soft drink, that will offset the loss.

CAFFEINE CONTENT

BEVERAGE	8-OUNCE SERVING
Espresso	350 to 400 milligrams
Drip coffee	178 to 200 milligrams
Percolated coffee	80 to 156 milligrams
Instant coffee	90 112 milligrams

CAFFEINE WITHDRAWAL

If you decide to give up caffeine, be prepared to go through a withdrawal period of about twelve to sixteen hours. Symptoms can include headaches, irritability, depression, runny nose, dizziness, and fatigue. It's best if you cut back gradually, unless you leave home for a couple of days and spare your family the aggravation.

CAFFEINE CAN KILL

The lethal dosage of caffeine for 50 percent of the population is about 10 grams if administered orally. This varies widely depending on a person's weight, though a dosage of 15 grams is capable of killing most people. The lethal dose for coffee varies from fifty to two hundred cups. Since no one drinks that much regular coffee per day, I don't think we need to worry. Children can show signs of toxicity after only 3.5 grams per day and should not be given highly caffeinated drinks.

PREGNANCY AND CAFFEINE

Evidence shows that excessive caffeine ingestion will cause malformations in rats when they ingest the equivalent of seventy cups of coffee per day for a human. Since this is more than anyone ever drinks there is probably no harm in consuming a reasonable level of coffee per day until better scientific evidence is released. Studies have shown that caffeine will reduce sperm motility, which may lead to reduced fertility.

OSTEOPOROSIS AND CAFFEINE

Studies have shown that the more caffeine ingested, the lower your bone density is at the hips and spine. However, if a person's calcium consumption is kept up, there is no difference. One glass of milk a day can help.

COFFEE DRINKING AND SUICIDES

Studies have shown that there are fewer suicides among coffee drinkers than those who do not drink the beverage. This study was performed on 130,000 northern Californians with records of forty-five hundred who died.

CAFFEINE MAY INCREASE METABOLISM

Caffeine tends to cause an increase in the level of circulating fatty acids in the bloodstream. This leads to an increase in the oxidation of these fats for fuel. Caffeine is used by some runners to enhance fatty acid metabolism and increase endurance levels. This is one reason why caffeine is included in a number of diet pills.

CAFFEINE AND MIGRANES

Migraine sufferers have been aware for years that consuming a cup or two of regular coffee lessens the severity of the headaches. The reason for this is that caffeine tends to increase the effectiveness of the drugs used to treat migraines, mainly ergot alkaloids.

COFFEE GLOSSARY

ACERBIC

Describes an acidic, somewhat sour sensation on your tongue from poorly brewed coffee. This results from chemical compounds that are released if the coffee is allowed to sit for too long a period.

AFTERTASTE

A taste that remains in the mouth after drinking a beverage. It is the result of residues left behind, usually from the acid or spices used.

ARABICA

A species of coffee tree that may be grown in different countries. The name was given to the particular species by a European botanist when he was categorizing the trees and flora of the Arabian peninsula.

BAGGY

Applied to an "off" taste in coffee produced from a weak roast or one that may have been stored for too long a period in poor conditions.

BEANY

Describes coffee that has not been roasted to its fullest and does not have the complete aroma that it should.

BITTER

Describes a taste caused by a combination of quinine, caffeine, and possibly other alkaloids. The bitterness will be isolated at the back of the tongue.

BLACK BEANS

Coffee beans that have fallen to the ground before they are harvested. When used they will make a poor-tasting coffee.

BRACKISH

Describes a poor taste in coffee that produces a salty or alkaline sensation. This usually the result of inorganic residues caused by excessive heating after the coffee is already brewed.

BRINY

Describes coffee that has been overroasted.

CARAMELLY

Having the aroma of caramel caused by the sugary compounds being heated.

CHICORY

A taste that is somewhat sweet, yet a bit bitter and even acidic.

ALKALINITY

A sensation of dryness toward the back of the tongue. This is usually produced by the presence of alkaloid compounds.

ACIDITY

A normal characteristic of coffee. An expert coffee taster can recognize three variables in acidic tastes: natural and desirable, sour and undesirable, and too acidic with a bite and a puckering sensation.

CREAMY

Describes a coffee that has oil suspended in it, which means that the beans used had a high oil content.

EARTHY

Describes a dirtlike taste from a faulty drying process caused by the fat absorbing organic matter from the grounds.

FERMENTED COFFEE

Coffee that has a taste abnormality in the bean, causing a sour sensation on the tongue. Enzymes in the green bean have converted the sugars to acids.

GRASSY

Describes an aroma in coffee similar to that of freshly cut alfalfa or grass. Usually occurs only when the nitrogen content of green beans is high.

INSIPID

Describes a poor aroma caused by the loss of organic matter in the coffee bean. Usually the result of excess oxygen and moisture entering the bean after it has been roasted.

MELLOW

Describes a common taste created as the salts combine with the sugars in coffee and increase the overall sweetness.

MUDDY

Describes a coffee that contains numerous pieces of particulate matter in suspension.

NUTTY

Describes an aroma caused by the reaction of aldehydes and ketones that is similar to roasted nuts.

ORGANIC

Describes coffee that must be grown without the use of fertilizers, pesticides, or herbicides. Usually sold at a higher price.

POTATO COFFEE

Coffee with the flavor of raw potatoes, which is the result of poor processing techniques.

PULPING

The first step after the pickling procedure when coffee is produced from the wet method. The outer skin is removed and machines scrape the pulp off without crushing the bean.

RIO

Coffee from Brazil that may have an iodinelike taste and is very pungent.

ROBUSTA

Coffee that contains a high caffeine content and is somewhat bitter with a weak aroma.

SOUR

Describes a normal flavor caused by acids in the coffee that are created by the presence of one or all of the following compounds: tartaric acid, citric acid, or malic acid.

TARRY

Describes a burnt flavor after the coffee has been brewed that is caused by the condensation and burning of the coffee proteins.

WEAK COFFEE

Coffee that is not actually flat but lacks sufficient body.

Chapter 11

Hot Chocolate

WHY AREN'T I DISSOLVING?

Cocoa does not mix well with water and tends to remain in suspension for only a short period of time. The heat from the water will cause the particles to remain in suspension only as long as the drink is hot. As the drink cools, a percentage of the particles will fall to the bottom of the cup. When mixed with hot milk, however, the fat in the milk tends to hold the chocolate better.

THIS CHILLER WON'T SCARE YOU

A great drink in the summer is to blend a cup of ice, 1 cup of whole milk, and 3 tablespoons of a quality cocoa until the ice cubes are gone. This makes a great chocolate chiller.

Homemade Hot Chocolate
6 ounces semisweet chocolate bits or finely grated bittersweet chocolate
1 pint heavy cream
¼ cup whole milk
1 teaspoon pure vanilla extract (not imitation)

Using a double boiler, melt the chocolate, then slowly stir in the cream, milk, and vanilla. Continue to heat the mixture to a point just below boiling, stirring continually. Serve topped with whipped cream.

CAN MIXES BE USED TO COOK WITH?

Mixes should be used only to prepare hot chocolate drinks. They contain milk or cream powder and sugar or a substitute. Only pure cocoa or real chocolate should be used in recipes.

WHAT IS DUTCHED COCOA POWDER?

The actual process of dutching the cocoa powder involves adding an alkali to the powder, which mellows the taste. Dutching will improve the color and flavor of the powder.

WHAT'S NEW IN HOT CHOCOLATE MIXES?

There are new chemicals being added to some cocoas used for hot drinks. These new ingredients are called texturing agents and are tapioca-based products that help keep the cocoa powder in suspension, providing you with a smoother, more enjoyable drink. A new product is called Textra, manufactured by National Starch Company, which actually gives the product a mouthfeel similar to that of fat without the fat calories.

DOES HOT CHOCOLATE HAVE CAFFEINE?

Hot chocolate does have caffeine, though only about one-tenth the amount found in a cup of regular coffee.

HOW IS HOT CHOCOLATE SWEETENED?

The better grades of powder are sweetened with sugar; however, there is a sugar-free hot chocolate available that uses Nutrasweet™. The amount of sugar is low in a hot chocolate, and real sugar is preferred to an artificial sweetener.

THE DIFFERENCE IN EUROPEAN COCOA

Most European cocoas are less sweet than the American varieties. Europeans prefer a cocoa that does not have the sweet taste so that they can enjoy the flavor of the chocolate more.

WHAT IS WHITE HOT CHOCOLATE?

White hot chocolate is hot chocolate without the chocolate liqueur, which makes real chocolate "real." It does have a smooth, creamy flavor and is a favorite of many hot chocolate connoisseurs.

TO MILK OR NOT TO MILK

Most hot chocolate recipes or powders can be made with either hot water or milk. Milk will give the beverage a more creamy taste and will also add a number of calories. Whole milk is preferred, since the fat is what makes the flavor stand out.

HOW LONG WILL COCOA POWDER LAST?

If you purchase one of the better brands of cocoa powder, such as Mont Blanc, it should be fresh for at least a year.

WHAT NEXT, A KIDS' MR. COFFEE?

A new item from the Sunbeam Company is now being sold called the Cocomotion, a European-designed machine that is capable of heating, aerating, and blending four cups worth of hot chocolate in ten minutes. The machine has a clear plastic chamber that allows the children to view the mixture being prepared. The price of the unit is $49.95, which includes a recipe book.

BEAT ME, BEAT ME

If you want to stop the skin from forming on top of your hot chocolate, just beat the drink for a few seconds until it gets frothy.

A DEFINITE IMPROVEMENT

Try mixing a teaspoon of cornstarch and a pinch of salt in a small amount of water and adding it to the pot of hot chocolate to improve the taste and texture.

Chapter 12
Dairy Products

COW'S MILK

Milk is sold in many forms and consistencies, such as powdered, dried, dehydrated, evaporated, condensed, whole, raw, 1 percent milk, 2 percent milk, buttermilk, chocolate, acidophilus, and nonfat. Then we have all the products that are made from milk, such as butter, sour cream, and cheese, yogurt.

We can trace the history of dairy milk back only about four thousand years. The yellowish color of milk is caused by the presence of carotene, which is the same chemical that gives carrots their color. That is why whole milk with fat is yellower than other milks that lack the fat. Curds and whey are mentioned in a fairy tale; the little girl must have been eating a milk product since these are two common milk proteins.

WHY DOES MILK TURN SOUR?

Fresh milk contains about 5 percent milk sugar, or lactose, which gives milk a somewhat sweet taste. However, as the milk ages, bacteria feed on the sugar and convert the sugar into lactic acid, which sours the milk.

DOES BUTTERMILK CONTAIN BUTTER?

Buttermilk sold today is not the same as your grandmother used to make. It is prepared from a culture of skim milk. However, if a recipe calls for buttermilk, it would be best to find a dairy and purchase the "real" thing. Real buttermilk has a fuller body, contains butter, and has a much richer flavor, which is what the recipe calls for.

OUCH! DON'T SCALD ME

Scalding milk is heating the milk to just below its boiling point. To prevent scorching, which is a common problem, use a double boiler. There are two reasons that a recipe would call for scalded milk: it will kill any microorganisms that may be present and will also kill enzymes that would interfere with emulsifying agents in the milk and retard thickening. Scalding is needed only if you use raw milk. Since almost all milk is now pasteurized, it is not necessary to scald milk, even if the recipe calls for it.

HELP, I'M STUCK

Milk is easy to scorch if it is somewhat stale. Fresh milk is the best choice to avoid scorching as well as using a thick-bottomed pot. A double boiler is still the best choice, though you may prefer a faster method. Never heat the milk for too long at a high temperature or too fast. Milk proteins tend to get very sticky as they break down and will almost glue themselves to the bottom of the pot when over-heated.

WHY DOES POWDERED MILK NEED AGING?

Powdered nonfat dry milk is dehydrated, though it still contains about 35 percent protein, or casein, and about 50 percent lactose. When you add water to reconstitute the milk, the taste is somewhat gritty. However, if you allow the milk to remain in the refrigerator for four to five hours, the constituents will have a chance to blend more thoroughly and provide you with a better- tasting product.

THE LEVITATING FILM

A common problem when cooking with milk is the formation of a film of milk protein that rises to the top, coating the surface. Stirring the milk frequently and watching the pot should lessen the risk of this film forming. Milk should always be cooked below 140°F; above that, the proteins tend to coagulate. If the film does form, air bubbles may form between the film and the milk, pushing the film up and possibly over the top of the pot.

CAN I STOP VINEGAR FROM CURDLING MY MILK?

This is one problem you can't do much about. When milk comes into contact with a mild acid such as vinegar, the acid actually "cooks" the protein and turns the milk into what looks like scrambled eggs. Heavy cream, however, will usually not curdle since the high fat content protects the small amount of protein. If you must make a dish with vinegar and milk, try adding a teaspoon of cornstarch to the cold milk and heat it before adding the vinegar.

SOMETHING ELSE TO BLAME ON EL NIÑO

Milk production fell during 1998, and of course it was blamed on the weather phenomenon El Niño. Since the spring was unusually wet, there was an increase in biting flies, causing many cows to expend a lot of energy scratching instead of concentrating on producing milk. They also failed to conceive when bred due to the stress of scratching.

HOW ABOUT A SILLY SYLLABUB DRINK

This is an old English drink made from milk and flavored with wine or cider, then sweetened with sugar, honey, and spices. It is whisked until it has a good head on it and then drunk like a "nog."

TURN OUT THE LIGHTS, YOU'RE KILLING MY MILK

When purchasing milk, buy it in a container that is not clear plastic. If milk is exposed to the ultraviolet rays emitted from fluorescent lights for four hours, 1 percent milk will lose 45 percent of the vitamin A content, while 2 percent milk will lose 32 percent. Manufacturers are now starting to sell milk in yellow-tinted containers.

MILK VS. HOT PEPPERS

Capsaicin, the substance in hot peppers that causes discomfort and can even produce a burn in your mouth and on your hands, can be neutralized by milk. Milk contains a protein that binds to the capsaicin and removes it from your tongue.

Milk Vs Hot Pepper

GOOD BREEDING EQUALS GOOD MILK

For a cow to give milk she must first have a calf. Then she will give milk for about ten months before getting pregnant again. After the next calf, she will produce milk for another ten months, and so on.

I'M ALIVE!

If you want your milk to have a longer shelf life, just add a pinch of baking soda to the carton. A small amount of baking soda has the ability to reduce the acidity level in milk just enough to add a few more days to the expiration date. However, milk will normally last for a week after the expiration date and still be usable if stored properly and no one drinks out of the carton. Another method is to transfer the milk from a carton to a screw-top glass jar to reduce the effects of oxidation.

NO NEED TO REFRIGERATE, NOW THERE'S PARMALAT

A milk that has recently been added to the nonrefrigerated dairy products on the shelf, Parmalat is an ultrahigh-temperature milk that has a long shelf life without refrigeration. It is perfectly safe, and you can save refrigerator space.

POWDERED MILK NEEDS REFRIGERATION

If you purchase powdered whole milk, it should be refrigerated due to the high fat content. The powder will go rancid if not refrigerated after a short period of time. Once any powdered milk is reconstituted, it must be refrigerated and will last only about three or four days.

COW'S K-RATIONS

Milk cows are fed eight times per day with feed consisting of hay and silage, which is composed of grass, corn, barley, cotton seed, and of course bakery and grocery by-products. Cows consume about 80 pounds of food each day at a cost of about $3.50. Cows also drink about 35 gallons of water daily.

CHOCOLATE MILK VS. CALCIUM ABSORPTION

While many nutritionists tell people not to drink chocolate milk, they neglect to give you the whole story. The truth is that there is not enough chocolate in chocolate milk to affect your calcium absorption because milk has a high level of calcium, so the loss from the chocolate is minimal.

It is true that chocolate does contain oxalic acid, which is a known calcium binder and will reduce the total amount of calcium absorbed. However, if an adult or child will drink milk only if it has chocolate in it, give him chocolate milk; it's better than no milk at all.

One cup of low-fat chocolate milk contains about 250 milligrams of calcium. The loss due to the chocolate is about 6 milligrams, which ends up as calcium oxalate. There is a small amount of sugar increase, but it is only minor compared to the nutrients obtained by drinking the milk.

There are new studies showing that calcium from milk is not as easily absorbed as we have thought for years and may actually be one of the causes of osteoporosis, since many women rely on milk as their main source of calcium. For additional information on this study call (888) 668-6455.

I'M STUCK! SLIP ME THE BUTTER

If you are going to heat milk in a pot, spread a very thin layer of unsalted butter on the bottom of the pot. This will stop the milk from sticking. Salted butter will not work.

FAT IN MILK—JUST THE FACTS

After you remove the water, whole milk contains 50 percent fat, 2 percent milk contains 34 percent fat, and 1 percent milk contains 18 percent fat. The percentages are meant to confuse you; if they placed the actual fat content on the package many people would not buy milk.

UDDERLY WORN OUT

More milk is produced by California cows than cows in any other state. California cows produce almost 20,000 pounds of milk annually, about 2,500 gallons. One cow can produce enough milk to provide 130 people with a 10-ounce glass of milk every day. California has 800,000 cows producing milk.

THE THREE BEARS WOULD HAVE LIKED THIS

Liquid porridge is an ideal food for babies in Sweden, where it is called *valling*. It is normally used to wean babies off the bottle or mother from about six months on. The porridge is composed of cereal and milk and is so popular with children

that they usually have the porridge until they are four or five years old. It is sold in three varieties: oat and wheat, oat, and multigrain. It can also be fed through a bottle that has a large hole in the nipple. For information call (203) 637-5151.

THE NEW WHEY: EDIBLE SHAVING CREAM

The cheese industry produces large quantities of this liquid protein, which is discarded. However, science has now found a number of uses, such as adding alcohol to the whey and making an edible shaving cream (patent pending). Pure alcohol tends to uncoil the amino acids of whey, which produces foam that traps air molecules. Whey is also being developed as an egg substitute and a dessert topping like whipped cream, and when it is placed on frozen pizza dough, the dough doesn't get soggy.

EVAPORATED MILK VS. CONDENSED MILK

Evaporated milk is processed in its can at temperatures above 200°F to sterilize it. This results in a somewhat burnt taste that can be eliminated by mixing it into a recipe. Condensed milk does not require high heat sterilization since it contains more than 40 percent sugar, which acts as a preservative, thus reducing bacterial growth.

EVAPORATED MILK FACTS
- It may be sold in whole, nonfat, or low-fat types.
- If you do not use the whole can, refrigerate the remainder in a well-sealed glass jar.
- If the milk is slightly frozen, it can be whipped and used as a low-fat ice cream topping. When whipped it will remain stable for about forty-five minutes if refrigerated.
- The stability of evaporated milk can be improved by stirring in 1 tablespoon of lemon juice into 1 cup of milk.
- Evaporated milk can be sweetened by adding 3 tablespoons of sugar.

CONDENSED MILK FACTS
- Condensed milk can be stored at room temperature for up to six months.
- After opening a can it must be stored in a glass jar as airtight as possible, then refrigerated.
- Heated condensed milk will turn thick and golden brown and tastes a little like caramel.
- Never heat a can of condensed milk unopened or it may end up in your neighbor's house. It may explode.
- Condensed milk cannot be substituted for evaporated milk in recipes.

THE COW NEEDS TO BE RELAXED

If you have ever purchased milk that has a somewhat cooked taste, the milk may have been poorly pasteurized. This happens only occasionally. If the milk has a grassy or garliclike flavor, it was because the cows were milked too close to their mealtime and not allowed to rest after they ate.

NEW MILK STERILIZATION FOR THE MILLENIUM?

A new and improved method of sterilizing milk to kill bacteria has been invented in Canada. Electrical-pulse sterilization may be the answer to eliminating the expensive process of pasteurization. The process involves passing an electrical current through liquid food by moving the food between two stainless steel electrodes. The electrodes emit pulses, which perforate the microorganisms' cell walls, permanently damaging them. This process destroys all the viable microbes and basically sterilizes the milk without high heat, which destroys nutrients. The liquids retain almost all of their nutrients and the process does not alter the taste of the food while utilizing only 1 percent of the energy used in pasteurization.

MILK ON THE ROAD

Since fresh milk is difficult to transport in a car, just bring along some powdered milk. When the children want their milk, add water and shake or go over a bumpy road for a few minutes to make a milk shake.

KEEPING COOL

Milk will last longer and remain fresher if it stored at about 34°F. The average refrigerator temperature is about 40°F if the door does not get opened too frequently.

NOT SOMETHING TO BRAG ABOUT

In 1998 Americans spent almost four times more on soda and almost seven times more on alcoholic beverages than they did on milk.

HUMAN MILK

CAN'T SLEEP? ON THE PILL?

Studies have shown that it can take up to 50 percent longer for the effects of caffeine to wear off if you are pregnant or are taking a birth control pill. Caffeine can concentrate in larger amounts in breast milk than in the blood. This may cause a nursing baby to show signs of caffeine addiction, which can result in crankiness, inability to sleep, and even colic.

THE ONLY WAY—BREAST FEED, THEN EXERCISE

Studies show that if you are nursing your baby it is wise to feed the baby before exercising. Lactic acid tends to build up during exercise and will give the breast milk a sour taste. The lactic acid levels will remain high for about ninety minutes after an exercise period before the body can clear it out. If you really need to feed during this period, have the milk prepared beforehand.

YOUR BABY IS NOT A CALF

If you are not going to nurse, remember that cow's milk must be diluted with water, and sugar should be added to sweeten it. Human babies do not require the concentrated protein content of cow's milk. A calf has a growth rate twice that of human babies and needs the extra protein. Cow's milk can be hard to digest and may irritate a baby's delicate digestive system. The addition of sugar makes it taste more like mother's milk. Check with your physician regarding the use of goat's milk.

A few comparisons between human milk and cow's milk:

INGREDIENT	HUMAN MILK	DAIRY COW'S MILK
Water	87 percent	87 percent
Casein	40 percent	82 percent
Whey	60 percent	18 percent
Lactose	6.8 percent	4.9 percent
Mineral content	0.2 percent	0.7 percent

THE X FACTOR

There is a factor in human milk called the bifidus factor. Scientists have not identified the actual chemical compound related to this factor, but they do know what the factor does. When an infant consumes mother's milk, the factor enhances the growth of a harmless bacterium called *Lactobacillus bifidus* in the infant's digestive system. The bacteria excretes a by-product called lactic acid, which has the ability to inhibit the growth of potentially harmful microorganisms.

PROBLEM WITH TEENS BREAST FEEDING

Since they are not fully developed physically, a teenager needs a doctor's supervision if she plans to breast-feed. Teens produce 37 to 54 percent less milk and require 23 percent more calories, additional vitamin B6, and 40 percent more protein than adults.

USE IT OR LOSE IT

Prepared formula is good only once and should be discarded, not saved and reheated. The bacteria that may be present in the baby's mouth can enter the formula through the nipple and cause illness. Only fill the bottle with enough formula for one feeding. The method of storage does not matter, and the temperatures needed to kill the bacteria are too high and will destroy nutrients.

MOTHER'S MILK MATE™

This is the most convenient method of storing breast milk available. It is a complete containment and storage system to preserve fresh breast milk. The unit fits right into the refrigerator and stores the milk in 5-ounce bottles, which can easily be rotated. All plastic components have been approved by the FDA. For further information call (800) 327-4382.

MILK AND MILK SUBSTITUTES—A COMPARISON

MILK(3½ oz)	CALORIES	PROTEIN(g)	FAT(g)	CALCIUM(mg)	PHOSPHORUS(mg)
Human	96	1	4.2	32	13.7
Goat	68	3.6	3.9	135	110
Cow (whole milk)	64	3.3	3.5	119	93
Enfamil®	66	1.4	3.5	51	35
Prosobee®	66	2.0	3.5	69	54

The carbohydrate content of the milks does not vary enough to be significant. Human milk does have the highest carbohydrate content, 6.9 grams per 3½-ounce serving.

GOAT'S MILK

Goat's milk has a protein and mineral ratio closer to mother's milk than cow's milk. It also contains higher levels of niacin and thiamine. The protein is of a better quality, and there is a lower incidence of allergic reactions than to cow's milk or soy milk. Goat's milk contains 13 percent more calcium, 25 percent more vitamin B6, 47 percent more vitamin A, and 134 percent more potassium than cow's milk.

Supermarkets are starting to carry more goat's milk products. If there aren't any in your favorite market, just have them call the Meyenberg Goat Milk Products Company. Evaporated goat's milk is available that has been pasteurized and homogenized.

CREAM

CURDLING UP OVER FRUIT

Cream has the tendency to curdle when poured over acidic fruits. To eliminate this problem, try adding a small amount of baking soda to the cream, then mixing it well before pouring it over the fruit. Baking soda is capable of reducing the acidity level in fruits.

CAN EVAPORATED MILK SUB FOR HEAVY CREAM?

This substitution will work well only in baked goods, cream soups, custards, and cream-based sauces. However, you may notice a somewhat "off" flavor in dishes that are not heavily spiced and rely on the cream for some flavor. If you are going to substitute evaporated milk for heavy cream in foods that are not cooked, such as mousse or a whipped topping, it would be best to substitute cottage cheese or part-skim ricotta cheese.

I'M COLD, WHIP ME NOW

Light cream can be whipped just like heavy cream if you place a metal bowl and metal mixing utensils in the freezer before using them to beat the cream. Also, try adding 1 tablespoon of unflavored gelatin that has been dissolved in 1 tablespoon of hot water to 2 cups of light cream to help it whip up and keep its shape. After it whips up, refrigerate it for two hours. If you are using heavy cream and want it to set faster, just add seven drops of lemon juice to each pint of cream.

WHY CREAM CAN BE WHIPPED

When cream is whipped, the fat globules are released into the milk and congregate. Air is also forced into the mixture by the force of the whipping action and is then trapped between the fat globules, creating a full-bodied mixture.

JOLLY GOOD, THAT HORSERADISH CREAM

The British make a great horseradish cream sauce. Just blend together ¼ cup of horseradish into ½ cup of lightly whipped cream. Add a small amount of salt and pepper, about ¾ teaspoon of sugar, and a few drops of vinegar.

TURNING CREAM INTO SOUR CREAM

Sour cream can be made from heavy cream by placing four drops of lemon juice concentrate into ¾ cup of heavy cream. Allow the mixture to stand at room temperature for about twenty minutes before refrigerating.

"REAL" SOUR CREAM

Sour cream should never be added to a recipe if the dish is still hot. The sour cream will usually separate and ruin the dish. Add the sour cream just before serving.

GOING ROUND IN CIRCLES

Cream is no longer made the "old-fashioned" way, which was to allow it to separate to the top of the milk and skim it off. Cream is now produced using a centrifuge, which allows the fat globules to be released in a liquid, concentrated, and easily removed. Light cream is 20 to 30 percent butterfat, light whipping cream is 30 to 36 percent butterfat, and heavy whipping cream is 36 to 40 percent butterfat. Half-and-half is 11 percent butterfat and is produced from half cream and half milk.

BAKING SODA TO THE RESCUE

If your sour cream is starting to have an "off" odor but is not really bad, just add 1/8 teaspoon of baking soda to neutralize the lactic acid that is starting to build up. However, if the odor persists, throw it out!

Crème Fraîche

This has a velvety smooth texture. Do not use yogurt in place of the sour cream or the mixture will curdle when heated.

2 tablespoons standard sour cream or buttermilk
1 cup whipping cream

Blend the ingredients in a standard pie plate, then cover as tightly as possible and allow to remain at room temperature for 1 to 2 days or until it becomes thick. To be sure that it is done, tip the pie plate just slightly; if the cream flows just a little, it is ready. The consistency should be similar to half-set gelatin and will last for 7 to 10 days in the refrigerator.

HOW TO PREPARE FLAVORED WHIPPED CREAMS

• chocolate: add 1 tablespoon of cocoa, 1 teaspoon of real vanilla extract, and, if you would like to sweeten it further, 3 tablespoons of sugar.
• coffee: add 1 teaspoon of a quality instant coffee and 2 tablespoons of sugar.
• lemon: add 1 teaspoon of pure lemon juice and 2 tablespoons of sugar.

NONDAIRY CREAMERS

Most nondairy creamers are made from corn syrup and oil, possibly coconut or palm oil. In moderation these will not give you enough sugar or saturated fat to really matter. A new product that will be sold shortly is a nondairy creamer with a new ingredient called N-Creamer™ 46, which is a modified food starch that can replace sodium caseinate in nondairy creamers. This should eliminate the problem of proteins coagulating and rising to the top of your coffee, especially if hard water is used to make the coffee. Mocha Mix, however, would be my first choice as a cream substitute.

CLOTTED CREAM

If you are ever working from a British recipe and it calls for Devonshire or clotted cream, allow nonpasteurized cream to stand in a saucepan for twelve hours in winter or six hours in summer at room temperature. Then place the pan over very low heat (without boiling) until small rings of foam come to the surface, which will show that the cream is scalded. Remove immediately from the heat and refrigerate for ten to twelve hours. Skin off the thick clotted cream and serve as a garnish for berries, or do as the English do and spread it on scones with a dollop of jam or preserves.

ICE CREAM

A BRIEF HISTORY OF ICE CREAM

200 B.C.	Chinese invent ice cream when a mixture of goat's and rice milk is flavored and packed in snow.
1050 A.D.	Roman emperor Nero sends his slaves to the mountains to return with fresh fallen snow, which is flavored with honey and juices.
1200	Marco Polo brings sherbet back from the Far East.

1700	Cookbooks print ice cream recipes and a written record of the first Maryland governor mentioning ice cream. (George Washington and Thomas Jefferson loved cherry ice cream.)
1812	Dolly Madison serves ice cream at the White House.
1846	The hand-crank ice cream machine is invented by Nancy Johnson.
1851	A commercial milk company owned by Jacob Fussell in Baltimore, Maryland, is converted into the first ice cream production plant in the United States.
1890	The ice cream sundae is invented when carbonated water, which was considered sinful, was not allowed to be included in a soda on Sundays.
1904	The ice cream cone is invented at the St. Louis World's Fair.
1921	Ellis Island immigrants are treated to ice cream cones, an American original.

WORLD RECORD FOR EATING ICE CREAM

The record for eating ice cream, which may never be broken, was set on August 7, 1977, by Dennett D'Angelo, who ate 3 pounds 6 ounces in just ninety seconds. Talk about a cold rush.

ICE CREAM SNEAKERS

One out of every five regular ice cream eaters will have a midnight binge. Men do it more frequently, especially those between the ages of eighteen and twenty-four.

ICE CREAM IS REALLY FROZEN FOAM

We are used to seeing ice cream in a solid or semisolid form; however, ice cream is really just a foam solidified by freezing a large percentage of the liquid it contains. Ice cream is composed of ice crystals, milk fat, water containing salts and sugars, and air pockets. The liquid in ice cream that contains the sugar keeps the ice cream from freezing into a solid block of ice. Ice cream must be well sealed, or it will pick up odors from other foods very readily.

REAL COMMERCIAL ICE CREAM

Regulations regarding the percentage of ingredients in commercial ice cream are strict. Ice cream must meet the following government standards by having:

- at least 10 percent milk fat. Premiums usually have at least 16 percent. Ice milk contains 3 to 5 percent milk fat.
- 9 to 12 percent nonfat milk solids, which contain the proteins and carbohydrates found in milk.
- 12 to 16 percent sweeteners—usually corn syrup and sucrose.
- 0.2 to 0.5 percent stabilizers and emulsifiers.
- 55 to 64 percent water, which comes from the milk or added ingredients.

BEN & JERRY'S TOP SELLERS

1. Chocolate Chip Cookie Dough
2. Cherry Garcia
3. Chocolate Fudge Brownie
4. New York Super Fudge Chunk
5. English Toffee Crunch

ICE CREAM CAPITAL OF THE WORLD

Americans consume 23 quarts of ice cream per person annually.

THE PLASTIC BLANKET

Some of the higher-quality ice creams now come with a thin plastic covering that can be placed over the exposed surface of the ice cream as it is removed to provide a degree of protection from odors. If your brand does not have the plastic sheet, just use a doubled sheet of plastic wrap.

LOW-FAT CHOCOLATE ICE CREAM CHIPS?

A new product called Benfat has produced a chocolate chip that has 50 percent fewer calories than a real chocolate chip. You will have a hard time telling the difference, especially in ice cream, which is what the product was designed for.

THE TOP 10 MOST POPULAR ICE CREAM FLAVORS

The following percentages refer to the people worldwide choosing that flavor:

1.Vanilla	29	percent
2.Chocolate	8.9	percent
3.Butter pecan	5.4	percent
4.Strawberry	5.3	percent
5.Neapolitan	4.1	percent
6.Chocolate chip	3.9	percent
7.French vanilla	3.8	percent
8.Cookies and cream	3.5	percent
9.Cherry	2.0	percent
10. Coffee	1.8	percent

Black Cow

2 scoops vanilla ice cream (or reduced-fat substitute)

Real root beer (or diet)

Combine ingredients in a tall glass.

Malted Milk Shake

1 tablespoon favorite syrup

1 cup whole milk

2 scoops ice cream

1 teaspoon unflavored malt

Blend all ingredients for 45 seconds.

NUTRITIONAL INFORMATION

CALCIUM VS. HIGH-FAT DIET

Studies have shown that if you consume a diet high in fat of any type, you will lose excess calcium through urination. This is also true of a diet with a lot of meat, probably because of the amount of fat in most beef products.

CHIPS AWAY

One of the fattiest snack foods is potato chips, which contain about 16 to 20 teaspoons of fat, mostly saturated, in just 8 ounces.

DO KIDS NEED WHOLE MILK?

The American Academy of Pediatricians recommends mother's milk or an iron-rich formula for the first year. The second-year recommendation is whole milk, which allows the child to get the essential fatty acids in sufficient amounts. After two years, low-fat milk can be used if the child's growth patterns are normal and if there are no medical concerns.

TESTING FOR LACTOSE INTOLERENCE

If you think that you have lactose intolerance but are not sure, your doctor can give you a simple test to measure the amount of hydrogen in your breath after you have consumed lactose. If the amount of hydrogen is elevated, this will indicate that you are having problems digesting lactose.

NEW MILK SUBSTITUTES

There is a new product out called Vitamite®, which is lactose-free and has only 2 percent fat. It is sold in 1-quart containers and tastes similar to milk, especially when used on cereal. It contains milk protein and is low in sodium and high in calcium.

Another product gaining in popularity is Vitasoy®, an enriched soy drink that is being teamed up with coffee. The drink may also be sold at a number of coffeehouses as a stand-alone drink. The health claims for soy are numerous and include reducing the incidence of heart disease, fighting certain cancers, lowering the incidence of osteoporosis, and reducing the severity of hot flashes associated with menopause.

WELL, POWDER MY PROTEIN

It seems like everyone is making a protein powder these days. There are so many brands on the market that is impossible to analyze them. As a general rule, most are made from soy or milk solids, calcium, egg, sugar, and added vitamins and herbs. They are mixed with milk or juice, and most supply about 15 grams of protein per serving.

SHOULD WE WORRY ABOUT ANTIBIOTICS IN MILK?

If antibiotics are given to cows, they must be kept out of milk production until the antibiotics are withdrawn and the cow gets a clean bill of health. There is also no evidence linking bovine growth hormone (BGH) to mad cow disease.

NONDAIRY MILK SUBSTITUTES

There are numerous milk substitutes on the market, most of which can be found in health food stores.

▯ SOY MILK

This nondairy milk is produced from ground cooked soybeans. The milk must be fortified with calcium to bring it closer nutritionally to cow's milk since it is naturally low in calcium; however, it is high in iron, is low in fat, and has no cholesterol. If you have an allergy to milk or are lactose-intolerant, soy milk is a good substitute.

▯ RICE MILK

This is produced from brown rice and water. Starch in the brown rice is transformed into a sugar by an enzyme. Since it does not taste very sweet, some companies add a small amount of rice syrup as a sweetener. The milk must be enriched with calcium and a number of vitamins.

▯ OAT MILK

Produced from oats and sold in aseptic containers, most oat milk is fortified to bring the nutritional level close to that of cow's milk.

▯ COCONUT MILK

This is not the watery liquid found in the center of coconuts. It is a liquid extracted from the coconut meat and is very high in saturated fat. Most coconut milk is diluted with water and is usually only found in Asian markets.

▯ BETTER THAN MILK™

This is a dairy-free tofu substitute beverage mix. It is a good-tasting beverage sold in a canister similar to other milk substitutes. The product is caseinate-free, cholesterol-free, lactose-free, and gluten-free, has B12, and contains 50 percent of the RDA of calcium in every serving. The ingredients are maltodextrim (rice source), soy milk, calcium carbonate, soy protein isolate, fructose, tofu powder, sea salt, titanium dioxide (natural mineral for color), potassium chloride, carrageenan gum, natural flavors, soy lecithin, and cyanocobalamin (source of B12). For information call (800) 227-2320.

▯ VEGILICIOUS™ A.K.A. DARIFREE™

This is one of the best-tasting dairy-free drinks available. It is sold in powdered form and mixed with water. The original name was Vegilicious, but that was too hard for most people to say, so the name was changed to DariFree. This is an excellent substitute for dry milk in baked goods. A liquid chocolate drink as well as a fat-free drink are due out shortly. DariFree's ingredients are maltodextrim (potato source), cereal solids (potato source), high oleic sunflower oil, cereal solids (corn source), dehydrated honey, di-calcium phosphate, calcium carbonate, tricalcium phosphate, natural flavors, sea salt, titanium dioxide, carrageenan, potassium citrate, citric acid, monoglycerides, diglycerides, and lecithin. It does not contain any gluten or MSG and has as much calcium per serving as milk. It is also hypoallergenic.

ENER-G NUTQUIK™ POWDER

This product can substitute for milk in many recipes and is made from almonds. When dry milk is called for in a baked-goods recipe, you might want to try this instead of milk, especially if you are avoiding lactose or soy.

RICE MOO BEVERAGE MIX™

This beverage is gluten-free, soy-free, animal product–free, cholesterol-free, and fat-free. It has a pleasant taste and supplies a number of nutrients.

ACIDOPHILUS—A FRIENDLY BACTERIA

There are times when you are ill or taking medication such as penicillin, which can destroy the good bacteria in your intestinal tract. These good bacteria have a number of functions; one important one is the production of B vitamins. Acidophilus is one of these friendly bacteria and eating live-culture yogurt or aciphophilus-enhanced milk will replenish your supply.

BACTERIA IN EVERY GLASS

When you purchase half a gallon of milk the bacteria count is about 50 million, give or take a million. If milk is left at room temperature for two to three hours, the bacteria will multiply to more than 300 million and the milk will go sour.

HORMONAL MILK IS A PROBLEM

Monsanto may be recalling their BGH that was given to cows to increase milk production. Scientists are finding an increase in breast and prostate cancers, and the problem may be linked to the hormonal milk.

EGGS

CREATING A FOAM

Many recipes call for beaten egg whites. They are used to add rising power, lightness, and puffiness to foods. Creating foam is an art and there are many pitfalls that you should be aware of as well as methods of repairing a foam problem. The following are some of the more common problems and their solutions.

• The slightest bit of fat can affect the foam developing and retaining its shape. This usually is a problem of a small bit of egg yolk being left in with the whites.

• Adding a small amount of an acid, such as lemon juice or cream of tartar, will cause the volume to increase.

• Eggs will develop better foam if they are allowed to remain at room temperature for 1 hour before they are used.

• Never overbeat; the more you beat, the more the whites will look dry and curdled.

• Add a small amount of sugar and the whites will remain stiffer for a longer period.

• Beating too much will cause the peaks to be too fragile.

STORING LIQUID EGG SUBSTITUTES

Liquid pasteurized egg substitutes can be refrigerated for three days after they are opened, but do not freeze well.

WHIP ME, WHIP ME, BUT USE A COPPER BOWL

Always use a copper bowl when whipping eggs. The copper will absorb the heat friction caused by the beating action, which tends to stop the formation of air pockets needed to form bubbles of air. The copper also releases ions during the beating process that cause the protein in the mixture to become stiffer. When a copper bowl is used, it will not be necessary to use cream of tartar. If you don't have a copper bowl, the next best is stainless steel; however, a pinch of cream of tartar needs to be added to stabilize the mixture.

Be sure that either bowl has a rounded bottom to allow the mixture to fall easily to the bottom and come into equal contact with the mixing blades.

HAVING TROUBLE MAKING YOUR PEAKS PERKY?

If you want your meringue to be world-class, you need to adhere to all the little tips.

• Make sure the egg whites are at room temperature, then add a small amount of baking powder to them and as you are beating them.

• Add 2 to 3 tablespoons of sugar for each egg used.

• Beat only until they stand up. If you want the peaks to stand up for a long period of time, add 1/4 teaspoon of white vinegar for every three eggs (whites only) while beating. Adding 4 or 5 drops of lemon juice for every cup of cream also helps.

• If the weather outside is gloomy or rainy or if the humidity is high, you will have droopy peaks no matter what you do.

EGG WHITES—A HEALTHY ALTERNATIVE

A number of companies are selling egg whites. These products can be used the same way as you would ordinarily use eggs. If you are making scrambled eggs or any dish that calls for egg whites alone, there should be no problem using these products. Be sure that the label states the product is pasteurized and salmonella-free. The pasteurization process does utilize high heat, so the products may not respond as well as fresh egg whites in certain recipes. For more information call (888) 669-6557.

Perfect Eggnog
2 large eggs (egg substitutes will do)
2 cups whole milk
1/4 teaspoon pure vanilla (no imitation)
4 tablespoons granulated sugar

In a small bowl, beat the eggs well, then beat in the milk, vanilla, and sugar. Chill and serve. If you do not use egg substitutes, then the eggs should be sterilized using the same procedure when preparing hollandaise sauce. (see page 332.) For chocolate eggnog replace the sugar with 2 tablespoons of chocolate syrup.

CUSTARD

MAKING THE PERFECT CUSTARD

When you heat custard containing egg yolks and whites, the protein solidifies and causes thickening. The egg-to-milk ratio, however, is very important if you really want to prepare a great custard. The perfect milk-based custard should use 1 whole egg for every 2/3 cup of whole milk. If sugar is added, add more egg. If you use a starch such as rice (a good thickener), you will need to reduce the amount of egg. After placing the custard in the oven, ***never*** open the oven door. The retained heat is needed to cook the center of the custard.

Custard
2 cups whole milk or cream
3 large eggs
⅓ cup granulated sugar
1½ teaspoons pure vanilla

In a small saucepan, heat the milk over medium heat until small bubbles appear around the sides of the pan. Remove the pan from the heat and set aside. In a medium bowl, whisk the eggs, sugar, and vanilla until they are well blended but not frothy. Place the mixture into the hot milk and stir, then allow to cool for about 2 to 3 minutes. Place the custard into individual dishes or one large dish. Bake by placing the dish or dishes into a large shallow pan that has been filled with about 1½ inches of boiling water. Bake for 25 minutes for small dishes or 45 minutes for one large dish at 350°F.

HOW SOFT I AM

If you would like to make very soft custard, make it on a stove top as opposed to the oven. To keep the consistency loose, you will need to reduce the amount of binding that will occur in the egg protein by stirring the custard continually. Remove the custard from the heat as soon as it reaches the desired consistency.

TAPIOCA

YUM, YUM, CASSAVA ROOT

Tapioca is extracted from cassava root and is a starch that can be found in three forms. Pearl tapioca, which is available in small and large sizes, is commonly used to prepare puddings and needs to be soaked for several hours to soften it before it can be cooked. Quick-cooking tapioca is normally sold in a granular form as a thickener for soups and stews and does not require a lengthy presoaking.

Plain old tapioca flour or starch, usually only found in health food stores, is excellent for thickening soups, glazes, fruit fillings, and stews. Tapioca flour has the advantage over cornstarch in that it won't break down when frozen and then reheated. When thickening, always prepare a thick paste first and gradually add it to the liquid to be thickened. If added to a liquid, the liquid should not boil or the tapioca may become stringy. If you stir too much, a mixture that has been thickened with tapioca flour may become somewhat gelatinous.

YOGURT

Basically, yogurt is prepared by fermenting milk and coagulating it with lactic bacteria, which produces a semisolid, custardlike consistency. Yogurt was invented in the Balkans about four hundred years ago. A number of animal milks can be used to make yogurt; cow's milk is the most common. If you want to make your own yogurt, bring milk to a boil, cool it to 98°F, then add a teaspoon of any plain commercial yogurt to act as a starter. The mixture must then be maintained at a steady temperature of 72°F for 2 to 3 hours before being refrigerated.

BOY, AM I FRESH

Yogurt should be as fresh as possible at all times. Always purchase the freshest by checking the pull date. Yogurt will last for 7 to 10 days in the refrigerator after the pull date.

MY YOGURT IS DROWNING

If you have ever opened up yogurt or cottage cheese and noticed a liquid that looked like water and thought that it was seepage, you were wrong. The liquid that has separated is whey, which is a good protein that has problems remaining in suspension after air gets in the package. Stir the whey back in—it's good for you.

EASY DOES IT

Be gentle when you are stirring yogurt. When yogurt is stirred vigorously, the whey is released and the yogurt becomes runny and watery.

WHERE'S MY YOGURT BLANKIE?

Yogurt needs to be brought up to room temperature before you add it to any hot mixture to avoid separation. If it gets too hot and boils it will separate, unless it is a flour-based mixture.

I'M ALWAYS A SUB

When a baked-goods recipe calls for sour cream, yogurt may be substituted in its place.

HOW DOES FERMENTED MARE'S MILK SOUND?

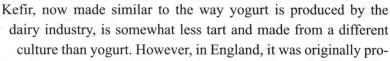

Kefir, now made similar to the way yogurt is produced by the dairy industry, is somewhat less tart and made from a different culture than yogurt. However, in England, it was originally produced from mare's milk, which was fermented with a starter similar to a sourdough starter. The original product was closer to a liquid beverage than to the semiliquid we can now purchase in the supermarket. Kefir is available in many different flavors and is even sold in a low-fat version.

THAT'S IT, I'M DEAD

If you heat yogurt to 120°F you will destroy the good bacteria that is a benefit of yogurt. If you are adding yogurt to a hot dish or liquid, add it toward the end of the cooking time. There are many other nutrients, however, that will survive the heat, such as protein and calcium.

I'M ON FIRE—QUICK, BRING ME A LASSI

A lassi is a yogurt beverage usually served with spicy Indian meals to relieve the spicy bite. It is prepared from yogurt, ice, mint, and fresh fruit. All dairy products have the ability to neutralize the bite of hot and spicy foods to a certain degree.

Chapter 13
Sweet Treats

SYRUPS AND ICINGS

PUTTING ON A COAT

A common coating for desserts and confections is a glaze, which is usually brushed or poured on and is prepared by combining a jam or jelly with a liquid, such as water or liqueur. The mixture is then strained to remove any pulp and warmed before use. One of the more common glazes is a chocolate glaze, which is prepared from melted chocolate, cream, butter, and corn syrup. Confectioners' sugar glaze is prepared by mixing confectioners' sugar with liquid, such as lemon juice or even water.

HEAT ME, HEAT ME

A commonly used icing is called boiled icing. It is prepared by cooking sugar with whipped egg whites, then beating the mixture until it is smooth, syrupy, and glossy. It may also be called Italian meringue.

CARAMEL

Caramel sauce is prepared from sugar and water. The mixture is cooked until it is dark brown. Caramel candy is prepared from sugar, milk or cream, honey or corn syrup, and butter. Additional ingredients can also be included such as nuts and chocolate bits.

CORN SYRUP

Corn syrup has been produced in the United States since the mid-1800s and is made by extracting starch granules from the kernels. The starch is then treated with an acid, bacterial, or malt enzyme, which turns it into sweet syrup. Corn syrup is important commercially because of its unique sweetness properties—it can be changed into a sweet substance that does not register on our sweet taste buds. When using corn syrup, remember that there are two colors, dark and light, that can be used interchangeably. The dark, however, will impart a dark color to your food.

SUGAR IS ATTRACTIVE

When using sugar to prepare syrups, remember that sugar has the tendency to attract moisture from the air and thus keeps foods moist. Cakes are lighter because the sugar keeps the gluten from becoming stiff. Sugar has the tendency to lower the freezing point of most liquids, which keeps ice cream in a semisolid state. When used on meats it will help retain the natural moisture. Sugar syrups are easy to prepare and very popular.

EASY-TO-PREPARE SUGAR SYRUPS

- thin sugar syrup: . . . . . .1 cup granulated sugar plus 2 cups water
- medium sugar syrup: . .1 cup granulated sugar plus 1 cup water
- heavy sugar syrup: . . . .1 cup granulated sugar plus ¾ cup water
- thick sugar syrup: . . . . .1 cup granulated sugar plus ½ cup water

In a small saucepan, add the sugar to the water and stir gently over low heat. Do not allow the mixture to boil until the sugar is completely dissolved. When boiling begins, stop stirring and continue to boil uncovered for about 1 minute. Flavorings can be added either before or after cooking. If you overcook the syrup, just add ¼ cup of boiling water and cook again.

▽ THREAD STAGES OF SUGAR SYRUP

The thread stage is used to determine the actual temperature of the sugar syrup. In order for the candy to set, it must crystallize into sugar syrup. Cook the syrup in a small saucepan over medium heat until it reaches the desired temperature. If you do not have a thermometer, use the following guidelines:

- thread stage—230 to 234°F: Syrup will form a soft light thread.
- soft ball—234 to 240°F: Syrup will form a small ball that will flatten out by itself when removed.
- firm ball—244 to 248°F: Syrup will form a firm ball that tends to flatten out when pressed between your fingers.
- hard ball—250 to 265°F: Syrup will form a hard ball that has just a little give to it when squeezed.
- soft crack—270 to 290°F: Syrup tends to separate into hard threads that are bendable.
- hard crack—300 to 310°F: Syrup will separate into threads that are hard and very brittle.
- caramelized sugar—310 to 338°F: Syrup will become a golden color.

NOTE: When sugar is cooked above 350°F, it will turn black and burn.

TINY BUBBLES

When preparing sugar syrup, always watch the bubbles. Bubbles tend to get smaller as the sugar syrup thickens. If the syrup bubbles get too small, it's time to start over.

I'LL HAVE SOME ORGEAT ON MY ICE CREAM, PLEASE

If you like the taste of almonds, try a syrup called orgeat, which is prepared from almonds and rosewater. Orgeat is also used in mai-tais and scorpions.

HONEY

TYPES OF HONEY

☑ LIQUID HONEY

Honey extracted from the honeycomb, then strained for clarity. All liquid honey will granulate very easily, but it can still be used.

☑ CREAMED HONEY

Honey produced by the crystallization of liquid honey under controlled conditions.

☑ COMB HONEY

Honey in the original wrapper and packaged by the bees. It is taken from the hive and sold in its original "wax cell" form.

☑ PASTEURIZED HONEY

Honey that has been high heat–processed to destroy yeasts, which can cause honey to ferment as well as melt the dextrose crystals that cause honey to granulate.

HONEY IS A SAP

Honey nectar is actually a flower or plant sap that is released from the plant to regulate the plant fluids. A human releases fluids through the kidneys in a similar fashion. Honey nectars all vary somewhat in their nutritional makeup. Some have more vitamins and minerals, while some are higher in sugar. Honey can vary in its sugar content as well as the types of sugars it contains. The sugars commonly found in honey are sucrose, glucose, and fructose.

OVERWORKED AND UNDERPAID

The average worker bee will forage up to 1 mile from the hive and make about twenty-five trips each day. Each bee can carry a load equal to half its weight and in a lifetime will consume 1 gallon of honey, which is about 7 million miles to the gallon. During their lifetime they provide the hive with less than 1 ounce of honey.

BACTERIA HATES HONEY

When the nectar reaches the hive, the bee has diluted it and the nectar must then be concentrated to resist bacteria and molds. The nectar goes through a processing in the hive that returns it to its original level of concentration. The sugar concentration in honey is so high that it kills any microbe that tries to eat it by drawing the moisture from its cells.

HONEY-COLORED

The color of honey is determined by the floral source the bees choose. There are three main colors. White honey, gathered from clover or basswood, is the mildest honey and the most desired by honey connoisseurs. Golden honey, gathered from goldenrod and other flowers that grow in the fall, has a stronger flavor than white honey. Amber honey, usually gathered from buckwheat flowers, is the darkest and strongest honey, and not one of the more desired unless you acquire a taste for it.

HONEY VS. BABIES

While honey has been good for many uses both in cooking and medicine through the ages, it is not recommended for children less than a year old. Honey has for many years been known to be a source of bacterial spores, which may produce a toxin that can result in infant botulism. This form of food poisoning can produce symptoms such as weakness in the neck and extremities, no ability to suck or cry normally, difficulty in eating and swallowing, and constipation. Researchers are even looking for a link between sudden infant death syndrome and botulism. Honey should never be added to an infant's formula as a sweetener.

MYSTERIES OF HONEY

There are still scientific investigations that are ongoing regarding honey. While more than two hundred different substances have been identified, there are still more that have not been found, especially the enzymes that are responsible for synthesizing long-chain sugars.

BAKING WITH HONEY

The best honey for baking is a milder-flavored honey, white or golden. When honey is added to a batter, it should be added in a slow stream with continuous stirring. If you use honey in baked goods they will brown faster, so you may want to reduce the oven heat by about 25°F. The addition of honey will also produce baked goods that will remain moist for a longer period of time.

A GREAT SUBSTITUTE

When preparing jams and jellies, honey can be substituted for sugar. If the recipe calls for 4 cups of sugar, use 2 cups of honey and cook the jelly just a little longer. Always use liquid honey and powdered pectin for the best results.

BUY ONLY THE BEST

The highest-quality honey will be labeled "100 percent pure unfiltered," "raw," or "uncooked" and will not be heat processed.

DANGEROUS HONEY?

There are areas of the world where honey bees forage that may contain plants with nectars that can be harmful to humans. Farmers call this honey "mad honey." Mad honey is harvested by bees from flowers such as the rhododendron, azalea, and laurel. The symptoms that may occur from consuming this honey include numbness in the extremities, nausea, and muscle weakness.

STORING HONEY

Honey should be stored in as airtight a container as possible, since the sugars will absorb moisture from the air, especially if the humidity is above 60 percent. If the water content of honey goes above 17 percent, the yeast will activate, the honey will ferment, and the sugars will change the honey to alcohol and carbon dioxide.

MAPLE SUGAR

RUN, SAP, RUN

The "sap run" occurs only in the spring, from the first major thaw to the time when the first leaf buds appear on the rock maple trees. If the tree's roots didn't freeze during the winter, the run will not be good. The sugar is stored in the trunk from the previous season. Maple tree sap contains about 3 percent sucrose, with each tree producing about 10 to 12 gallons of sap. To produce 1 gallon of "real" maple syrup, you need 35 gallons of sap. The final syrup is composed of 62 percent sucrose, 35 percent water, and 1 percent each glucose, fructose, and malic acid.

THE REAL THING

When a product is labeled "maple sugar" it must contain a minimum of 35 percent "real" maple syrup. Maple syrup should be stored in the refrigerator after it is opened to retard the growth of mold and to retain its flavor. If the label says "maple-flavored," "maple-blended," or "imitation" then it is not the real thing. The typical pancake syrup is made from corn syrup and artificial maple flavoring.

ARTIFICIAL LIQUID SWEETENERS

ACESULFAME K®

This noncaloric sweetener is sold under two brand names, Sunette™ and Sweetone™. The body is unable to break down the sweetener, which passes through harmlessly. The sweetener has an advantage over Equal® in that it can be used for high-temperature cooking and baking. It is two hundred times sweeter than sugar and is presently being used in chewing gums, beverage mixes, candies, puddings, and custards worldwide after being approved by the FDA in 1989.

ALITAME™

This sweetener, produced from the amino acids L-aspartic and D-alanine, has two thousand times the sweetness of sugar. Alitame™ is broken down by the body and contains almost no caloric value. It is a good all-around sweetener that may be used in most recipes and baked goods.

ASPARTAME (NUTRASWEET® OR EQUAL®)

Produced from two amino acids and methanol, aspartame may have negative effects on the body if consumed in too large a quantity. It cannot be used in any dishes that require high cooking temperatures. Excessive use may lower the acidity level of urine, leading to an increased susceptibility to disease.

STEVIA™

A new sweetener to the United States, Stevia™ has been used in South America and Japan for a number of years. It is calorie-free and is produced from an herbal extract from a member of the chrysanthemum family. The product has not been approved by the FDA and is being sold as a natural herbal product. The sweetener is two hundred to three hundred times sweeter than sugar.

SUCRALOSE™

Sucralose™ is refined from ordinary table sugar, but has been concentrated and is six hundred times sweeter than sugar, with no calories. It is a very stable product in foods and carbonated beverages and is sold in Canada under the brand name Spelda™.

SUBSTITUTING SWEETENERS FOR SUGAR

SWEETENER	COMPARISON	SUGGESTED USE
Equal® (contains aspartame)	1 pkt. = 2 tsp. sugar	cold liquids or hot foods (do not boil)
Sucaryl® liquid (contains saccharin)	⅛ tsp. = 1 tsp. sugar	table use & cooking
Sugar Twin® (contains saccharin)	1 tsp. = 1 tsp sugar	table use and baking
Sweet & Low® (contains saccharin)	1 tsp. = ¼ cup sugar	canning, baking, & cooking
Fructose (contains calories)	1 pkt. = 1 tsp sugar	table use and cooking
Sweetone™ (contains acesulfame K)	1 pkt. = 2 tsp. sugar	table use, cooking, & baking

MOLASSES

Molasses is produced from sugar cane through a complex processing, which removes all the nutrients, resulting in white sugar. The residue that remains after processing is called blackstrap molasses. Blackstrap molasses is collected from the top layer of the residue and is higher in nutrients than other types of molasses.

The key nutrients are iron, calcium, and potassium. When a recipe calls for dark molasses you can substitute light molasses without any noticeable difference in the flavor; the color will be somewhat lighter. The acidity of molasses can be reduced by adding 1 teaspoon of baking soda to the dry ingredients for every cup of molasses used.

SORGHUM

Sorghum is sometimes classified with molasses, but there is a distinct difference between the two. Molasses is produced from the juice of the sugar cane stalk, while sorghum is produced from a different variety called the sweet-sorghum cane and is normally used for animal feed. While molasses is usually darker and slightly bitter since most of its sugar is refined out, sorghum tends to retain most of its sugar and has a higher nutrient value. Sorghum contains more calcium, iron, and potassium than honey, molasses, or any other commercial syrup.

SWEET FACTS

BEAT ME, PLEASE!

Fudge should be stirred or beaten with a wooden spoon. Beating is important to produce a slightly thick, glossy consistency. The fudge will set better if you add 1 teaspoon of cornstarch when you first begin mixing.

HOW CLEAR I AM

When adding water to a candy recipe, always add very hot water for a crystal-clear candy. Cold water may contain contaminants that cause cloudiness. Freshly prepared candy will keep for about two to three weeks.

HOW ABOUT GRITTY JELLY

Jellies should never be placed in the freezer. They tend to lose their consistency and turn very granular.

HUMIDITY: A JELLY KILLER

Always remember to never prepare jellies or preserves on a day when the humidity is above 50 percent. High humidity causes the gelatin or pectin to absorb excess moisture, leaving the product too watery.

SMALL BATCHES ARE BEST

It is always best to prepare jellies in small batches. Large batches use large quantities of juices, so you have to boil the jellies longer, resulting in a loss of flavor. The jellies may also darken and become somewhat tough.

COME ON SLOWPOKE, BOIL ME FAST

Always boil jelly as fast as possible. When jellies are boiled slowly, the pectin in the fruit juice may be destroyed.

HIC—MY JELLIED FRUIT FERMENTED

Jellied fruit may ferment because yeast is allowed to multiply. This usually occurs only when the product is poorly processed and the jar poorly sealed. It may also occur if the sugar content is too low. If this occurs, don't try and save the batch; just throw it away.

LOOK, THERE ARE BEAUTIFUL CRYSTALS IN MY JELLY

There are a number of reasons why crystals form in jellies, such as when too much sugar is used. Test the fruit juice with a Jelmeter (sweetness tester) to be sure that you have the proper proportions of sugar. Crystals can form if there is sugar that has not been dissolved and is stuck to the sides of the saucepan. Make sure you wipe the sides of the pan clean and free of crystals with a damp rag before you fill the jars.

The grape juice you are using may have tartrate crystals in it. To resolve this, just extract the grape juice and allow the tartrate crystals to settle down, which can be done by refrigerating the juice overnight and then straining to remove the crystals. Crystals can also form from cooking the mixture too slowly or too long. The juice should be cooked at a rapid boil; when it reaches the jellying point, remove it from the heat immediately.

DOTH YOUR SYRUP RUN OVER?

If you place a small amount of vegetable oil on the threads of a syrup bottle top, it will stop the syrup from running down the sides of the bottle.

BUBBLE, BUBBLE, TOIL AND TROUBLE

When jelly is poured into a jar from the pot, the pot must be close to the top of the jar. If it isn't, or if the jelly is poured slowly, air becomes trapped in the hot jelly and bubbles will form. Bubbles may also indicate that the jelly has spoiled. When there are bubbles that move, throw out the jelly.

JUST AN OLD SOFTY

One of the most common problems when preparing jelly is that of the jelly being too soft. There are a number of reasons for this problem. One of the more common problems is overcooking the fruit to extract the juice. Overcooking tends to lower the pectin level and thus reduce the capacity of the jelly to thicken properly. The use of too much water when extracting the juice will produce a jelly that is too runny. Follow instructions as to the proper amount to be used. The wrong proportions of sugar and juice will also cause the jelly to be too soft.

When jelly is undercooked, it tends to be soft due to insufficient concentrations. Too little acid can also be the culprit. If the fruit is low in acid, try adding a small amount of lemon juice. Making too large a batch can also cause the jelly to have difficulty setting properly. Never use more than 4 to 6 cups of juice for each batch.

HELP, IT'S GETTING DARK IN HERE

When you overcook jelly, some of the sugar and juice tend to burn and cause a darker color than you may be used to. Boiling too long because you are making too large a batch is usually the cause of the darkness. If the jelly is stored for too long at too high a temperature, that may also cause darkening to occur.

MY JELLY IS WEEPING

There are a number of reasons that jelly will "weep." Too much acid will cause a tear or two. The pectin used may be unstable and old. The proper acidity level is very important. If the jelly is stored in too warm a location or if the temperature fluctuates too much, it may shed a tear as well. Jelly should always be stored in a dry, cool location

CLOUDY JELLY—NOT TOO APPETIZING

If the fruit you are using is green or not ripe enough, the jelly may be cloudy. Other reasons for cloudiness may be poor straining, which means that you may have forced the fruit through the strainer instead of allowing it to drip naturally, or not allowing the juice to stand before it was poured into the jars.

TOUGH JELLY

Jellies tend to get tough and stiff because of overcooking. Jelly should be cooked to 220°F or until it flows from a spoon in a "sheet." Too much pectin or too little sugar in the juice will also contribute to the problem. When pectin is added, you should use only ¾ cup of sugar for every 1 cup of juice for the majority of the fruits.

SWEETIE, YOUR CANDY IS BOILING OVER

If you have a problem with candy boiling over, try placing a wooden spoon across the top of the pot to break the bubbles.

NAUGHTY, NAUGHTY, FAKE CHOCOLATE

To be called chocolate, the product must contain chocolate liqueur. White chocolate does not and thus is not "real" chocolate; it is produced from sugar, milk powder, and cocoa butter. Cocoa butter is derived from chocolate liqueur but loses its chocolate flavor during processing.

HELP! MY SYRUP IS CRYSTALLIZING

When boiling syrup, the most frequent problem is that of the syrup crystallizing. The easiest way to avoid this problem is to place a pinch of baking soda in the syrup while it is cooking.

Chapter 14

Low-Fat Recipes for Liquids

SOUPS

Mom's Chili Vegetable Soup

1	pound potatoes, peeled and diced
1	cup zucchini, sliced
1	cup celery, chopped
1	cup corn kernels, canned
½	cup carrots, sliced
1	cup red onions, diced
3	cloves garlic, crushed
1	cup water
2	cups defatted chicken or turkey broth (low-sodium if possible)
½	cup nonfat milk
½	tablespoon mild chili powder (or hot if preferred)
	Salt and ground fresh pepper to taste

Combine all the vegetables and the garlic in a large pot. Add the water, poultry broth, milk, chili powder, and other seasonings and bring to a slow boil over medium heat. Cover the pot and reduce heat to a low simmer until the vegetables are tender (about 15 minutes). Remove the pot from the heat and allow the soup to cool for about 15 minutes.

Puree 2 cups of the soup, including some of the vegetables, in a blender or food processor. Stir back in the pureed soup and reheat for 5 minutes.

Nutrition facts per serving:

Calories 115	Sodium . . . . . .198 mg	Vitamin C . . . . .17 mg
Total fat . . . . . .0.6 g	Potassium . . . .597 mg	Calcium . . . . . .59 mg
Saturated fat . . .0 g	Soluble fiber . . .3.6 g	Iron . . . . .1.1 mg
Cholesterol . . . .trace	Beta-carotene . .3.2 mg	

Creamy Mushroom and Barley Soup

2	cups defatted chicken or turkey stock (low-sodium if possible)
2	cups water
½	pound onions, chopped
3	cloves garlic, chopped
6	tablespoons barley
½	pound fresh mushrooms, chopped
2	tablespoons dill, chopped
¼	cup fresh parsley, finely chopped

Boil the water and stock in a large pot over medium heat, then add the onions, garlic, and barley. Stir and cover, simmering for 40 minutes. Add the mushrooms, then cover and simmer for another 15 minutes. Remove the solids only and puree them in a blender or food processor. Place the pureed mixture back into the pot and add the dill and parsley. Bring the soup to a boil over medium heat.

Nutrition facts per serving:

Calories 116	Sodium . . . . .92 mg	Vitamin C . . . . . .12 mg
Total fat . . . . .1 g	Potassium . . . . . .516 mg	Calcium . . . . . . .34 mg
Saturated fat . . . .0 g	Soluble fiber . . . .4.2 g	Iron . . . . .2 mg
Cholesterol . . . . .0 mg	Beta-carotene . . .trace	

Old-Fashioned Cream of Tomato Soup

1	14-ounce can whole tomatoes, including liquid
1	cup plain tomato juice
1¾	cups red or yellow bell pepper, diced
1	cup red onions, finely chopped
2	tablespoons coriander, chopped
2	cloves garlic, crushed
¼	teaspoon fresh ground black pepper
¼	teaspoon salt
½	pound red potatoes, peeled and diced
¾	cup nonfat milk

In a medium saucepan, combine the whole tomatoes, their liquid, tomato juice, bell peppers, onions, 2 tablespoons of coriander, garlic, black pepper, salt, and potatoes. Bring the mixture to a slow boil over medium heat, then cover the pan. Reduce heat and allow to simmer for 15 minutes. Remove the pan from the heat and allow to cool for 6 minutes, then place the mixture in a food processor and puree for about 1 minute or until smooth. Add the milk very slowly during the processing. Return the pureed mixture to the pan and cook only until it is hot (do not boil).

Nutrition facts per serving:

Calories	130	Soluble fiber	4.1 g
Total fat	1 g	Beta-carotene	0.9 g
Saturated fat	0.2 g	Vitamin C	111 mg
Cholesterol	trace	Calcium	114 mg
Sodium	479 g.	Iron	2.2 mg
Potassium	748 g.	Vitamin E	trace

STEWS

New Orleans Shrimp and Sweet Potato Stew

¾   teaspoon ground coriander
¼   teaspoon fresh ground black pepper
2½ teaspoons cumin
½   teaspoon ground ginger
¼   teaspoon mild chili powder (hot if you prefer)
1   pound medium shrimp, cooked and cubed
1½ pounds sweet potatoes (yams are okay)
1½ cups defatted chicken broth (low-sodium if possible)
4   cloves garlic, crushed
1   red onion, chopped
1   tablespoon lemon or lime juice (not concentrate)

In a small bowl, mix the coriander, pepper, cumin, ginger, and chili powder. In a large bowl, mix the shrimp with 1 teaspoon of the spice mixture, then set aside. In a medium saucepan, combine the sweet potatoes, chicken broth, garlic, and onion. Cover and bring to a boil over high heat. Reduce heat and allow to simmer for about 20 minutes or until the potatoes are tender.

Remove 1 cup of the potatoes and mash, then stir the potatoes back into the stew. Add the shrimp mixture, cover, and cook for 3 to 4 minutes, stirring occasionally. Mix in the lemon or lime juice and serve hot.

Nutrition facts per serving:

Calories 252	Soluble fiber . . . . . .5.1 grams
Total fat . . . . .2.3 grams	Seta-carotene . . . . .15 milligrams
Saturated fat . . . . . .0.3 gram	Vitamin C . . . . .61 milligrams
Cholesterol . . . . . . .112 milligrams	Calcium . . . . .97 milligrams
Sodium . . . . .320 milligrams	Iron . . . . .3.6 milligrams
Potassium . . . . . . .trace	Vitamin E . . . . .0 IU

Chicken, Barley, and Carrot Stew
2   cups defatted chicken broth diluted with 1½ cups water
3   cloves garlic, crushed
⅓   cup fresh pearl barley
¼   teaspoon fresh ground black pepper
½   teaspoon thyme
3   cups carrots, sliced
3   celery stalks, chopped
1   red onion, chopped
2   teaspoons extra virgin olive oil
14   ounces chicken breast, cubed
1   bay leaf
2   cups fresh tomatoes, chopped
¼   cup parsley, finely chopped

In a large saucepan, combine the diluted chicken broth, garlic, barley, pepper, and thyme. Cover and bring to a slow boil on medium heat. Reduce heat and allow to simmer for 15 minutes, then add the carrots, celery, and onion. Increase the heat and return to a boil, then reduce the heat, cover, and simmer for about 10 minutes or until the barley and carrots are tender.

In another pan, warm the olive oil over high heat with ½ teaspoon of canola oil added to lower the smoke point, and sauté the chicken until browned and cooked through. This should take about 10 minutes depending on the size of the pieces. Add the chicken to the stew and bring to a boil. Reduce heat and allow to simmer for about 5 minutes. Remove from heat, add the tomatoes and parsley, and serve.

Nutrition facts per serving:

Calories 240	Soluble fiber . . . . . .8 g
Total fat . . . . .4.2 g	Beta-carotene . . . . .16 mg
Saturated fat . . . . . .0.6 mg	Vitamin C . . . . .38 mg
Cholesterol . . . . . . .28 mg	Calcium . . . . .64 mg
Sodium . . . . .490 mg	Iron . . . . .2.4 mg

DESSERTS

South of the Border Quinoa Pudding

Quinoa is a grain grown in South America and is one of the best grain (or vegetable) sources of protein.

½   **cup fresh quinoa**
1   **cup water**
2   **large eggs**
½   **cup dried figs, chopped**
1   **cup cooked brown rice**
¼   **cup rolled oats**
1   **cup nonfat milk**
3   **tablespoons brown sugar**
1   **teaspoon almond extract**
¼   **cup raisins**

Place the quinoa into a large bowl and rinse thoroughly several times with cold water. If any grains float to the top, discard them. In a medium saucepan, combine the quinoa and water, and bring to a slow boil over medium heat. Cover, reduce heat, and simmer for 15 minutes or until the grain is somewhat transparent. Remove the pan from the heat and allow to cool for a few minutes. In a medium-size bowl, beat the eggs.

Add the quinoa, figs, rice, oats, and remaining ingredients while continually stir-ring. Transfer the mixture to a baking dish with high sides, and add boiling water to about ½ inch from the top. Cook the dish in a 375°F oven for 45 minutes or until the top is golden brown.

Nutrition facts per serving:

Calories	218	Soluble fiber	3.2 g
Total fat	3.1 g	Beta-carotene	0 mg
Saturated fat	0.9 g	Vitamin C	trace
Cholesterol	75 mg	Calcium	102 mg
Sodium	48 mg	Iron	2 mg
Potassium	369 mg	Vitamin E	trace

Florida Lemon-Lime Sherbet

2 **limes**
2 **lemons**
⅓ **cup nonfat dry milk**
1 **cup nonfat milk**
¼ **cup granulated sugar**

Grate 1 teaspoon of lemon and lime zest each, then squeeze the juice from the fruit. In a large bowl, combine the dry milk, juices, and zest. Slowly whisk in the nonfat milk and sugar until very smooth. Freeze the mixture in a divided ice cube tray for about 3 hours or until firm. Place the mixture into a blender or food processor and blend until it is loose enough to spoon.

Nutrition facts per serving:

Calories	112	Potassium	257 mg
Total fat	0.3 g	Soluble fiber	trace
Saturated fat	0.1 g	Beta-carotene	0 mg
Cholesterol	2 mg	Vitamin C	31 mg
Sodium	58 mg	Calcium	149 mg

Grandmother's Honey Cream Topping

1   **cup 2 percent fat–reduced cottage cheese**
2   **teaspoons pure honey**
5   **tablespoons nonfat sour cream**

Puree the cottage cheese until smooth, then place in a medium bowl. Fold in the honey and sour cream. Cover the bowl with plastic wrap and refrigerate for 1 hour or until ready to use. The mixture will be very similar to real whipped cream, but without the fat.

Nutrition facts per serving:

Calories	15	Sodium	65 mg
Total fat	0.1 g	Potassium	13 mg
Saturated fat	0 g	Calcium	10 mg
Cholesterol	trace	Iron	trace

SAUCES AND SALSAS

Yogurt Sauce

1   **cup low-fat plain yogurt**
1½   **cup cucumber, peeled, seeded, and chopped**
2   **scallions, chopped**
1   **tomato, peeled, seeded, and chopped**
1   **teaspoon curry powder (or mild chili powder)**
1   **teaspoon cilantro, finely chopped**
    Salt and pepper to taste

Combine all ingredients in a medium bowl and allow to chill for 6 to 8 hours. Taste to see if additional salt or pepper is required.

Brooklyn Smoked Salmon (Lox) Sauce

1   **cup dry white wine or white grape juice**
1   **cup light cream**
5   **scallions, chopped (white and light green parts only)**
2   **tablespoons salmon caviar or finely chopped capers**

1   teaspoon fresh dill, finely chopped
Salt and fresh ground pepper to taste
3-4 ounces smoked salmon (Nova if possible)

Slice the salmon into bite size pieces. In a medium saucepan over high heat, boil the wine or juice, cream, and scallions for about 7 minutes until the liquid is about one-third of the original amount. Remove from heat and add the caviar, seasonings, and smoked salmon. Mix thoroughly and serve over pasta, such as fettuccini.

Wild Cranberry Salsa

3½ cups of frozen cranberries
3   chopped Tamed™ Whole Jalape
heat, boil the wine or juice,1 red onion, chopped
2   tablespoons lemon juice (not concentrate)
2   tablespoons orange zest
2   tablespoons honey
2   tablespoons orange juice (no pulp)
½   cup fresh coriander, chopped

Mix all the ingredients in a large bowl. Cover and refrigerate for 6 to 8 hours before serving.

HOW GREEN IS MY GUACAMOLE?

Avocado contains phenolic compounds, which tend to turn brown as soon as the air hits them. However, they can be neutralized by spraying the guacamole with a solution of powdered vitamin C and water, then placing a piece of plastic wrap on the surface of the guacamole to keep the air out.

Chapter 15
Cold Facts

FREEZING FACTS

THERE ARE ICICLES IN MY ICE CREAM

Icicles or ice crystals in ice cream are usually formed from opening the door to the freezer too often. It doesn't take very much of a temperature drop to force the water molecules out of some of the ice cream cells. If the ice cream is stored for a prolonged period of time at 0°F, the crystals will change form again. Just scrape the crystals away; they are harmless.

WHY ICE MUST FLOAT

When water freezes, the hydrogen and oxygen molecules combine in a loose fashion, creating air pockets. When water remains in its liquid form, the air pockets do not exist, making water denser than ice.

SCRUB THOSE ICE CUBES

When ice cubes remain in the freezer tray or the ice maker for more than a few days, they may pick up odors or contaminants from the air when the door is opened. It would be best to wash the ice cubes before using them for the best taste.

IT'S PARTY TIME

If you are buying ice cubes for a party, just figure 1 pound of ice per person and you will probably be okay (unless you have some very heavy drinkers).

A COLD SOLUTION

When you place a bowl of ice cubes out for a party and don't want them to melt too fast, place a larger bowl with dry ice under the cubes. The ice cubes will last through the entire party.

NO DILUTION HERE

One of the easiest methods of keeping punch cold is to make a large ice cube from an empty milk carton. The larger the ice cube, the slower it will melt.

HOW CLEAR I AM

To make clear ice cubes, boil the water before placing it in the ice cube trays. This will eliminate the impurities that make the cubes cloudy. Never use cloudy ice cubes in a gin and tonic. This is probably against the law somewhere.

BOY, AM I SHAPELY

If you would like to make different-shaped ice cubes, just freeze water in small cookie cutters, then place the frozen shapes into a pan of very hot water for a few seconds to loosen them up.

SPEEDY ICE CUBES

Believe it or not, if you use boiling water to make ice cubes, they will freeze faster. Even though cold water is closer to the freezing point, the hot water evaporates faster, leaving less water to freeze. The evaporation also creates an air current over the ice cube tray, which tends to actually blow on the water, similar to the cooling effect when you blow on a spoonful of hot soup before tasting it.

YOU'RE FREEZING MY ENZYMES

When foods are frozen the enzymes go into hibernation, but they are not destroyed. If enzymes were not inactivated by freezing, they would cause flavor and color changes in the foods. When blanching, the enzymes are destroyed. Blanching must be done if you want to produce top-quality vegetables. Enzymes in fruits are the cause of browning and can be neutralized with the use of ascorbic acid.

RANCIDITY CONTROL WHEN FREEZING

Products with high fat contents that are frozen can become rancid to a certain degree and ruin the flavor of the food. Air is the guilty party, which means that the food must be wrapped properly to avoid air coming into contact with the food. If you use a freezer bag, squeeze as much of the air out of the bag as possible.

HELP! MY TEXTURE IS CHANGING

When you freeze food, you are actually freezing the water in the food cells. As the water freezes it expands and a number of the cell walls rupture, releasing their liquid, which then freezes into ice crystals. This results in the food becoming softer. These changes in texture are more noticeable in fruits and vegetables since they have a higher water content than most other foods. Certain vegetables such as tomatoes, lettuce, and celery are so high in water content that they literally turn into mush when frozen.

When cooked products are frozen, their cell walls are already softened, so they do not burst as easily. This is especially true with high-starch vegetables such as corn, lima beans, and peas.

QUICK, FREEZE ME FASTER

The damage to foods when freezing them can be controlled to some degree by freezing as fast as possible. When foods are frozen more rapidly, the ice crystals that are formed are smaller and cause less cell-wall rupture. If you know you will be freezing a number of items or a food that you really want to keep in good shape, try setting the freezer at the coldest setting a few hours before you place the food in. Some freezer manuals also will advise you which shelves are in the coldest area.

IT FEELS LIKE A ROLLER COASTER IN HERE

The temperature of your freezer should never fluctuate more than a few degrees to keep foods at their best. The temperature should be kept at 0°F or below for the best results. Thawing and refreezing is the worst thing you can do to food. Every time the temperature drops in the freezer, some of those small ice crystals will convert to larger ice crystals, and little by little the dish will be ruined.

MICROBE ALERT

Most microorganisms are not destroyed by freezing and may even be present on fruits and vegetables. Blanching does help lower the microorganism count significantly, but enough of them do survive and are ready and waiting to destroy the food as soon as it thaws. Inspect all frozen foods, which may have accidentally thawed by leaving the freezer door open or from an electrical failure. The botulism microorganism does not reproduce at 0°F.

GET THE ALOE, I'VE GOT FREEZER BURN

Poorly wrapped food or slow freezing allows moisture to evaporate and cause freezer burn. This produces a grainy brown spot on the food, and that area becomes dry and very tough. The area will lose its flavor; however, the food is still safe to eat (if you really want to).

YOU WON'T LIKE ME IF YOU FREEZE ME

There are number of foods that have a high liquid content. When these foods are frozen they are not very palatable.

FOOD	PROBLEM AFTER FREEZING
Cooked egg whites	soft, tough, rubbery
Cooked macaroni and rice	mushy, loss of taste
Cheese in blocks	tends to crumble too easily
Crumbled cheese	soggy
Cucumbers	limp, waterlogged, poor flavor
Custards	watery
Custard fillings	easily separate, watery
Cream pies	watery
Fried foods	loss of crispness, soggy
Gelatin	weep
Gravy	needs to be reheated if fat separates
Icings made with egg whites	weepy
Jelly on bread	jelly will soak into the bread
Lettuce	loses shape, very limp
Mayonnaise	separates
Meringue	toughens
Raw onions	watery and very limp, but ok for cooking
Raw potatoes	texture is lost, may darken
Radishes	texture is poor, pithy
Sauces with milk or cream	separate
Sour cream	separates, watery
Raw tomatoes	watery, loss of shape
Whole milk	separates
Yogurt	separates

THAWING 101

Thawing is best done in the refrigerator at about 41°F. This will not expose foods to the temperature danger zone. Many foods can be thawed under warm water at about 70°F providing it takes less than 2 hours. This method is usually reserved for poultry.

If you thaw in the microwave, the food should be cooked immediately to be on the safe side. Room temperature thawing should never be done since it allows the food to reach a temperature that may cause bacterial growth.

PROTECT ME, I'M VALUABLE

It is necessary to use the proper packaging materials if you want to keep your food in good condition. Foods will lose color, flavor, nutrients, and moisture unless you are careful. The wrapping material or container will vary depending on the type of food or dish you are freezing. Never freeze fruits or vegetables in containers bigger than ½ gallon, since they tend to freeze too slowly and usually do very poorly. If you wish to have the best results use packaging with the following characteristics:

- resistant to oils, grease and water
- strong and leakproof
- easy to seal
- has a space to write the date
- not too porous
- should not become brittle and crack at freezing temperatures

FOILED AGAIN

Aluminum foil should never be used next to a warm or hot meat product and frozen. It keeps the food warm for too long a period and bacteria may grow, and if the food is not reheated to a high enough temperature, the bacteria may be reactivated. Aluminum foil develops microcracks and is good only next to a cold food in the refrigerator for no more than 1 to 2 days.

Never place aluminum foil on top of a meatloaf with tomato sauce. It will deteriorate from the acid in the tomato sauce. The acid in citrus fruits will also eat away aluminum foil.

WE'RE BREAKING UP—ALL FOOD OVERBOARD

Standard glass jars are not recommended for the freezer because they break very easily. If you do use glass jars, use only ones made specially for freezing. Plastic containers are very good for freezing. When using a plastic container, remember to place a piece of plastic wrap next to the food after it has cooled or is newly frozen. This will slow any moisture loss and may prevent the formation of larger ice crystals. Use freezer tape whenever possible to seal around the lids of all containers.

I'M EXPANDING—I HOPE I DON'T BURST

Other than most vegetables that will normally pack loose, most foods should have a small air space to allow for expansion.

THE POWER'S GONE

If you lose power, never open the freezer door unless you really have to. If the freezer is full, the foods will remain frozen for up to two to four days depending on the size of the freezer. Food in a half-filled freezer will remain frozen only for about twenty-four hours. Cover the freezer with a blanket and tape around it as best you can. Tape all around the door after placing aluminum foil in the door cracks. Keep a plastic bag with ice cubes in the freezer to alert you in case it has thawed and refrozen the food.

WELL, ZIP MY LOCK

Zip-type bags should not be used for freezer storage unless they specifically state that they are made for freezer use. Most are too porous and the seal is not airtight enough to really do the job.

YOU CAN GROW OLD IN HERE

When foods are kept past the recommended freezer storage time, the food is still safe to eat, but the taste, texture, and nutritional quality will be reduced significantly. Rotating frozen foods is a must.

I WANT MY SWEETS

Fruits can be frozen without sugar. Sugar is used only to maintain the sweet flavor, help retain the texture, and stabilize the color, and is not needed as a preservative.

I'M NOT ALL ARTIFICIAL

It's okay to use a sugar substitute with foods that are going to be frozen, but you should follow the directions for equivalents very closely. While the artificial sweeteners do provide sweetness, they do not provide the syrup and color stabilization that the real thing will.

BROWNOUT

The best method of reducing or eliminating the browning of fruits is to use ascorbic acid or vitamin C. Pure ascorbic acid is available in most supermarkets or drugstores. While some people use lemon juice, it is not as effective and may impart more of a lemon flavor, which may not be desirable for many foods.

I DIDN'T BLANCH AT ALL

Vegetables that are frozen and not blanched are still good to eat, but the quality, color, texture, and flavor will be considerably lower than those that have been blanched before freezing. If you choose to blanch in a microwave, I suggest you read up on the procedure in your manual. It is not as efficient as blanching in boiling water, and cold spots are possible, which will not kill the enzymes that must be destroyed.

FREEZING YOUR CORN

Corn must be handled just right or it will not be very edible. Corn should be blanched according to directions and chilled immediately in a bowl of ice water until the cobs are completely cooled down. Before you cook the ears, allow them to partially thaw at room temperature and place a small amount of sugar in the water.

COOKING FROZEN VEGGIES

Vegetables should be cooked right from the freezer for the best results. The only exceptions are corn on the cob and leafy greens.

COOKING MEATS THAT HAVE BEEN FROZEN

Meat and fish should be cooked directly from the freezer.

FREEZE THAT COMMERCIAL

Commercial fruit juice concentrates can be frozen at 0°F for one year and most vegetables for eight months. Bread can be frozen for three months, ground beef for four months, and roasts and steaks for one year. Whole chicken can be frozen for one year, while parts are good for only six months.

TO REFREEZE OR NOT TO REFREEZE, THAT IS A HEALTH QUESTION

MEAT AND POULTRY

May be refrozen if freezer temperature was maintained at 40°F or below and the meat has no odor or discoloration.

VEGETABLES

May be refrozen only if ice crystals are present or if the freezer temperature was 40°F or below.

FRUITS

May be refrozen providing they do not show any signs of spoilage. If they have fully thawed, it would be best to use them in cooking or preserves.

COOKED FOODS

May be refrozen only if ice crystals are present or if the freezer was 40°F or below. If questionable, the food should be discarded.

ICE CREAM

If even partially thawed, discard it. If the freezer temperature was above 40°F, the ice cream could be dangerous.

FREEZER AND REFRIGERATOR STORAGE TIMES

PRODUCT	DAYS IN REFRIGERATOR (40°F)	MONTHS IN FREEZER (0°F)
Butter	45–90	7–8
Clarified butter	60–90	7–8
Buttermilk	7–14	3
Cream	3–5	3
Half-and-half	3–4	4
Eggnog	3–5	6
Frozen desserts	—	1–2
Ice cream (commercial)	—	2–3
Margarine (all types)	90–120	12
Milk (all types)	3–7	3
Nondairy creamer	21	12
Sour cream	14	do not freeze
Yogurt	14	2
Whipped cream (commercial)	30	do not freeze

Chapter 16
Fats and Oils

THE DIFFERENCE BETWEEN FATS AND OILS

Fat is usually solid at room temperature and an oil is liquid. If the fat is from an animal source, it is usually solid; from a vegetable source, it is usually liquid. However, all fats are similar in their chemical structure and vary more due to the type of fat saturation.

Shortening is solid fat at room temperature and can be either animal or vegetable fat. The best shortenings will have the word "pure" on the label; otherwise the product may contain a number of additives that are capable of lowering the smoke point (see page 279).

Fats and oils should be as pure as possible to obtain the best results when preparing any dish.

VEGETABLE OILS

The best vegetable oils to use for cooking are those lowest in saturated fat. However, some dishes require that certain oils or fats be used to produce the desired flavor. In those instances, the recommended oil should be used. In all other instances, olive oil is highly recommended since it is high in monounsaturated fat, which is fat the body prefers over other types. Throughout this book, when recipes call for cooking with olive oil, note that a small amount of canola oil is usually recommended along with it. The canola oil raises the smoke point of olive oil just enough so that it slows down the breakdown of the olive oil.

SPRAY OILS ARE A MONEY SAVER

For many years the only spray oil that was sold was Pam. The markets now sell many different brands as well as different oils available in spray containers. The latest to hit the shelves is olive oil. If you find these products too pricey, all you have to do is stop by a kitchen supply store and purchase an oil spray bottle. These are small pump-action spray bottles that you can easily fill. Use any oil and an equal amount of lecithin to keep the oil in suspension. Lecithin may be found in the vitamin section of your market or any health food store. Most market brands contain lecithin, which helps keep the propellant and the oil from separating, though it is best to purchase the pump-type sprays to protect the ozone layer. Never spray the oils on too hot a surface or an open flame since they are flammable. Also, be careful of inhaling the oil spray, as it is capable of coating the lungs and could be fatal.

OLIVE OIL STATISTICS

The United States presently imports about 140,000 tons of olive oil annually. The United States has only 0.02 percent of all olive trees worldwide, while the Mediterranean basin has 95 percent. Italy produces almost 600,000 tons of olive oil and uses more than 800,000 tons. The surplus comes from Greece, Spain, and Tunisia.

OILS ARE NOT FRIENDLY TO BAKED GOODS

Because of their liquid nature, oils tend to collect instead of evenly distributing throughout the dough. The baked goods may then become grainy when baked. If you use solid fat, such as shortening, the fat can be more evenly distributed and the baked goods will retain their moisture and be fluffier.

GARLIC/OLIVE OIL ALERT

The government has issued an alert regarding placing raw garlic in olive oil for more than twenty-four hours. Garlic may harbor bacteria that multiply in an atmosphere that lacks oxygen. Even though the risks are minimal it would be wise not to store garlic in this manner. For additional information regarding this problem call (800) 232-6548.

NUTTY OILS

THE HAWAIIAN NUT

Macadamia nut oil is now becoming more available. The oil is high in monounsaturated fat and is great in salad dressings and to sauté many dishes in for a great flavor. The smoke point is somewhat higher than olive oil, so you may not have to add canola oil.

TOP OF THE NUT HEAP

If you wish to use nut oil, one of the best would be walnut oil. Walnuts are lower in saturated fat than the other nuts and high in polyunsaturated fatty acids. Peanut oil has twice the saturated fat of walnut oil.

ARE MY TASTE BUDS WORKING?

Peanut oil has very little flavor when used for cooking. It has a relatively high smoke point, which makes it a good choice for frying. The mild nut flavor is popular with Asian cooks, but it is not flavorful enough for most American dishes. The oil will remain fresh for about a year under refrigeration, and if it becomes cloudy it will clear up in a short period of time if allowed to remain at room temperature.

GRAVY

Gravy is always best if you use the pan drippings, which contain the flavor of the meat or poultry. Many people avoid using the drippings because of the high fat content, but this can easily be significantly reduced by separating the fat from the flavorful liquid with a separating cup. Other methods include placing ice cubes in a piece of cheesecloth and swirling that around to trap the fat, or if time allows, the drippings can be placed into the freezer for a few minutes until the fat rises and can be removed.

A LEGAL SEPARATION

A common problem with gravy is that it almost always separates, especially as it cools down. To keep the gravy in suspension, all you have to do is add a pinch or two of baking soda to the gravy and stir.

GETTING RID OF YOUR LUMPS

You will never have lumpy gravy if you just mix in a pinch of salt to the flour before adding any liquid.

QUICK, PUT ME IN A SUNTAN BOOTH

If your gravy is not brown enough and you need a quick fix, just add 1 teaspoon of hot instant coffee. There will not be any flavor of coffee in the gravy.

THIS SALT IS KILLING ME

To improve the taste of oversalted gravy, just add ¼ teaspoon of brown sugar.

REPAIRING BURNT GRAVY

If you accidentally burn gravy, all you have to do is add 1 teaspoon of peanut butter. You won't notice the taste of the peanut butter at all.

GRAVY PERKER-UPPER

If you would like your gravy to have a rich, dark brown color, just spread the flour on a cookie sheet and cook over a low heat, stirring occasionally until the flour browns. Just before serving the gravy, add 1 teaspoon of coffee to firm up the color permanently. Another method of browning the gravy is to add onion skins during cooking.

Grandmother's Gravy

The rule of thumb is to use the same number of tablespoons of fat drippings (you need to use a little) as flour. The pan drippings should be taken from the pan before you remove the fat. The following recipe yields about 2½ cups of gravy and should be adjusted depending on the number of people to be served. This amount usually serves 8 people comfortably. Unsalted butter may be used in place of the fat drippings, but be sure to start with the butter at room temperature; do not microwave it.

4   tablespoons pan drippings
4   tablespoons all-purpose flour
2   cups defatted drippings

In a medium saucepan, combine pan drippings and flour. Cook over low heat until brown, stirring occasionally. Add defatted drippings and continue to cook over low heat until the desired thickness is achieved.

FAT FACTS

GREECE-ING UP FOR HEALTH

In Greece, people consume 40 percent of their calories as fat, though their risk of heart disease is low. They consume most of their fat as olive oil.

HOW MUCH FAT WILL A STOMACH STOMACH?

The time it takes for fat to clear the stomach is about 10 grams per hour. If your breakfast consists of two eggs, two slices of bacon, bread and butter, orange juice, and coffee, it will take the stomach almost seven hours to clear the 70 grams of fat completely.

THE QUALITY OF BUTTER

Butter is sold in three grades depending on the flavor rating and milk fat content. The best grade is U.S. Grade AA; next is U.S. Grade A, which has a lower flavor rating; and last is U.S. Grade B, which is made from sour cream. The milk fat rating of butter must be at least 80 percent.

SQUEEZING THE LAST DROP FROM A CAN

If you want to get the last drop of shortening from a can, just pour boiling water in the can and place it in the refrigerator for an hour or until the fat rises to the top, then just skim off the fat.

GOING UP IN SMOKE

Oil will deteriorate very quickly depending on the smoke point of that particular oil. When any oil deteriorates it starts smoking and develops into bad fat called a trans-fatty acid. To check on the level of deterioration while the oil is hot, just drop a piece of white bread in the oil. If the bread develops dark spots, the oil has gone bad.

NEVER REUSE FRYING OIL

A common practice is to clean out frying oil and store it in the freezer for future use. While the oil can be cleaned using a raw potato, the oil is not healthy oil once it has been used at a high temperature. A percentage of the oil breaks down into trans-fatty acid, and the more you use that oil, the more acid it contains.

TURN OUT THE LIGHTS

When purchasing liquid oil, only purchase oil that is packaged in opaque containers. Oil deteriorates very quickly and the light will hasten the process.

THE HOTTER THE OIL, THE FEWER THE CALORIES

Tests have been conducted that prove that the hotter the oil, the less oil that will be absorbed by the food. The frying time is also lessened, which contributes to the fewer fat calories retained.

THE HIGHER THE FRYER, THE LOWER THE TEMPERATURE

When you fry above sea level, it is necessary to lower the frying temperature 3°F for every 1,000-foot increase in elevation. If you live in Denver, Colorado, you will need to lower your frying temperature by 15°F.

LEAF LARD IS BEST FOR PIES

Leaf lard has large fat crystals, which will produce a flakier pie crust. The lard is derived from the kidney area of pigs instead of the abdomen, which is where lard is usually derived from. When substituting lard for butter or shortening in a recipe, reduce the amount by 25 percent.

FAT IN MARGARINES

The average margarine sold contains about 90 percent fat. Diet margarine contains 80 percent fat, 16 percent water, 2 percent salt, and 2 percent nonfat milk solids. Liquid margarine may contain only 40 percent fat and more air and water than other diet margarine.

FAT SUBSTITUTES

The 1990s were the decade when a number of fat substitutes were invented. The requirements for these substitutes were that they have the mouthfeel of real fat and be able to enhance other flavors. Most of these are still in use today but found only in certain products with which they are compatible.

 SIMPLEASE™

Whey protein concentrates that are subjected to microparticulation. Used in Simple Pleasures frozen desserts and may be used in other frozen foods. Contains 1-2kcal/g and is digestible.

 STELLAR™

Modified cornstarch with water sheared into a smooth cream. Used in salad dressings, Danish pastry, hot dogs, and sausage. Contains 1kcal/g and is digestible.

 SLENDID™

Pectin, calcium chloride, and water sheared to form a gel. Used in cookies and cheese products. Contains 0kcal/g and is digestible.

OATRIM™

Oat starch, fiber, and water that is sheared. Used mainly for Healthy Choice beef products. Contains 1kcal/g and is digestible.

CAPRENIN™

Derived from canola, coconut, and palm oils and contains fatty acids that are longer than those found naturally. Used in Milky Way II candy bars. Contains 5kcal/g and is partially digestible.

OLESTRA™

Sucrose polyester with fatty acids attached. Used in chips and cookies. May appear in other products. Contains 0kcal/g and is indigestible. A government warning is placed on the label.

NUTRILIPIDS™

Composed of high-oleic sunflower oil, medium-chain triglycerides, and soy protein. Used in beverage mixes to improve the flavor and texture. The product is trans-acid and lactose-free. It provides a good source of protein, calcium, and iron. Look for it on the label; this is an excellent product.

NEW FAT REPLACER

PAC-TILLA™ is being used to produce nonfat baked goods. Produced from specially processed rice flour and used primarily in wheat flour tortillas, it provides a smooth texture and a similar mouthfeel to that of real fat. The new fat substitute will also provide a longer shelf life for the products.

APPETIZE®

This is a new natural shortening made from a patented blend of cholesterol-free meat fat and vegetable oils. Appetize® provides a believable taste of "real" meat fat shortenings combined with an excellent nutritional profile. For more information call (800) 828-0800.

THE LEGAL FAT: SUET

Suet is fat that is derived from the kidneys of sheep and cattle. It may be substituted for lard in many recipes and has large fat crystals similar to lard, which is why suet is very popular in certain baked goods such as pie crust.

MASHED POTATOES WITH SCHMALTZ AND GRIBENES (UFOS)

Schmaltz is a traditional Jewish food prepared from rendering down chicken fat and skin. The fat has an excellent flavor and after it has finished rendering, the small UFOs (unidentified fried objects) are called gribenes. The gribenes are actually the remains of the skin that has been turned into small, crunchy fat balls. In moderation these fats are very tasty when added to mashed potatoes. Don't knock it till you've tried it.

BROWNOUT

When greasing a pan with oil or butter, try not to overdo it. Overbrowning baked goods and some foods is often caused by placing too much oil in the pan.

HOW TO STOP UP YOUR DRAIN

Fat should never be poured down the drain unless you pour at least 1 quart of boiling water after the fat. Cold pipes will solidify animal fat very quickly.

SALAD AND COOKING OIL USE

In 1909 Americans used 1.5 pounds of salad and cooking oil per person annually. Corn oil and lard were the most popular oils. In 1998 Americans used 35 pounds per person. Margarine use increased from 6 pounds per person in 1950, when it was invented, to 21 pounds per person in 1998.

WHY FAT IS USED IN BAKED GOODS

Fat is used to produce tender baked goods by coating the gluten strands. The more the strands are coated, the more tender the product. Fat is also needed to add texture to baked goods and other products. Chilled solid fat is recommended when preparing flaky pastry dough since it does not combine with the flour. This creates a flaky effect of alternating layers of fat and flour, which is why lard is the preferred fat for pie crusts.

FRIED FOOD PROTECTOR

Fried foods will not pick up and retain as much fat if you add 1 tablespoon of vinegar to the fryer or skillet before adding the oil. Coat the pan as best you can and leave the balance of the vinegar on the pan.

TRAPPING AIR

Room-temperature fat, when creamed with sugar, has the capability of trapping air in a cake batter, creating very light-textured cakes.

FRYING FOODS? HIDE THE SALT SHAKER

Never salt a food before placing it into a fryer. The salt tends to draw moisture out of the food and will cause splattering. The moisture will also cause the oil to decompose more readily.

TOGETHERNESS

When you shake oil and vinegar together, the oil breaks into smaller particles, which allows the two to mix together temporarily. As soon as you stop shaking, the fat droplets start to combine again and come out of suspension, rising back to the surface. However, if you use an emulsifying agent it will hold the oil and vinegar in permanent suspension. The best substance to keep these two together is lecithin. Just break open two lecithin ampules and mix the liquid into the oil and vinegar. The shaking will break down the fat globules into very small particles and the lecithin will grab them, encircle them, and keep them from combining again. Lecithin is the emulsifying agent in egg yolks, which keeps hollandaise sauce in suspension.

GOING UP IN SMOKE?

Knowing the smoke point of the oil you are going to cook or fry with is very important. Since certain foods need to be fried or cooked at certain temperatures, the last thing you want is for the oil to break down and ruin the dish. The following are the smoke points of the more common oils used for frying:

OIL	SMOKE POINT
Canola	525°F
Safflower	510°F
Soybean	495°F
Corn	475°F
Peanut	440°F
Sesame	420°F
Olive (blend)	375°F
Vegetable shortening	375°F
Clarified butter	350°F
Butter	250°F

THERE GO THE EYEBROWS AGAIN

The danger level of oil is called the flash point, which is about 600°F. At this point the oil will start to show signs of catching fire; the actual fire point is around 700°F. The easiest way to avoid this is just to cover the pan and eliminate the oxygen. Another method is to pour baking soda on the fire to suffocate it.

NOT JUST HOT—REALLY HOT

Frying at too low a temperature will cause the breading to fall off many foods. Also, too much of the oil will enter the food since the hot frying oil is supposed to seal the food. If the oil is too hot, the food may burn or not be fully cooked. Breaded foods need to be fried at 375°F. Chicken needs to be fried at 365°F for ten to twenty minutes depending on the thickness of the piece. Meats should be fried at 360°F.

FORCING YOUR BREADING TO STAY PUT

Chefs never have a problem making breading stay on a food. Here are a few secrets that will really make the difference.

• When using eggs, make sure they are at room temperature.
• Always place the breaded food in the refrigerator for forty-five minutes, then allow it to return to room temperature before placing it in the fryer.
• Never overbeat the eggs; the more air you put in, the lower the binding ability of the egg.
• Always use the smallest bread crumbs you can purchase; large bread crumbs do not adhere well.
• Homemade bread crumbs are coarser and always adhere better.

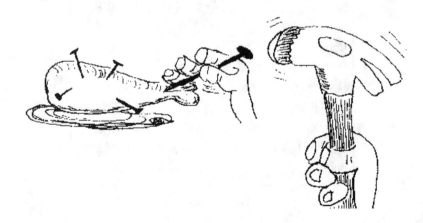

FAT FROM DOWN UNDER

Copha is a coconut shortening commonly found in Australia. If your recipe calls for copha, just use a solid shortening.

STOP CROWDING ME, WAIT YOUR TURN

One of the first rules a chef learns is not to place too much food in a deep-fat fryer. Smaller batches will not cause the frying temperature to drop too low. When you do fry, remember to make sure that the oil is about 15°F above the temperature you want to fry in. Foods that are placed into the fryer at room temperature will cause a drop of about 15°F. Never place food directly from the refrigerator into the fryer, since this will cause splattering and may cause a 30°F drop in temperature.

CANOLA OIL BEING KILLED BY BIOTECHNOLOGY

Canola oil, a good oil high in monounsaturated fat, which the body prefers, is now being altered into a more saturated fat through the addition of laurate. When you see canola oil on the baked-goods package, be aware that it is probably not the good canola oil, but an altered one. Initially, the new oil is being used in nondairy creamers and whipped cream.

PURE OR VIRGIN—WHAT'S THE DIFFERENCE?

Law has set the standards for olive oil and the saturated fat levels it contains. Extra virgin olive oil must not contain more than 1 percent unsaturated fatty acid, and virgin olive oil must not contain more than 3.3 percent. Pure olive oil is a combination of both oils.

CLARIFIED BUTTER

Clarified butter is far superior to regular butter because you are able to fry with it at higher temperatures and it will store longer, even at room temperature. One of the drawbacks, however, is that you do have to give up some of the butter flavor that comes from the casein in the part of the butter that is lost during the clarification process. The smoke point of butter will be raised from 250°F to 350°F since it is the protein that tends to cause the butter to scorch and smoke. The protein also reduces the storage time of butter.

When you clarify butter you separate the fat from the nonfat ingredients. When butter is heated it tends to break down into three different ingredients: a layer of foam, the thick middle layer of fat (the clarified butter), and a light-colored bottom layer of water, carbohydrates, and protein. The bottom layer contains no fat at all. The top layer contains ingredients similar to the bottom layer; trapped air keeps it from falling to the bottom.

To make clarified butter, cut ¼ pound of unsalted butter into very small chunks. Place the butter into a clear ovenproof bowl. Cover and place in the oven on the lowest temperature setting possible. After the butter has completely melt-ed, place the bowl in the refrigerator for an hour. The middle fat layer should solidify. Remove the top foam and the bottom slimy layer, then rinse the middle layer under cold water. Dry the fat layer gently with paper towels. It will keep in the refrigerator for three to four weeks.

GHEE, ITS BUTTER

Ghee is similar to clarified butter and is made using real butter. Ghee has a big advantage over butter in that you can cook and especially sauté with it without it breaking down and burning too easily. Therefore, you are able to treat ghee sim-ilar to oil. The smoke point of ghee is around 375°F, which is still lower than most oils but it is still much better than plain butter. Ghee tends to impart a great flavor to many sautéed foods, which is not possible with standard butter.

To prepare ghee, just place some butter in a saucepan on high heat and heat until all the water evaporates. Butter is approximately 19 percent water. Continue cooking on the lowest heat until the milk solids start to coagulate and caramelize (turn a light brown). The excellent flavor is released into the ghee when the milk solids turn brown. The milk solids can be easily skimmed off, leaving you with the ghee. Strain the final mixture through a few pieces of cheesecloth to remove any remaining milk solids.

POPCORN WITH GHEE

If you want to give popcorn a new taste treat, just use ghee instead of the oil you are presently using. There will be no heavy oil taste and the popcorn will have a new light buttery flavor.

DRAWN BUTTER

Drawn butter is clarified butter with the sediment drawn off. It is a very clear but-ter that has a refrigerator life of about two weeks.

COMPOUND BUTTER

A compound butter is just a butter that has added ingredients and flavorings. It is usually prepared from unsalted butter, butunless you prefer a sweet, slightly sour taste, you might prefer using salted butter for most recipe variations. Basically, the butter is softened and beaten to add air and create a degree of fluffiness before adding any ingredients. When preparing a compound butter, it would be best to use the highest-quality butter available. Many pasta dishes are served using a flavored compound butter instead of a sauce.

BROWN BUTTER

Basically, this is an unsalted butter that has been heated until it is light brown and has a somewhat nutty aroma. It is prepared just before serving the dish and usually used on vegetables and fish dishes. The butter is easily burned and should not sit after it is prepared since it may deteriorate very quickly.

BLACK BUTTER

Black butter is prepared the same as brown butter, except it is heated a little bit more and has a few drops of apple cider vinegar added and possibly a few capers. Care is necessary so that the vinegar will not cause splattering.

STORING MARGARINE

Margarine readily absorbs odors from the refrigerator and should always be stored in a tightly sealed container. Margarine will store under refrigeration for four to six months if not contaminated by someone placing a spoon in it that had been in his or her mouth. Margarine will freeze for up to a year if the temperature is kept at 0°F.

BUTTERY SECRETS

Always allow the butter to soften at room temperature. The butter should be soft enough to be stirred with a wooden spoon. Never soften butter in a microwave or in a pan on top of the stove, since these methods will affect the flavor of the butter.

When adding other ingredients, never use a blender, mixer, or food processor. This will affect the overall texture of the final product.

Italian Garlic Butter
2-3 cloves garlic, finely chopped
¼   pound salted butter, softened
1-2 tablespoons parsley
1   tablespoons lemon juice
     Salt and fresh ground black pepper to taste (if desired)

Crush the garlic into a paste. Stir the garlic into the butter, then add the parsley and lemon juice. Season additionally if desired with salt and pepper. Roll in a ball or cylinder, place in a piece of waxed paper, and chill for 1 to 2 hours or until ready to use. Allow the mixture to remain at room temperature for 20 minutes before serving or placing on lightly toasted French bread.

Florida Orange Butter
¼   **pound sweet unsalted butter**
2   **tablespoons orange liqueur (if desired)**
3   **tablespoons orange zest, finely grated**
1   **teaspoon pure orange juice**

Blend all ingredients well in a small bowl and form into a cylinder. Wrap the mixture in a piece of waxed paper and refrigerate for 1 to 2 hours before serving to allow the orange flavor to penetrate the butter.

Alaskan Smoked Salmon Butter
¼   **pound sweet unsalted butter, softened**
2–3 **ounces smoked salmon (Nova lox)**
    Pinch onion salt

Combine all ingredients until very smooth. Roll into a cylinder, wrap in waxed paper, and refrigerate until ready to use. Allow to remain at room temperature for 15 minutes before serving.

WOULD SOMEONE CAUL FAT

A caul fat is a strip of fat used to wrap meats. It is sold in French, Asian, and Italian markets. A good substitute would be bacon strips.

SAUTÉING SECRETS

- Chefs will never use salted butter when they are sautéing. The salt may separate from the butter and impart a somewhat bitter taste to the food being sautéed. Always use unsalted butter.
- Always use a small amount of oil, and heat the oil to a high temperature before adding the food. Try placing a small sample of the food (at room temperature) into the pan; if it sizzles the fat is hot enough.
- If the food is cold it will stick to the pan.
- Move the pan gently back and forth while sautéing.

- Parboil any dense foods such as carrots or potatoes first. This will assure that all the food will be done at the same time.
- Never salt food that is to be sautéed; this will retard the browning.
- Before sautéing meat, sprinkle a small amount of sugar on it. The sugar will help the browning and caramelization and will also improve the taste.
- Never overcrowd the pan.
- Remove any excess fat with a bulb baster.
- Never cover the pan or the food will become mushy.

ONE POUND OF FAT

One pound of solid shortening is equal to 2 cups.

Chapter 17
Condiments

HOT PEPPER SAUCES

One of the most common hot sauces is salsa. These sauces are very popular in Mexico and most of South America. They may be served either hot or cold.

CHEF'S SECRETS

When handling hot peppers, always wear light rubber gloves and be careful not to touch your eyes. The chemical capsaicin in peppers can be very irritating to your skin and especially eyes. The same chemical is used in police pepper sprays. One drop of pure capsaicin diluted in 100,000 drops of water is still strong enough to blister your tongue.

To reduce the hotness, remove the seeds and the ribs, then wash the peppers in cold water.

TABASCO—THE WORLD'S FAVORITE

Only three ingredients go into producing the most popular hot sauce in the world: fiery hot Tabasco peppers, vinegar, and salt. Sales total more than 76 million bottles annually. The Tabasco pepper seeds were originally planted in the United States at Avery Island, Louisiana, around 1865 and today's Tabasco sauce is made from peppers planted from the first strain. The salt used in Tabasco sauce is from the same island. The peppers need to be fermented for three years before they can be used in the sauce. Tabasco was first marketed in 1868.

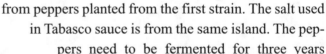

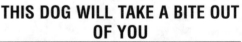

THIS DOG WILL TAKE A BITE OUT OF YOU

If you really want fiery hot sauce, try Mad Dog Liquid Fire Hot Sauce. Just use it a drop at a time or it will take your toupee off and send it flying. The product contains jalapeño peppers and African bird's-eye chile pepper, plus a few other secret ingredients. (I think it's best we don't know what they are.)

HOT CAN BE ICE COLD

Salsa can be frozen, but it must be uncooked and freshly prepared. Drain as much liquid as you can from the tomatoes or a layer of ice will form on the top.

HOW HOT IS HOT?

The following peppers have been graded as to their level of hotness. A grade of 10 will knock your socks off and curl your toes; 6 to 9 will only knock your socks off; and those below 6 will still give you a pretty good kick but are palatable for most people. If your mouth is on fire, try to drink a small amount of milk or beer, since both will neutralize the hot bite. Most dairy products will also work well, or try a bite of bread. Peppers are graded on the Scoville Scale.

PEPPER	GRADE	SCOVILLE SCALE
Habanero	10+	200,000–300,000
Thai piquin	10	100,000
Jalapeño	10	100
Cayenne	8+	50,000
De arbol	8	25,000
Hungarian wax	7	20,000
Serrano	6+	12,000
Cherry	6	7,500
Cascabel	5	5,000
Ancho	3+	1,500
Anaheim	3	1,000
Pimiento	2	500
Pepperoncini	1	100

Classic Red Chile Salsa

4   large ripe tomatoes, peeled, seeded, and chopped
3   ancho or casabel chiles, with stems, seeds, and ribs removed, finely chopped
8   scallions, chopped (do not use scallions with dark green stems)
3   tablespoons extra virgin olive oil (cold-pressed)
½   cup fresh coriander, minced
4   tablespoons red wine vinegar
    Salt and ground black pepper to taste

In a medium bowl, combine all ingredients and stir well. Place a piece of plastic wrap over the bowl and refrigerate for at least eight to ten hours to allow the flavors to blend well.

South of the Border Jalapeño Vinaigrette

¾   cup extra virgin olive oil (cold pressed)
1   tablespoon quality yellow mustard
2   cloves garlic, finely chopped
¼   cup red wine vinegar
1   teaspoon jalapeño peppers, finely chopped (remove seeds and ribs and rinse in cold water)
¼   cup fresh cilantro, minced
    salt and ground black pepper to taste

Thoroughly mix all the ingredients and allow to stand at room temperature for about 30 minutes. Refrigerate if not used immediately, but allow the mixture to return to room temperature before using.

Taco Sauce

2   cans whole tomatoes, chopped, with liquid
1   red onion, chopped
1   cup green chili, chopped
1   whole Tamed™ Jalapeno, chopped
2   teaspoon cumin
1   teaspoon oregano
1   teaspoon salt

Simmer all ingredients in a large saucepan for 1½ hours.

KETCHUP

Ketchup was originally called ***ketsiap*** and was invented by the Chinese in the 1600s. It was used as a sauce for fish and was composed of fish entrails, vinegar, and hot spices. The sauce was exported to Malaysia; the Malayans then sold the sauce to English sailors during the 1700s. In 1792 tomatoes were added and it was renamed catsup. The sauce became popular in the United States in 1830, and H.J. Heinz started producing the commercial product in 1870.

Cranberry Ketchup

4½   cups fresh or frozen cranberries
1½   cups red onions, chopped
1   cup dry white wine (optional)
2   cups pure water
2   cups apple cider vinegar
3¼   cups granulated sugar
1   tablespoon powdered cinnamon
½   tablespoon ground cloves
1   tablespoon ground allspice
1¼   tablespoon celery seed
1   teaspoon ground black pepper
¾   teaspoon sea salt
½   teaspoon quality dry mustard

Combine the cranberries, onions, wine, and water in a large saucepan and cook over medium heat until the cranberries pop, then allow the mixture to cool slightly. Puree the mixture in a blender. Return the puree to the saucepan and add in the balance of the ingredients. Simmer over low heat for 25 minutes or until it starts to thicken, stirring frequently. Allow the mixture to cool and use or freeze.

VINEGAR

The earliest record of vinegar use dates back almost seven thousand years to ancient Babylonia when dates were made into wine and vinegar. Vinegar was used as a medicinal as well as a flavoring for a number of dishes. Other fruits became popular around the same period, including grapes and figs. Laborers in ancient times were given small amounts of wine vinegar and water with a dash of salt to pep them up and work more hours. The Roman army was given vinegar rations to give them more stamina. In World War I vinegar was used to treat wounds. Vinegar does have certain antibacterial and antiseptic properties.

JUST THE FACTS

Vinegar can be purchased in a number of different varieties depending on the food source used to produce it. Vinegar is a mild acid called acetic acid. The actual amount of acid in vinegar varies from 4 to 7 percent, with the average being 5 percent. By law in the United States, vinegar needs to be at least 4 percent acetic acid. The most common types are apple cider, white, red and white wine, barley, malt, rice, and balsamic, which is made from grapes.

The acetic acid content of vinegar is referred to as grains. A 5 percent acetic acid content is known as 50-grain vinegar. The 50-grain means that the product is 50 percent water and 50 percent vinegar. A 6 to 7 percent vinegar will keep foods fresher for a longer period due to its higher acid content. The shelf life of vinegar is about eighteen months.

Studies have found that excessive use of vinegar that contains acetic acid may cause digestive problems, liver disorders, and ulcers and can destroy red blood cells prematurely. In moderation there should be no problem; however, if you can substitute apple cider vinegar in a recipe it would be healthier. Apple cider vinegar contains malic acid, which is actually friendly to the human digestive process.

One cup of vinegar is composed of 98.8 percent water, hardly any protein, no fat, 14.2 grams of carbohydrates, 14 milligrams of calcium, 22 milligrams of phosphorus, 1.4 milligrams of iron, 2 milligrams of sodium, and 34 calories.

SOME DIFFERENT TYPES OF COMMERCIAL VINEGAR

CANE VINEGAR

This is produced from sugar cane extract and water that has been fermented. The acidity level is just barely within the legal limit of 4 percent. It can only be purchased in some Oriental groceries and is mainly used in the Philippines.

CHAMPAGNE VINEGAR

This is really not made from champagne, but from the grapes that are used to make champagne. These include chardonnay and pinot noir. The methods used are the same used to produce wine vinegar. The acidity level in champagne vinegar is relatively high, around 6 percent. Most have excellent flavors and are usually used in delicate sauces. Flavoring herbs are lemon balm, lemongrass, and lemon zest.

CIDER VINEGAR

Produced from whole apples that have been ground into pulp, then cold-pressed and fermented in wooden barrels, cider vinegar can be used in salad dressings, pickling, and any dish that calls for white vinegar. Purchase a good brand since some apple cider vinegar is produced from apple cores and peelings and poorly processed. The best flavoring herb combination is dill, garlic, and bay.

COCONUT VINEGAR

This tends to leave an aftertaste and has an acidity level of 4 percent. It may only be found in Asian grocery stores and is frequently used in Thai cooking.

DISTILLED VINEGAR

Distilled vinegar may be prepared from grain, wood pulp, or oil by-products. It has a somewhat harsh flavor and an acidity level of 5 percent. Usually used in the commercial processing of pickles and related foods, it is best used for cleaning purposes around the house.

MALT VINEGAR

Originally prepared using soured beer and called alegar in Europe, malt vinegar is traditionally used on fish and chips in England. Presently it is produced from malted barley, grain, and mash, which is fermented and combined with wood shavings, then placed into large vats with vinegar bacteria. The acidity level in malt vinegar is normally 5 percent. The best flavorings are a combination of tarragon, whole cloves, and garlic.

RASPBERRY VINEGAR

Prepared from raspberries, this is one of the more popular vinegars on the market. Vinegar can be produced from almost any fruit, but the flavor of raspberry vinegar seems to be the most acceptable for a large majority of the public.

RICE VINEGAR

The Chinese have produced rice vinegar for more than five thousand years. It has a mild, somewhat sweet taste and is produced from rice wine or sake. This is a very robust vinegar that is somewhat bitter. The Japanese produce rice vinegar that is sweeter and much milder by using cooked rice. The Japanese rice vinegar is capable of neutralizing lactic acid in the body, which may relate to increasing endurance levels for athletes.

SHERRY VINEGAR

This is a very mellow vinegar with a somewhat nutty flavor. A more expensive vinegar, it is produced similar to the methods of producing balsamic vinegar. The acidity level in sherry vinegar is 6 to 7 percent, and it blends especially well with olive oil in salad dressings. Chefs use the vinegar to deglaze pans. The best flavoring combination is thyme, rosemary, oregano, and basil.

WINE VINEGAR

Wine vinegar is produced from white, red, or rosé wine and is common in salad dressings. White wine vinegar is milder than red and goes well with fish and lighter dishes. The best flavoring combination for red wine vinegar is rosemary, savory sage, bay leaf, garlic, and basil. The best for white wine is dill, tarragon, basil, and lemon balm.

I'LL HAVE A SHOT OF VINEGAR WITH MY PEARLS

Cleopatra is said to have dissolved pearls in a glass of vinegar and drank it to win a wager that she could consume the most expensive meal ever.

I WAS PUNGENT

Vinegar has the tendency to lose its pungency when heated. For this reason, when you add vinegar to a dish, it should be added only when you remove the dish from the heat. If the level of acidity in vinegar is not desired, just add the vinegar while the dish is cooking and the acidity will dissipate.

I can't wait for my little vinegar

MOTHER CAN BE A PRODUCER

If you purchase a better-quality wine, cider, or malt vinegar, it may be used as a starter if the vinegar has not been filtered or pasteurized. Bacteria or "mother" may form on the surface, then sink to the bottom. If this occurs, the "mother" can be used to prepare another batch of vinegar similar to a sourdough starter.

A VINEGAR-TASTING PARTY REALLY SUCKS

One method of tasting vinegar is to place a sugar cube into the vinegar for about five seconds, then suck out the vinegar. It is best not to taste more than four or five different varieties before drinking a small amount of pure mineral water to clear your taste buds.

LIVENING IT UP

If the dish you are preparing lacks the flavor you would like it to have, just add 1 to 2 teaspoons of balsamic vinegar to it.

I'M TOO SWEET FOR YOU

If you oversweeten a dish, add vinegar until the flavor is more to your liking.

VINEGARCOPTER

If you want to eliminate cigarette smoke from a room, very lightly dampen a dishtowel and swirl it around over your head, keeping your feet on the floor. This will clear the room of cigarette smoke as well as the smoker.

PHOOEY, I FORGOT TO ADD VINEGAR

When cooking cabbage, add a small amount of vinegar to the cooking water to eliminate about 70 percent of the cooking odor. If you get a fish or onion smell on your hands, just rub a small amount of vinegar on it to remove the odor (lemon juice works, too).

OLD-FASHIONED REVIVAL

When vegetables become slightly wilted, they can be revived by placing them into a vinegar and water bath. Make sure the water is ice cold.

FRESHER WATER WITH VINEGAR

Next time you go on a camping trip and want your water to remain fresher longer, just add a few drops of cider vinegar to the water. It will also have a cleaner taste.

NICE LITTLE MOLD, HAVE A SUGAR CUBE

If you want to store cheese for a long time, to keep the cheese from becoming moldy, just place the cheese brick into a well-sealed plastic container with a piece of paper towel on the bottom that has been lightly soaked with vinegar, then add three or four sugar cubes. If any mold spores are lurking around after you seal it, they will be killed by the vinegar or go to the sugar cube.

BALSAMIC GRAPE BREW

There are two varieties of balsamic vinegar: artisan-made and commercial. True balsamic vinegar is more of a liqueur than vinegar and is almost like syrup. True balsamic vinegar can be produced only in the provinces of Modena and Reggio in northern Italy.

Artisan-made balsamic vinegar can be traced back more than one thousand years. It is made from boiled-down grape must and legally cannot contain any wine vinegar. The aging process is complex and the juice must be passed down through a series of progressively smaller wooden barrels, which are kept in a cool, dry location. These special wooden barrels have small holes in their tops, which encourages evaporation, thus allowing the flavors to concentrate. This process also allows special enzymes to assist in the production of complex flavors. The vinegar must be aged between twelve and twenty years, and the cost for a ½ ounce bottle is between $60 and $250. The best brands to purchase are Malpighi, Cavalli, Mamma Balducci, and Giusti.

Commercial balsamic vinegar is not regulated and the amount of aging can vary. It may be a blend of artisan-made or even boiled grape must combined with good-quality wine vinegar. The really inexpensive commercial balsamic is produced from cheap wine vinegar colored and flavored with caramel. The poor quality can be compared to a quality paint remover and might substitute for one.

HOUSEHOLD CLEANING USES FOR VINEGAR

REMOVE WATER RINGS
Mix vinegar and olive oil in a one-to-one ratio and apply with a soft cloth, using slight pressure in a circular motion.

POLISH LEATHER FURNITURE
Boil 2 cups of linseed oil for one minute, allow to cool, and stir in 1 cup of white vinegar. Apply with a soft cloth, allow to stand for one to two minutes, and then rub off gently.

REMOVE CARPET STAINS
This only works well if the stain is fresh. Combine one part white vinegar with three parts water and allow to remain on the stain for three to four minutes. Using a sponge, rub the area gently from the center out, then dry with a clean soft cloth. Try an area that is out of the way to be sure that the carpet is colorfast.

REMOVE CHEWING GUM
White vinegar is capable of dissolving and softening chewing gum from a number of fabrics and carpeting.

☙ REMOVE DECALS

Apply warm vinegar on a sponge, allow to stand for a few minutes, then wipe with a soft dry cloth.

☙ REMOVE MILDEW

For severe buildup of mildew, use white vinegar full strength. For all other mildew buildup, use a solution of vinegar and water.

☙ CLEAN PLASTIC UPHOLSTERY

Combine vinegar and water one-to-one and wipe the furniture with a dampened soft cloth. Follow with a dry cloth to buff.

☙ CLEAN METAL

Use a small amount of vinegar, baking soda, or salt to prepare a paste and use the paste to clean bronze, copper, or brass pots or utensils.

☙ CLEAN ALUMINUM POT STAINS

Black stains on aluminum pots can be removed by boiling white vinegar in the pot up to the area of the stain. For large pots, boil the vinegar in a small pot and pour it on the stain.

☙ WASH WINDOWS

Mix 1 tablespoon of white vinegar in 1 quart of water.

☙ CUT GREASE

Place a capful of vinegar in the dishwasher to cut grease.

☙ CLEAN GLASSWARE

If you want your crystal to sparkle, just rinse it in a solution of one part white vinegar to three parts warm water.

☙ REMOVE LIME RESIDUE

Coffeepots, tea kettles, and irons are notorious for hard water residue buildup. When they get really bad, fill with white vinegar and run a cycle.

☙ CLEAN DRAINS

Boil 2 cups of vinegar and pour it down the drain a small amount at a time. Allow the vinegar to remain in the drain for five to ten minutes before pouring a pot of very hot water down the drain. Or use ½ cup of baking soda poured into the drain followed by ½ cup of warm vinegar, cover the drain, and allow to stand for five to ten minutes before running cold water down the drain.

CLEAN SHOWER HEAD

Remove the head and place it in a container that will allow you to cover the head with vinegar. Allow to soak overnight, rinse, and replace.

KILL WEEDS

Pour white vinegar on weeds in sidewalk or driveway cracks and they will die.

KILL PET FLEAS

Add 1 teaspoon of cider vinegar to 1 quart of water. Fleas will not go near your pet.

REMOVE CEMENT

When you are working with concrete or cement, clean your hands with vinegar—works great.

REMOVE ANTS

If you are having a problem with ants, just wipe your counters off with a solution prepared from equal parts of vinegar and water. Crawling insects hate vinegar.

REMOVE SCORCH MARKS

Rub a scorched mark with a clean soft cloth that has been lightly dampened with vinegar; the mark may disappear if it is not too badly imbedded.

BRIGHTEN CLOTHES

If you add 1½ cups of white vinegar to your rinse water, it will brighten the colors. If you are dying a fabric, add 1 cup of vinegar to the final rinse to set the color.

REMOVE CRAYON STAINS

Moisten a toothbrush with white vinegar and rub the area lightly until the crayon is removed.

ELIMINATE DEODORANT STAINS

Perspiration stains can be removed by rubbing the area with vinegar before laundering.

REMOVE INK STAIN

Vinegar will remove most ink stains if they are fresh.

🍾 REMOVE RUST

To remove rust, just moisten the fabric with white vinegar, then rub the area lightly with salt. Place the garment in the sun to dry, then launder.

MEDICINAL USES FOR VINEGAR

🍾 ELIMINATE DANDRUFF

Three to four times per week, massage white vinegar into the scalp, then shampoo.

🍾 SAVE NAIL POLISH

To make nail polish last longer, just soak the fingernails in a solution of 2 teaspoons of white vinegar and ½cup of warm water for one to two minutes before applying the polish.

🍾 RELIEVE SUNBURN

Place a piece of cloth that has been lightly dampened with apple cider vinegar on the burn. Replace every twenty to thirty minutes.

🍾 RELIEVE ATHLETE'S FOOT

Rinse your feet three to four times per day in apple cider vinegar.

🍾 RELIEVE MORNING SICKNESS

When morning sickness occurs, just add 1 teaspoon of apple cider vinegar to a glass of water and drink it.

🍾 RELIEVE INDIGESTION

To relieve indigestion, place 2 teaspoons of apple cider vinegar into a glass of water and drink during a meal.

A BUNION SANDWICH

In a small bowl, soak two slices of white bread and two slices of red onion in 1 cup of vinegar for twenty-four hours. Place the bread on the bunion and place a slice of onion on top. Wrap with a bandage and allow to remain overnight.

AROUND THE KITCHEN WITH VINEGAR

STORE PIMIENTOS

If you want to store pimiento peppers after opening a can or jar, place them into a very small bowl, cover them with vinegar, and refrigerate. They will last for two to three weeks.

KEEP GINGER FRESH

Add grated ginger to a clean jar filled with balsamic vinegar, seal tight, and refrigerate.

ENHANCE FLAVORS

When preparing soup or tomato sauce, add 1 or 2 tablespoons of vinegar to the soup or sauce during the last five minutes of cooking.

HELP OVERSALTED FOODS

Add 1 teaspoon of vinegar and 1 teaspoon of sugar, then reheat the dish or sauce.

ELIMINATE MOLD

Always remember to wipe down the outside of canning jars with vinegar to eliminate the possibility of mold growing.

WASH VEGETABLES AND FRUITS

Mix 2½ tablespoons of vinegar in 1 gallon of water and use the mixture to wash the outsides of fruits and vegetables before peeling or slicing into them.

STOP FOOD DISCOLORING

If you add 1 to 2 teaspoons of vinegar to the water you are boiling potatoes in, they will not discolor for a longer period.

DO THE GREAT MASHED POTATO TRICK

Once you have mashed the potatoes and added the hot milk, try adding 1 teaspoon of vinegar and beat a little bit more. It will fluff the potatoes up and they will hold their shape.

FIRM GELATIN

In warmer weather, gelatin tends to lose its shape. Just add 1 teaspoon of vinegar to the gelatin to keep it firm.

BETTER WEAR DARK SHADES

If you would like the crust on your fresh baked bread to have a great sheen, brush the top of the bread with vinegar about five minutes before the bread has finished baking.

ALL CRACKED UP OVER EGGS

To keep the whites where they belong when an egg cracks during boiling, just add some vinegar to the boiling water.

FISH MASSAGE

Before you scale a fish, give the fish a vinegar massage; the scales will come off more easily, and your hands won't smell fishy.

VINEGAR RISES TO THE OCCASION

Next time you steam vegetables, try adding 2 teaspoons of vinegar to the water. It will prevent unwanted odors and stabilize the color of the vegetables.

WELL, PICKLE MY EGGS

Pickled eggs are found in every English pub and will be sitting in a big jar of malt vinegar and spices.

Old English Spiced Pickled Eggs

6   medium eggs, hard-boiled and peeled
1   tablespoon honey
1   medium onion, diced
3   cups red wine vinegar
1   long cinnamon stick
1   teaspoon whole cloves
1   teaspoon whole allspice
1   small piece fresh ginger
½   teaspoon coriander seed
1   fresh bay leaf

Cook all ingredients in a stainless steel or iron pot over medium heat. Slowly bring the mixture to a boil, then reduce the heat and simmer for 5 to 7 minutes. Place the eggs into a medium-size large-mouth jar and pour the hot mixture over the eggs. Seal well and refrigerate for 7 to 10 days before serving. The eggs will remain fresh for about 2 months in the refrigerator.

STEAK SAUCE

A-1 STEAK SAUCE—RATED ONE OF THE BEST

The ingredients are tomato puree, high fructose corn syrup, distilled vinegar, corn syrup, salt, raisins, spices, orange base (combination of orange, lemon, and grape-fruit juices), orange peel, dried onion and garlic, xanthan gum, and caramel color.

NEW KID ON THE BLOCK

Grande Gusto™ is a new flavor enhancer approved by the FDA that contains all-natural flavor and has no yeast or MSG.

WHO INVENTED WORCESTERSHIRE SAUCE?

John Lea and William Perrins invented Worcestershire sauce in England in 1835 by accident. They were managing a small drugstore in Worcester when a customer, Lord Marcus Sandys, asked them to reproduce his favorite Indian sauce that he had liked when he was in Bengal. They mixed up a batch of sauce prepared from vegetables and fish but didn't like the aroma it gave off, so they placed the mixture in their cellar for storage.

While cleaning the cellar two years later they accidentally found the mixture and were surprised at the taste. Lea & Perrins Worcestershire Sauce is now one of the most popular steak sauces in the world. The recipe has barely changed from the original, using anchovies layered in brine, tamarinds in molasses, garlic in vinegar, chilies, cloves, shallots, and sugar to sweeten it. The mixture must still age for two years before being sold. The solids are filtered out and preservatives and citric acid are added.

SOY SAUCE

Soy sauce is one of the most popular condiments in the world. It is prepared from wheat (or barley) and roasted soybeans that have been fermented. The Chinese claim that ketchup was originally produced from a Chinese soy sauce recipe. There are four varieties: light soy sauce, which we normally see in supermarkets; dark soy sauce, which is not as salty but has a very strong flavor; Chinese black soy sauce, which is very thick and the color of blackstrap molasses; and Japanese tamari soy sauce, which is very dark and thick and has a lower salt content than the Chinese variety.

THE SOY SAUCE LEADER

Kikkoman International, Inc., is the largest producer of soy sauce in the world. Their latest product is a clear soy sauce that can be used in recipes without altering the color of the food. The company also produces soy sauce that is preservative-free and low in sodium; both are available in either powered or liquid forms.

MUSTARD

The mustard we know today can be traced back to 1726 and was produced by Adam Bernhard Bergrath in Dusseldorf. He combined strong brown mustard seeds with a milder yellow seed and added vinegar, water, and salt. One of the finest-quality mustards produced in the world is made by Appel & Frenzel under the name Lowensenf Mustard.

Old-Fashioned Mustard Sauce

3   tablespoons quality mustard
1   cup heavy cream
3   tablespoons pure water
1½ teaspoon fresh cornstarch

Mix the mustard and heavy cream in a small pan and bring the mixture to a boil over high heat. Mix the water and cornstarch in a bowl and stir until it becomes a smooth paste. Add this to the mustard sauce and bring to a boil, stirring continuously. As soon as it starts to boil, it it done.

MARINADES

Marinades are usually prepared with one or more acidic foods, which are used to soften the food and allow the flavors to be more easily absorbed. They are usually thin liquids, but most utilize an oil as a carrier of the flavorings into the food. Marinades may be used for as little as thirty minutes and as long as two or three days, depending on the type of food and the recipe.

LOVE ME TENDER

Most marinades are used to both flavor food as well as tenderize it. The more common tenderizing acids are papaya (papain), pineapple (bromelain), kiwi, lemon or lime juice, apple cider vinegar, and wine.

A TASTY MORSEL

The number of seasonings used in marinades is endless and really depends on a person's taste. The most common are black or red pepper, garlic, and onion.

HELP! THE MARINADE IS DRYING OUT MY ROAST

Marinades will provide a small amount of moisture to a piece of meat, but one of the major components of a marinade is acid, which will reduce the ability of the meat to retain its natural moisture when the meat is cooked. In some meat, the addition of the marinade will balance this process and you will not notice any dryness. Always remember to allow your roast to stand for ten minutes after you remove it from the oven so that the liquids that are left can return to the surface.

CHEF'S SECRETS

Many chefs use a plastic bag to apply marinade to meats and fish. Just pour the marinade into the bag, add the food, and seal it well with a rubber band, plastic strap, or metal tie. The bag should be turned occasionally to ensure that all areas of the food are well marinated.

Sometimes a chef will simmer the marinade after removing the food, thus reducing it and concentrating the flavors to use the marinade as a sauce. One note of caution: if the marinade was used for raw meats of any kind or raw fish, it would be best not to use the marinade for a sauce unless it is boiled.

Garlic Marinade
¼   cup extra virgin olive oil (cold-pressed)
4   cloves garlic, crushed
4   tablespoons apple cider vinegar
5   tablespoons parsley
½   cup dry red wine
1   tablespoon red onion, finely chopped

Combine all ingredients in a bowl and mix thoroughly before placing the marinade into a plastic bag with the food. This marinade is best for meats; it does make a tasty chicken marinade.

MAYONNAISE

Mayonnaise may be made using any type of vegetable oil. The preferred oil is low in saturated fat and ideally one that is high in monounsaturated fat, which would be olive or canola oil. If you wish to have a somewhat nutty flavor, you can use walnut or almond oil. Always use the highest quality of the oil you choose.

STEP BY STEP, DROP BY DROP

When preparing mayonnaise, always remember to add the oil drop by drop, which gives the emulsification enough time to fully form. As soon as the mixture begins to become more solid and looks somewhat white, you can then add the oil in a slow, thin, steady stream. Adding the oil too quickly will result in separation.

CURING A SEPARATION

If the oil that is being added does cause a separation, the problem can be solved by adding either ½ teaspoon of prepared mustard or 1 teaspoon of vinegar to the mixture. If this doesn't work, try using an egg yolk that has been beaten well. Whisk the egg yolk into the mixture a small amount at a time just until the mixture is emulsified again. The balance of the oil then needs to be added a small amount at a time.

TASTY SENSATIONS

Once all the oil has been added to the mayonnaise, flavorings can be added if desired. If you would like a more tart sauce, just add 1 teaspoon of lemon juice. Additional mustard may be added, or you can use any other condiment that appeals to your taste. Always serve mayonnaise at room temperature for the best flavor.

I DON'T LIKE THE COLD

Emulsions such as mayonnaise do not freeze well. The water in the products tends to freeze into ice crystals and separates from the oil. The sauce breaks up when thawed and cannot be put back into suspension easily. Mayonnaise will stay fresh in the refrigerator after it is opened for about two months.

MAKING MAYONNAISE? CHECK THE WEATHER REPORT FIRST

When the temperature or humidity is high, the mayonnaise will come out heavier and greasier than normal.

SHORT LIFE SPAN

Fresh mayonnaise will remain fresh for only about three days under refrigeration and should not be frozen. After this time, the mayonnaise will start to separate.

Mayonnaise

6	large egg yolks
1	teaspoon lemon juice
1	teaspoon quality mustard
⅛	teaspoon crushed sea salt (if desired)
⅛	teaspoon freshly ground black pepper (if desired)
1	cup extra virgin olive oil (cold-pressed)

Combine the egg yolks, lemon juice, mustard, salt, and pepper in a bowl and whisk. After they are blended, add the oil a few drops at a time, allowing the mixture to thicken and obtain a yellow-white color. Continue to add the balance of the oil slowly in a thin stream. If the mixture becomes too thick, add a small amount of lemon juice to thin it out.

Russian Dressing

1	cup mayonnaise
⅓	cup quality mild chili sauce
2	tablespoons chives, finely chopped
½	teaspoon pimentos, finely minced

Combine all ingredients and refrigerate for 2 to 3 hours. This is best served chilled.

Tartar Sauce

1	cup mayonnaise
3	tablespoons dill pickle, chopped
2	tablespoons parsley, chopped
1	tablespoon tarragon
2	tablespoons scallions or red onions, finely chopped
2	tablespoons very dry white wine (optional)
	Ground sea salt and ground fresh black pepper to taste

Combine all ingredients in a medium bowl and refrigerate for 2 to 3 hours to allow the flavors to blend well. This is best served chilled.

SALAD DRESSING

CHEFS' SECRETS

The standard ratio followed by most chefs when preparing an oil and vinegar salad dressing is to use one part apple cider vinegar (or lemon/lime juice) to three parts of extra virgin olive oil (cold-pressed). A vinaigrette salad dressing can be made by just adding ½ teaspoon of quality mustard and using red wine vinegar instead of cider vinegar.

To prepare a creamy olive oil salad dressing, pour the oil very slowly into a running blender with a variety of seasonings and herbs already in it.

Thousand Island Dressing

1   cup mayonnaise
1   tablespoon green bell pepper, finely chopped
¼   tablespoon red bell pepper, finely chopped
1   cup canned whole tomatoes, seeded and chopped
¾   teaspoon chopped pimentos
1   hard-boiled egg, finely chopped
½   teaspoon Worcestershire sauce
3   tablespoons mild chili sauce

Combine all ingredients in a medium bowl and refrigerate for 2 to 3 hours. Whisk well before serving chilled.

Classic Caesar Dressing

1   large egg
½   cup extra virgin olive oil (cold-pressed)
6   anchovy fillets, cleaned, dried, and sliced
½   teaspoon sea salt
2   tablespoons fresh lemon juice
¼   teaspoon fresh ground black pepper
½   cup Parmesan cheese, grated

Sterilize the egg in the microwave. Combine all ingredients in a large bowl and whisk rapidly, but do not allow foam to appear.

Creamy Italian Dressing

1	cup standard mayonnaise
2	tablespoons white wine vinegar
2	cloves garlic, finely chopped
¼	cup heavy cream
2	tablespoons chopped fresh oregano or 1 tablespoon powdered
	Salt and ground black pepper to taste

Combine all ingredients and refrigerate for 1 hour. Serve at room temperature.

Chapter 18
Desserts

GELATINS

Gelatins are sold in two forms. Powdered gelatin is the most common, while leaf gelatin is sold only in bakery supply stores and is produced in brittle sheets. Leaf gelatin is rarely called for in most American recipes and is usually only required in European recipes. Leaf gelatin, however, does have a better flavor and produces a clearer gelatin. Both types are interchangeable. Gelatin dishes are at their best for only about twelve hours. They will keep for about two to three days when refrigerated, but allow them to stand at room temperature for thirty minutes to soften them before serving. Never freeze a gelatin dish, since it will crystallize and separate.

SOFTENING THEM UP

When using either powdered or leaf gelatin, it must first be softened in a cold liquid. Water is usually the liquid of choice.

To soften powdered gelatin, place it in a dish and gently drop cold water on it. For every tablespoon of gelatin, use ¼ cup of cold water. Allow to stand for five minutes or until rubbery.

To soften leaf gelatin, place the sheet in a bowl and cover with cold water. Allow the leaf to remain in the water for five minutes or until it is very soft. Remove the gelatin with your hand and squeeze out the excess water, then return it to a dry bowl. If the gelatin will be add to a hot liquid, it will not have to be melted further in hot water.

MELTING THE GELATIN

To melt either type of gelatin, just place the dish with the gelatin into a pan of hot water and heat over a burner. You can shake the mixture gently, but never stir the gelatin or it will become stringy. To check it, remove a small amount; there should be no visible crystals. Gelatin should never be dissolved over direct heat since it will stick to the pan.

THE THREE STAGES OF GELATIN

PARTIALLY SET
The gelatin appears syrupy and has the texture of beaten egg whites. Add additional ingredients, such as nuts, fruits, beaten eggs, or vegetables.

ALMOST FIRMED-UP
The gelatin is almost set but still able to flow when the pan is tipped. Add additional layers of gelatin if desired.

FIRM
The gelatin should remain fairly solid when the pan is tipped. If it does not lose its shape when sliced, it is ready to serve.

STIFFEN UP FOR ASPIC
Gelatin needs to be really stiff for aspic. If you are curious as to whether the gelatin will be set enough, just place a small amount in the freezer for five minutes. If it jells up, it will make good aspic.

LOOSENING UP
To release the gelatin from a mold or pan, just place the bottom of the mold in very warm (not hot) water for a few seconds to loosen the sides.

QUICK, SET ME UP
After completing the gelatin and placing it in the mold, try putting the mold in the freezer for twenty to thirty minutes before refrigerating. Gelatin will crystallize if frozen, so keep an eye on it.

WHOOPS, I MISSED MY STAGE
If you accidentally set gelatin to a stage that is not desired, just place the mold in a pan of very hot water and stir the gelatin until it melts. Refrigerate the gelatin and keep an eye on it until it jells to the stage you desire.

STAYING TOO LOOSE

There are a number of fruits and vegetables that will affect the setting of gelatin. They all posses an enzyme that has the tendency to keep the protein in a liquid state and not allow it to become a semisolid. These include pineapple, papaya, kiwi, ginger root, figs, and mangoes. If you would like to use any of these fruits, just cook them for about five minutes to destroy the enzyme. However, some of these fruits tend to lose their color and flavor when heated. If you use too much sugar, it will also stop the gelatin from setting.

THROW ME A LIFELINE, I'M SINKING

If you are having a problem with your ingredients sinking to the bottom and not staying put, they were probably added at the wrong time. When this occurs, try melting the gelatin until just syrupy; then stir the mixture until the fruits are back where they belong.

BOUNCY, BOUNCY

If your gelatin set too solid and rubbery, you probably used too much. When this occurs, the only way to fix it is to melt it and add more liquid.

WHAT'S THE DIFFERENCE BETWEEN SHERBET AND SORBET?

Very simply, sherbet has milk and sorbet doesn't. Sorbet is prepared from undiluted fruit, water, and sugar if the fruit is not sweet enough. Sherbet is made from milk, sugar, and flavorings or real fruit, depending on the brand.

PUDDINGS

There are two types of basic puddings: starch-thickened and baked. The starch-thickened puddings are often called boiled puddings since it is necessary to cook the starch to thicken the pudding to an acceptable consistency.

CORNSTARCH PUDDING

This consists of a mixture of sugar, milk, and some flavoring, and is usually thickened with cornstarch. The pudding may be thickened with enough cornstarch so that it is solid enough to be placed in a mold.

Cornstarch Chocolate Pudding

½ cup granulated sugar
2 tablespoons cornstarch
¼ teaspoon salt (lite salt if desired)
1 large egg
2 cups whole milk (reduced-fat if desired)
1 tablespoon unsalted butter or margarine
1½ teaspoons pure vanilla
2 ounces unsweetened chocolate, shaved

In a medium saucepan over low heat, combine the sugar, cornstarch, salt, and egg. When these are well blended, gradually add the milk, stirring continuously. Cook the mixture while stirring until it starts to boil, then blend in the butter, vanilla, and chocolate. Allow to cool for a few minutes, then place the pudding into individual serving dishes and refrigerate.

Baked Custard Pudding

2 large eggs
½ teaspoon pure vanilla
⅓ cup granulated sugar
¼ teaspoon salt
2 cups whole milk (reduced-fat if desired)

In a medium bowl, beat the eggs, vanilla, sugar, and salt until blended. In a small saucepan, scald the milk and gradually pour it into the egg mixture, stirring continuously. Place the mixture in individual custard cups and then in a pan of very hot water. Bake at 350°F for 30 minutes or until a knife comes out clean, then refrigerate.

Old England Bread Pudding

4 cups coarse bread crumbs
2 cups whole milk (reduced-fat if desired)
¼ cup unsalted butter, melted
½ cup granulated sugar
2 large eggs
½ cup raisins
¼ teaspoon salt
1 teaspoon cinnamon

Place the bread crumbs in a large bowl. Scald the milk, pour it over the bread crumbs, and allow to cool. Add the balance of the ingredients while gently stirring. Bake the mixture in a buttered, deep casserole pan at 350°F for 1 hour. When a knife comes out clean, the pudding is ready.

MOUSSE

Mousse is the French word for "foam." A mousse dessert is a smooth, somewhat spongy type of whipped cream mixture that is either consumed as is or used as a topping for fruits.

Cherry Chocolate Mousse

2   cups heavy whipping cream
½   cup 10X confectioners' sugar
¼   teaspoon salt
1   teaspoon gelatin
1   tablespoon maraschino cherry juice
1   cup Hershey's or U-Bet chocolate syrup

In a large bowl whip the cream until stiff, then beat in the sugar and salt. Soften the gelatin with 1 tablespoon of cold water, and in a separate bowl mix the gelatin, cherry juice, and chocolate syrup. Gently fold in the whipped cream and place the mixture into a container to freeze until firm or the consistency you desire.

MAKE YOUR OWN NUT AND SEED PASTES

ALMOND PASTE

Process 2 cups of almonds that have been blanched and toasted in a food processor or blender for two to three minutes. Add 1 teaspoon of salt, then continue processing for another one to two minutes. If you don't want to make the paste, just substitute peanut butter.

CHESTNUT PASTE

In a medium saucepan over low heat, simmer peeled chestnuts in whole milk (just enough to cover the chestnuts) for about one hour or until very tender. Add more milk as the milk is lost. Drain the chestnuts and process them in a blender or food processor until you have a paste.

PEANUT PASTE

Combine 1 cup of roasted peanuts and 2 tablespoons of peanut oil in a food processor until it is the consistency you desire.

SESAME PASTE

Process 1 cup of sesame seeds (or less) with ½ teaspoon of peanut oil (more if desired) in a blender until it is the consistency you desire.

Chapter 19
Soups, Stews, and Sauces

SOUPS

YOU WILL NEVER CURDLE AGAIN

It is not uncommon for tomato soup to curdle, since all the ingredients—cream, salt, and tomatoes—are capable of changing the ratio of acid to cream as the soup is heated. To avoid curdling, just heat the liquefied tomatoes separately from the cream. Add the hot tomato mixture to the cream very slowly, mixing constantly, just before you are finished cooking the soup. The salt should not be added until just before serving or this may also increase the risk of curdling.

FREEZE ME, FREEZE ME

Soups and stews can be refrigerated for three to four days safely and can be frozen with little or no problem for two to three months. A texture change can easily be corrected, though you should whisk in any dairy product after thawing to avoid curdling. That goes for egg yolks as well.

CANNING SOUPS

The best soups for canning are vegetable, dried bean, dried pea, meat-based, and seafood-based. Meats should be cooked in a liquid until tender, then strained to remove all debris. Vegetables should be fully cooked to the consistency desired. Cover the meat and vegetables with water and boil for five minutes. Never thicken soups to be canned, though you can add some salt to taste. Fill your jars halfway with the solid mixture, then add the remaining liquid, allowing 1 inch headroom for expansion.

☆   **CHEFS' SECRETS**   ☆

- When a chef needs to thicken soup, he will usually use flour, tapioca, tomato sauce, or cream of wheat depending on the type of soup.
- If you wish to blend flavors in the soup, cook the soup with the cover on.
- Always use salt and pepper toward the end of the cooking time. Both of these seasonings will intensify the more they are heated. If too much salt is added, just place a piece of raw potato in and swirl it around to absorb the salt, then discard it.
- Chefs usually prepare soups the day before they serve them to allow the flavors to blend.
- Always use a warmed bowl for hot soups.
- If the soup becomes lumpy, just place it into the blender for a few seconds and reheat it.

Old-Fashioned Beef and Barley Soup

1	pound lean beef round, cut into small pieces
3	cloves garlic, chopped
2	cups red onions, minced
5	cups pure water
2	cups brown stock
1	teaspoon paprika
½	cup barley
⅛	teaspoon marjoram
2	medium carrots, chopped
3	small stalks celery, chopped
3	medium potatoes, cut into small chunks
16	ounce can seasoned stewed tomatoes
¾	cup mushrooms, sliced
1	small package frozen peas
3	tablespoons vegetable oil
	Salt and ground black pepper to taste

Combine the beef, garlic and onions in a medium saucepan and sauté in the oil until just tender. Add the water, stock, paprika, barley, and marjoram, then simmer with the pan covered until the meat is tender. Add all the vegetables and continue to simmer until they are tender. Be careful not to overcook or the vegetables will become mushy.

Chicken Noodle Soup

3–4 pounds chicken, cut into quarters and washed in cold salted water

1 teaspoon salt

3 quarts pure cold water

½ cup red onions, sliced

2 large carrots, chopped

3 small celery stalks, chopped

1 bay leaf

2 cloves garlic

3 stalks parsley, chopped

Pepper to taste

2 ounces thin noodles

Bring the chicken and salt to a boil slowly in a large pot. Remove any foam or debris that rises to the surface. Simmer for about 1 hour uncovered and continue to add cold water as the water evaporates. Add the vegetables and seasonings, bring to a boil, and simmer for another hour. Strain the soup, cut up 1 cup of the chicken into small pieces, and add them to the soup. Refrigerate the soup until the fat rises, then remove the fat. Cook the noodles in salted boiling water, being careful not to overcook. Add them to the soup, heat, and serve.

SOUP FLOATERS AND BOBBERS

The best floaters to use to top off soups are croutons, small pieces of bacon, broccoli, small celery chunks, mushrooms, crushed hard-boiled egg, parsley, Parmesan cheese, miniature onions, a dollop of sour cream or yogurt, and chives.

COOLING OFF

Blowing on your soup when it is too hot will cool the soup about 50 percent faster than if the soup is left alone. Blowing on the hot liquid encourages evaporation at a faster rate.

CHOWDERS

Basically, chowders are very thick, chunky, and hearty soups. Many times they tend to resemble stews more than soups. The majority of chowders are prepared with shellfish, fish, or vegetables, or a combination of all three. Most chowder recipes call for the addition of potatoes and milk or cream. The vegetables most commonly used in chowders are corn, celery, and onions.

THE CLAMMIER, THE BETTER

New England clam chowder was first prepared in the United States by early colonists who were watching wild pigs dig up clams for food. They realized that these were a good food source and started making soup from them. Different groups made the chowder with milk and some with tomatoes, and neither agreed on which recipe was the best. The one thing they agreed on was that the chowder had to have a very strong clam flavor. Quahogs (named after the wild pigs) are hard-shelled clams and are preferred.

Old New England White Clam Chowder

4–5 dozen hard-shelled clams or 3 cups shucked clams, chopped into small bits

1	cup pure water
2	medium potatoes, diced
1	large red onion
2	cloves garlic
¼	teaspoon thyme
2½	quarts whole milk
1	teaspoon salt
¼	teaspoon fresh ground black pepper

Clean the clams thoroughly under running water with a brush. In a large steamer or covered kettle, cook the clams with the water over medium heat until all the shells open, stirring occasionally. Remove from heat and allow to cool. Cook the remaining broth until it is reduced to 1 to 2 cups and place aside as a reserve broth or clam liquor.

In a medium saucepan, cover the potatoes with water and boil with a small amount of salt. Cook just until tender. In a small covered saucepan cook the onion, garlic, and thyme in a small amount of butter slowly until they are transparent. Remove the lid and allow to brown slightly. Remove the clams from their shells and separate the harder meat from the soft center meat. Chop the harder meat only into very small pieces. Place the softer meat aside.

In a medium pot, heat the milk until it is just scalded and a thin skin forms on the top. Remove the skin and add the chopped clams, potatoes, and onion mixture. Increase the heat to scald the milk again, then strain the reserve broth through a double thickness of cheesecloth and add to the pot. Add the chopped-up soft clam pieces, salt, and pepper. Simmer for 3 minutes and add any additional seasonings you desire.

Old Manhattan Red Clam Chowder

1½ cups shucked clams, chopped into small pieces
1   cup red onions, chopped
3   large carrots, diced
3   stalks celery, diced
½   cup green or yellow bell pepper, chopped
2   tablespoons parsley, finely chopped
16 ounce can tomatoes
2   quarts pure water
1   bay leaf
8   peppercorns
½   teaspoon thyme
2   medium potatoes, cubed into bite-sized pieces
    Salt and pepper to taste

Use the same instructions for the red chowder as was given for the white chowder with the exception of chopping the tougher clam meat into pieces the size of corn kernels. The soft clam meat can be left in larger pieces since they are tender. Be sure that the vegetables are just tender, not mushy. Corn can also be added to the red chowder, if desired, 20 minutes before the end of the cooking time.

IF IT'S COLD, GO FOR IT!

When preparing cold soups you need to add additional seasonings, since heat increases the release of flavors in vegetables, seasonings, and herbs.

TO PREVENT SCORCHING, USE PLATFORM COOKING

To avoid scorching your soup when simmering for long periods, try placing two or three bricks under the pot. This slight elevation will prevent a boilover from occuring.

THE GARLIC MAGNET

If your soup or stew has been overpowered by garlic, just place some parsley in a tea ball and swirl it around for a minute or so. Garlic is attracted to parsley. Discard the garlic when done.

RAFTING ON THE COMSOMMÉ

Consommé should be crystal-clear when served. To clarify the consommé, egg whites are added to the stock, and the egg protein and the protein in the consommé stick together. When this occurs, they trap particles that cloud the soup and just are floating around. When you add the egg whites, whisk the mixture, and when it comes to a boil, stop whisking and allow the solids to rise to the top and take the shape of a "raft." Allow the raft to continue acting as a filter and growing as the soup simmers for about an hour. Ladle off the raft carefully so as not to unduly disturb it and release some of the unwanted materials.

THE TAIL OF THE SOUP

Oxtail soup is actually made from the tail of an ox, which is very flavorful. It is a clear soup that contains carrots, turnips, barley, and celery. Occasionally, whole soft-cooked chicken or duck eggs may be found floating in the soup, especially in Europe.

HELP! MY PEAS ARE DROWNING

Next time you prepare pea soup, try placing a piece of white bread in the water while the peas are cooking. The bread will prevent the peas from falling to the bottom and sticking or burning.

RATINGS OF THE TOP TEN LOW-FAT SOUPS

The following soups or brands all contain less than 3.5 grams of fat in a 1-cup serving, are low in sodium, and contain at least 10 percent of the RDA for at least four major vitamins or minerals.

SOUP	CALORIES	SODIUM (mg)	FIBER (g)
Health Valley Fat-Free	90	230	8
Pritikin Split Pea	160	290	7
Arrowhead Mills Red Lentil	100	320	3
Healthy Choice Garden Vegetable	110	400	3
Baxter's 99 Percent Fat Free Onion	70	420	3
Shari's Organic	130	420	3
Progresso 99%Fat Free Beef Barley	140	460	5
Campbell's Healthy Request Bean	150	480	7
Hain Healthy Naturals	120	480	4
Westbrae Natural Fat Free	190	580	7

BISQUES

Bisques are among the more difficult soups to prepare. They are thick, creamy soups, usually prepared with shellfish. Shrimp and lobster are the shellfish of choice for most chefs. Lobster bisque, when prepared properly, has no equal. Brandy is often used after it has been burnt and the alcohol heated and burned off.

New England Shrimp Bisque

1   **cup pure water**
1½ **teaspoons salt**
⅛   **teaspoon ground black pepper**
⅛   **teaspoon celery salt**
1   **tablespoon onion, finely minced**
2   **teaspoons parsley, minced**
1   **cup milk**
1   **tablespoon flour**
8   **ounces shrimp, diced with liquor**

Combine the water, salt, pepper, celery salt, onion, and parsley in a medium saucepan and simmer for 3 minutes. Add the milk and a roux paste prepared from flour and butter. Boil for 1 minute in the top of a double boiler, stirring constantly, then add the shrimp with liquor. Remove from heat until you are ready to serve. Do not allow the bisque to boil any further.

STOCKS

Stocks are the basis of many soups and sauces. There are four basic stocks: brown, white, poultry, and seafood. A stock is prepared from a liquid in which fish, meats, or poultry are cooked. The liquid is then seasoned and usually cooked for eight to ten hours to ensure that the flavors are adequately incorporated into

320 — Soups, Stews and Sauces

the stock. The liquid is then removed, leaving the flavored residue. Stocks may be frozen and used as needed.

Most quality stock bases are not sold in markets. A 1-pound jar of base is capable of making 5 gallons of stock. However, the better brands of bases are almost all sold directly to restaurants and chefs. One of the best stock bases is produced by the L.J. Minor Corporation in Cleveland, Ohio.

☞ BROWN STOCK

Usually prepared with beef and veal bones. The bones are grilled, producing a rich brown color, and should be included in the initial stages of preparation whenever possible.

Brown Stock

3	tablespoons vegetable oil
3½	pounds beef shank (butcher will easily supply)
3	red onions, sliced
3	medium carrots, sliced
4	fresh celery stalks, diced
1	cup boiling water
½	teaspoon dried thyme
2	bay leaves
8	fresh peppercorns
4	sprigs parsley
4	quarts pure water

Add if desired:

1¾	teaspoons sea salt (iodized salt is okay)
½	teaspoon ground black pepper

In a large pan with 1½ to 2-inch sides, combine the vegetable oil and the beef bones that have beef broken into chunks, and bake at 450°F until they are brown, turning occasionally. This should take about 10 minutes. When the bones are brown add the onions, carrots, and celery and bake until the vegetables start to brown. Remove from the oven.

Place the mixture into a large pot. Add the boiling water to the baking pan and scrape all the residues into the water. Add this to the large pot, then add the thyme, bay leaves, peppercorns, parsley, and pure water. Bring the stock to a slow boil over medium heat, reduce the heat, and allow the stock to simmer for 5 hours. Remove any fat that rises to the top for the first hour using a piece of white bread as a sponge or a thin wooden spoon. Remove from heat and strain.

Allow the stock to cool to room temperature. The stock will freeze for 6 to 8 months but will last for only a few days in the refrigerator. If any more fat rises to the top, allow it to remain until you are ready to use the stock, then remove it. The fat will protect the stock from outside contamination.

☞ CHICKEN STOCK

A clear stock prepared from chicken or other poultry parts and usually simmered with vegetables, herbs, and spices.

☞ FISH STOCK

Prepared from fish bones and poached fish or shellfish.

☞ VEGETABLE STOCK

Usually prepared from onions, carrots, and celery and flavored with garlic and other herbs. The formula for making the stock is 60-20-20: 60 percent onions, 20 percent celery, and 20 percent carrots. Strong-flavored vegetables such as broccoli and cabbage should be avoided.

☞ POULTRY STOCK

Prepared from any kind of poultry, but usually chicken. Vegetables used include onions, carrots, and celery.

☞ WHITE OR VEAL STOCK

Originally prepared with only veal bones, providing a clear stock that contains very little flavor of its own. The stock is now made with veal, beef, or poultry bones or a combination.

White Stock
4   pounds bones, broken into small chunks and meaty if possible
1   cup red onions, chopped
2   large carrots, chopped
5   celery stalks, chopped
3   cloves garlic, crushed
2   bay leaves
½   teaspoon thyme
3   cloves
1   teaspoon black peppercorns
     Small bunch parsley
     Salt to taste

Place the bones in a large stockpot and cover with water to about 4 inches above the bones. Cover and bring to a boil, then pour off water with foam and residues. Cover with water again to the same level and simmer for 7 hours, adding cold water as the water evaporates. Continually skim the surface to remove foam and debris. Stir occasionally to make sure that the bones do not stick to the bottom.

Add the vegetables about 2 hours before the cooking time is completed, then add all the seasonings 30 minutes before the end. Cover a large bowl with three layers of cheesecloth and strain the stock. Discard all the bones and vegetables. Cool the stock as rapidly as possible. The stock will keep for about 2 to 3 days in the refrigerator and may be frozen for 4 to 6 months.

☆ **CHEFS' SECRETS** ☆

- Never use salt; it will concentrate and ruin the stock as the liquid reduces. Salt may be added later if desired.
- Always simmer with the pot uncovered. Condensation may affect the final result. Stock should never be boiled or it may become cloudy.
- Gelatin from the bones is important, since the stock should become com pletely gelled when cooled down. The stock can be spooned as needed.
- Stocks should be kept frozen until needed, especially if they contain an animal product. If refrigerated for storage, stock can be kept for about six days. If it is refrigerated for more than six days, the stock should be boiled for eight to ten minutes before using.
- Brown stock can be reduced until it is syrupy or even very dark. Brown stock is usually very concentrated and very little is needed to flavor sauce. It is easy to overpower with a brown sauce and detract from the flavor of the dish. Any stock can be more concentrated the more you boil it down.
- All fat should be trimmed off before placing the meat and bones into the stock pot. The stock should be stirred only three times during the first hour or it may become cloudy.
- When dissolving dry gelatin, never pour hot water directly on the gelatin. This causes clumping and reduces the ability of the gelatin to dissolve prop erly. Try using a small amount of cold water until the gelatin is dissolved, then add the additional hot water.
- Hot water added to gelatin should never be more than 180°F. If your recipe calls for an equal amount of sugar to gelatin, the cold-water step is not required since the sugar will stop the clumping. However, you should still never pour hot water into gelatin; place the gelatin into the water.

☞ PURE SALT IS A MUST FOR A QUALITY STOCK

Kosher salt is the preferred salt that most chefs use when preparing a stock. Kosher salt contains no additives, which may cause the stock to become cloudy. Salt is important to stock but should be added after the stock has cooked for ten minutes. Salt will help draw albumin (a protein) from the bones to keep the stock clear.

☞ ONE OF THE TOP TEN TIPS

Next time you prepare soup or stock, try placing a pasta basket into the pot, or just use a large pasta pot. The basket can be removed and will contain many of the ingredients you may wish to dispose of or keep.

☞ WELL, SIMMER MY BONES

When you simmer bones to extract the flavor, they may create foam on the surface, which is composed of albumin and a number of impurities (mineral residues) that are released from the bones. This foam is usually bitter and needs to be completely removed. Even leaving a hint of the foam may alter the desired taste.

Speedy Stock

If you are really in a hurry and need a stock that can easily be prepared in about thirty minutes, the following should solve your problem.

2   **cans low-salt broth**
1   **teaspoon beef stock**
1½ **cans pure water**
1   **medium carrot, chopped small**
1   **large celery stalk, chopped**
½   **large onion, sliced**
⅛   **teaspoon thyme**
⅛   **teaspoon celery powder**

Place all the ingredients in a large saucepan and bring to a slow boil, then reduce the heat and simmer uncovered for twenty to thirty minutes. Strain the stock through a fine sieve.

☞ CLARIFICATION PLEASE!

All stocks need some degree of clarification. First strain the stock through a piece of cheesecloth or very fine sieve, then for each quart of stock add one slightly beaten egg and a crumpled-up eggshell. Stir the eggs and shell into the stock and bring to a slow simmer; do not stir. Foam will form on the surface as the heat rises. Allow the stock to simmer for fifteen minutes, remove from the heat, and let stand for thirty minutes. Gently move the crusty foam aside and spoon the stock into a sieve lined with three layers of lightly moistened cheesecloth.

☞ OLD COWS ARE IN DEMAND

The bones and meat from older cows will have more flavor for stock, and their bones will have eight times more gelatin than their meat. The bones are more important to making stock than the meat.

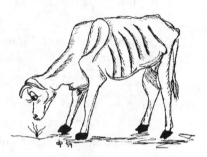

☞ DON'T STRAIN TOO MUCH

When the stock is finished, you should strain it once only through a fine mesh strainer before refrigerating for two to three hours. Remove the stock and skim off the fat that has risen to the top you will be left with an almost fat-free broth with the flavor intact. Stocks that are refrigerated for more than three days should be reboiled or they will spoil.

☞ A STOCK BY ANY OTHER NAME

If you prefer to purchase stock in the supermarket, it may be sold under a number of different names, including bouillon, broth, or consommé. There are two types of canned broth to choose from: ready-to-serve, which has liquid added, and condensed, which requires that you add the liquid. Canned broth should be placed into the refrigerator overnight to allow the fat to rise. Remove the fat before using for a low-fat broth.

☞ SAVE THAT CARCASS

An excellent poultry stock can be made using the turkey carcass from Thanksgiving dinner. If you don't have the time right away, just freeze the carcass well wrapped in freezer paper. Try to use it within two months for the best results.

☞ ALUMINUM POTS AND STOCK ARE ENEMIES

Preparing stocks in aluminum pots should be avoided. The aluminum tends to impart a bitter taste to stocks and will stain the pot if a stock is stored in it.

☞ DON'T USE HOT TAP WATER
Cold water is usually more pure than hot water. Hot water tends to leach more impurities from water pipes.

☞ VEAL BONES ARE NUMBER ONE
Chefs always prefer veal bones when preparing stocks since they tend to provide a more delicate flavor than beef bones. Veal bones contain more collagen and therefore have a better thickening ability.

GLAZES

Glazes are actually just stock that has been reduced to a point that it will coat the back of a spoon. They are used as flavorings in many sauces in moderation since they are a concentrated source of flavoring. Glazes are the original bases and are still thought of as a base.

Even though the glaze has been reduced from a stock, it will not taste like the stock. The types of glazes are basically the same as the stock from which they were prepared, such as chicken, meat, or fish.

☞ GUIDELINES FOR PREPARING A GLAZE
• The stock should be reduced over medium heat.
• The surface should be skimmed frequently to remove any debris or skin.
• When reducing by at least ½ a small saucepan should be used.
• Continue reducing over low heat until the glaze is syrupy and coats the back of the spoon.
• Glazes will store well in the refrigerator for at least three or four weeks if not contaminated and sealed well. Glazes may also be frozen for two to three months.

STEWS

Stews are basically prepared from almost any combination of meats, vegetables, and seasonings you enjoy. Stew should always be relatively thick and not watery.

TOUGH STEW MEAT—SHOULD HAVE USED COLD WATER

If you have a problem with tough stew meat, you may have added hot water instead of cold water. Studies have shown that hot water added to boiling or simmering stew may cause the meat to become tough. Cold water does not have the same effect.

TIMING IS EVERYTHING

Basil is a common spice used in stews, but it does not hold its flavor very long when subjected to heat for as little as fifteen minutes. Basil should be added during the last ten minutes of cooking.

STEW SAUCE NOT CHEWY ENOUGH?

To really thicken your stew sauce, just mix 2 tablespoons of potato starch in 3 tablespoons of water and add the mixture slowly while stirring. If you do this for every cup of liquid in the stew, you'll really make it thick and good.

THERE'S TEA IN MY STEW

Strong tea is a good source of tannic acid, which is an excellent meat tenderizer. Place ½ cup of strong tea in the stew and you will be amazed at how tender the beef will be.

RAW POTATO TO THE RESCUE

If you accidentally oversalt your stew, just place a peeled slice of raw potato in the stew and stir for a few minutes. The raw potato will attract the salt. Then just throw the potato away.

CARROTS—A SWEET TREAT

If you would like to sweeten up your stew or soup just a little, add a small amount of pureed carrots to the dish.

Mulligan's Irish Stew

2	pounds potatoes, sliced about ½ inch thick
4	large red onions, sliced into small chunks
3	pounds shoulder lamb, cut into 1-inch cubes
¼	teaspoon thyme
1	teaspoon freshly ground black pepper
2-3	teaspoons salt
2	cloves garlic
6	cups pure cold water
2	medium carrots, chopped
3	stalks celery, chopped

Irish stew is normally prepared in layers. Using a large stew pot (or preferably a large covered casserole that can go directly from the oven to the table), place a layer of potatoes on the bottom of the pot; then add a layer of onions, then lamb (or other meat). Sprinkle on the seasonings and add the garlic. Place any remaining onions on top of the lamb, then the rest of the potatoes on top of the onions. Add just enough water (about 4 to 5 cups) to cover the last layer of potatoes. Slowly bring the stew to a boil, cover, and reduce the heat to a low simmer for 1 to 2 hours. Stop cooking as soon as the meat and vegetables are just tender.

If the water is evaporating, add a small amount at a time as it is being lost. Preheat the oven to 350°F. Add the carrots and celery. Place the stew into the oven and check regularly to be sure that it is not boiling, only simmering, for 30 minutes.

Grandma's Chicken and Rice Stew

3   pounds broiler chicken, cut up in chunks with skin removed
    Salt and ground black pepper to taste
1   teaspoon dried oregano
¾   teaspoon ground coriander
2   cups pure water
16   ounces seasoned stewed tomatoes
2   cloves garlic, crushed
2   cups chicken stock
1½   cups uncooked rice
    Small package frozen peas
    Small package frozen corn
½   cup green olives, chopped (no pimentos)
½   cup Parmesan cheese, finely grated
1   cup red onion, minced

In a large skillet, season the chicken with salt, pepper, oregano, and coriander. Add the water, tomatoes, garlic, and stock. Bring to a boil, then simmer for 40 minutes. Add the rice, stir, and simmer until the chicken pieces are tender, about 15 minutes. Wash the peas and corn, drain well, and add them, the olives and onion. Stir and allow simmer for 5 minutes. Sprinkle the cheese on top and serve.

SAUCES

Sauces are meant to complement the flavor or provide moisture for the dish, and should never detract from the original flavor of the food. French cooking schools classify sauces in five categories: espagnole, a brown, stock-based sauce; velote, a light, stock-based sauce; bechamel, a white sauce that is usually milk-based; hollandaise or mayonnaise, emulsified sauces; and vinaigrette, considered an oil and vinegar sauce. However, we place mayonnaise in the condiment class because it is usually always purchased as a commercial product and vinaigrette as a salad dressing.

THICKENING 101

To thicken any sauce, you will need to increase the solids and reduce the amount of liquid. This can be accomplished by boiling away some of the liquid, though this will reduce the amount of usable sauce and may concentrate the flavors too much. If the sauce is high in water content, cooling it causes the water molecules to lose energy and relax, thus thickening the sauce. There are, however, a number of good substances that will thicken sauces; depending on the type of sauce you are preparing, one will surely be just right for the job. These include pureed vegetables, egg yolk, flour, gelatin, tapioca, pectin, okra, cornstarch, arrowroot, potato starch, kneaded butter, emulsified butter, cream, and peanut butter.

A FEW OF THE COMMON THICKENING AGENTS

☞ ARROWROOT

This is purchased as a fine powder derived from the roots and stalks of a tropical tuber. It is prepared by dissolving a small amount in water. These stems are mainly composed of complex carbohydrates, which have the tendency to thicken at a lower cooking temperature than most other starches. The advantage of arrowroot is that there is a less likely chance of burning the thickener due to its low protein content.

☞ CORNSTARCH

Produced from the endosperm of a kernel of corn, this should always be dissolved in water before using for the best results.

☞ PECTIN

When using pectin in preserves, use only the amount specified in the recipe. Different brands are prepared with different ingredients that will make a difference in the final product. Some pectin needs acid and sugar to set, while others never need acid or sugar.

☞ TAPIOCA

Tapioca is extracted from the tropical cassava root and best used as a thickener if it is diluted with water before being added to a dish just before serving. The roots are finely grated and left to ferment, then pressed into cakes and baked. The baked cakes are then powdered into a pure starch. Tapioca is best when it is moistened, then heated and immediately used.

☞ VEGETABLE PUREE

A healthier method of thickening gravies and sauces, a puree may be made with any assortment of vegetables that complement the dish. Vegetables need to be cooked first, some need to be sautéed first, then pureed in a blender or food processor. Once the vegetables are pureed, they should be put through a sieve or fine mesh before using.

REAL EASY AND THICK, TOO

A relatively new thickener, Thick & Easy® is now available. The thickener is made from modified food starch and maltodextrin with no additives or preservatives. The product can be used to thicken any type of cold or hot food, either solids or liquids. It can be frozen and reheated in the microwave. The thickening activity stops after one minute and it retains its consistency. It is fully digestible and does not bind fluids, releasing 98 percent for consumption, while most competitive products only release 50 percent. For additional information call (800) 866-7757.

COMMERCIAL THICKENERS

One of the better commercial thickeners is Textra™, a modified tapioca starch that has been designed to improve the mouthfeel and texture of foods. It does not impart any taste while providing thickening for drinks, sauces, and syrups. It is one of the more stable thickeners and will help particles such as fruit pulp to remain in suspension.

INSTANT STARCH

There are two "jel" products that do a great thickening job, ClearJel-310® and Rice Gel®. ClearJel-310 will thicken as soon as it is added to either water or milk and will provide a smooth, fully hydrated texture as well as being heat- and acid-resistant. Rice Gel is produced from precooked rice flour with no noticeable taste of its own. It has a high water capacity, blends well with dry foods, and is nonallergenic.

THICKENING A SAUCE OR MAKING GLUE FOR THE KIDS

The easiest method to thicken a sauce is to prepare a small amount of "paste." The paste should be prepared separately from the sauce. Never add the paste ingredients to the sauce to hasten the procedure. The paste needs to be smooth and the consistency will vary depending on the level of thickening needed. If the sauce is very thin, you will need a thick paste. Add the paste gradually, allow the sauce to boil, and stir until the desired texture is obtained. Use whatever liquid is compatible with the sauce you are preparing. These pastes will work especially well with gravy and most other sauces:

- thin paste: 1 tablespoon flour and 1 cup of liquid
- medium paste: 2 tablespoons flour and 1 cup of liquid
- thick paste: 3 tablespoons flour and 1 cup of liquid

HEAR YE, HEAR YE: HOT SAUCES HATE EGG YOLKS

If your recipe calls for egg yolks, never add them to a sauce that is hot. The instant change in temperature resulting from placing the cool egg into the hot liquid is enough to curdle the egg yolk and may ruin the sauce. To eliminate the possible problem, remove a small amount of the sauce and allow it to cool for a few minutes before mixing in the egg yolk. The cooled sauce can then be added to the hot mixture.

WHISK ME A RIBBON

When sauce is finished cooking, it should fall from the whisk in a wide ribbon or sheet. This should take about five minutes of cooking.

WHY DOES STARCH THICKEN A SAUCE?

Starch granules are a solid, which just by being there will cause a certain degree of thickening. However, the small starch granules tend to trap water molecules, thus reducing the percentage of free-flowing water that is in the sauce or soup. When you heat the starch it has the ability to expand and is capable of absorbing even more water.

NERVOUS PUDDING

Kids call gelatin "nervous pudding" because it is always shaking. Gelatin has been used as a primary thickener for hundreds of years and is capable of increasing to ten times its original size. Gelatin is the best water-trapping medium ever found. Care, however, must be taken when adding other ingredients to gelatin. Sugar reduces the absorption capacity of gelatin significantly, and fruits such as pineapple and papaya, which contains the enzymes bromelain and papain, will almost eliminate gelatin's thickening ability.

AVOIDING A SEPARATION

If your egg-based sauce separates, remove the pan from the heat and beat in 2 tablespoons of crushed ice to reduce the heat and place the eggs back into suspension, thus saving the emulsion. You can also change pans and add 1 tablespoon of ice water to a small amount of the sauce while slowly whisking back the balance of the separated sauce. Additional ice water can be added slowly, but only as needed.

TWO TIMES THE POWER OF FLOUR

Cornstarch, arrowroot, and potato starch should be used only just before you are finishing the sauce, since they have twice the thickening power of flour and can only be cooked for a few minutes before losing their power.

NEED KNEADED BUTTER?

This is an excellent thickener, especially at the last minute. If you wish to make a sauce from leftover liquids that have remained in the pan, just place an equal amount of unsalted butter and flour in another pan, then mix them together to make a thick paste. Use small amounts of the paste, adding it gradually to the leftover liquid.

THE FATS IN THE FLOUR

Flour will not lump if you add it to any fat that is already hot. In fact, you can add flour to any hot liquid without the flour lumping.

REGULAR FLOUR VS. INSTANT FLOUR

Regular flour tends to turn into a form of gelatin when it comes into contact with hot water and blocks the water from entering. Instant flour contains smaller irregular-shaped granules that allow space for the water to enter.

HOW ABOUT A QUICKIE?

If you would like a hollandaise sauce that can be prepared in ten minutes or less, try Knorr® Hollandaise Sauce Mix. The ingredients include modified food starch, wheat flour, nonfat dry milk, hydrolyzed vegetable protein, partially hydrogenated peanut oil, lactose, salt, fructose, onion and garlic powder, citric acid, vegetable gum, yeast extract, soup stock, spices, and natural flavor. It really doesn't taste too bad, but it's nothing like the made-from-scratch original.

DON'T MOCK MY HOLLANDAISE

To prepare a "mock" hollandaise sauce, just cook 1 cup of white sauce and 2 slightly beaten egg yolks until just two bubbles (not three or four) appear on the surface. Remove the pot from the heat and beat in 2 tablespoons of unsalted butter and 2 tablespoons of pure lemon juice. Voilà—fake hollandaise sauce that will fool everyone but a chef.

HOT IS NOT REALLY HOT—IT'S WARM!

Sauces are never served hot, only warm. High heat will melt the butter too fast and ruin the emulsification, causing separation. You want the butter to turn into a foamy mixture, not a liquid. Start with cold butter, which will keep the mixture cool and reduce the risk of the butter melting instead of foaming. Keep the pan moving on and off the heat if necessary while beating the butter with a whisk. You can also use a double boiler, which is easier for the person who is not used to making a white sauce.

I'M GOING BAD—MY STARCH IS FREEZING

Most sauces and custards that are thickened with flour or cornstarch do not freeze well. The starch amylase, commonly found in grain starches such as wheat flour and cornstarch, tends to freeze into a very firm, spongy texture and allows the liquid to drain out. If the food is thickened with a root starch, such as arrowroot or tapioca, it can be frozen and thawed without any problem.

I'LL NEVER COOK AGAIN

If you accidentally burn your dessert sauce, don't fret. Just add a small amount of pure vanilla or almond extract to it to cover up the burnt taste.

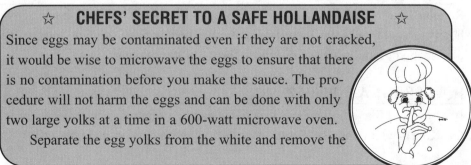

☆ **CHEFS' SECRET TO A SAFE HOLLANDAISE** ☆

Since eggs may be contaminated even if they are not cracked, it would be wise to microwave the eggs to ensure that there is no contamination before you make the sauce. The procedure will not harm the eggs and can be done with only two large yolks at a time in a 600-watt microwave oven.

Separate the egg yolks from the white and remove the

cord. Place the yolks in a small glass bowl and beat until well mixed. Add 2 teaspoons of real lemon juice and mix thoroughly. The bowl should then be covered and placed into the microwave on high and the surface observed. When the surface starts to move, allow the mixture to cook for no more than ten seconds. Remove the bowl and whisk with a clean whisk. Return the bowl to the microwave and cook until the surface moves again and then for another ten seconds. Remove and whisk again with a clean whisk. Allow the bowl to sit for one minute before you use it and it will be salmonella free.

ARE YOU GOING TO DO IT AGAIN?

There are a number of rules to remember when reheating soups, sauces, and stews. Foods that contain fats tend to oxidize more readily, and this may impart a less than desirable flavor. When reheating, never place the food in an aluminum or iron pot, and never add salt until the food is almost completely warmed up. Soups and gravies should be simmered for only about two minutes. Creamed soup should be reheated only at a slow simmer after it has reached a slow boil for about two minutes.

AM I REALLY THAT BITTER? I TRY TO BE SWEET

Occasionally, sauces tend to taste a bit bitter and the reason escapes you. It may be from a tomato seed or two that ended up not being strained out.

WHY IS MY MELTED CHEESE SOLID?

When melting cheese, never cook it for too long or at too high a temperature. When this occurs, the protein separates from the fat and the cheese gets tough and rubbery. Once a cheese hardens, especially in a sauce, it would be wise to discard the sauce and start over. When you melt cheese, grate it first. The cheese will then melt in less time.

MAKE YOUR CHEESE HAPPY—GIVE IT SOME WINE

The reason cheese tends to form lumps or strings is that the calcium phosphate present in the cheese binds with the protein. This can be avoided if a small amount of wine, which contains tartaric acid, is added to the melting cheese. The tartaric acid prevents the calcium phosphate from linking the cheese proteins. If you prefer not to use wine, just use a small amount of lemon juice and the citric acid will accomplish the same thing.

WHITE SAUCE THE RIGHT WAY

There are two types of white sauces: bechamels, made from whole milk or cream, and veloute, which is made from chicken or fish stock to be sure it retains a white color. All white sauces are made with a roux, which is made by combining flour in clarified butter (or almost any fat) while cooking slowly until it combines. This is always done before adding any liquid; however, be sure the mixture doesn't brown and that it does foam up slightly and remains a light color. As soon as this occurs, add the liquid at once and stir continually until it starts to boil, then reduce the heat and simmer for five to eight minutes. The simmering is important since it will remove the taste of the flour.

Cajun roux is cooked until the mixture of flour and fat turns black but does not burn. This is a very slow process.

☆ CHEFS' SECRETS TO THE PERFECT WHITE SAUCE ☆

- When you stir the liquid into the roux and lumps are formed, strain the mixture through a fine sieve before continuing.
- If the sauce is too thick, add a small amount of liquid while stirring slowly. If too thin, just simmer longer until it thickens.
- If you are preparing the white sauce and need to allow it to sit for a period of time, rub the top of the sauce lightly with the end of a stick of butter. This will result in a thin layer of melted butter on the top, which prevents a skin from forming.
- If a skin does form, skim it off carefully to remove it all.

FREEZING WHITE SAUCE

If you do not use cream or eggs, the sauce will freeze well for two weeks but will last for only one day in the refrigerator. If you do freeze the sauce with egg, the yolk will separate from the sauce when thawed. Cream in the sauce may be too thin when thawed and will require 1 to 2 teaspoons of arrowroot to be added.

WINE SAUCE TIP

When wine is added to any sauce, heat the sauce long enough for the alcohol to evaporate thus leaving the flavor only.

GIDDYUP, BUTTER

Mounted butter sauces gain body from both the emulsification process and the air that is beaten in.

SPEEDY SAUCES

☞ BEEF SAUCE

Whisk 1 cup of heavy cream with 2 tablespoons of a mild horseradish sauce, 1½ tablespoons of lemon juice, and salt and pepper to taste.

☞ CHICKEN SAUCE

In a small saucepan on low heat, whisk 8 ounces of sour cream with one can of cream of mushroom soup, then add 1 cup of defatted chicken broth.

☞ FISH SAUCE

Whisk together 1 cup of mayonnaise with 2 tablespoons of minced sweet pickles, 1 tablespoon of minced onions, and 1 tablespoon of minced stuffed green olives.

☞ LAMB SAUCE

In a small saucepan over low heat, melt 1 cup of mint jelly with 1 cup of pure, pulp-free orange juice and 1 tablespoon of mild prepared mustard. Serve warm.

☞ LOW-FAT SAUCE

Combine one can of quality light evaporated milk with one package of onion soup mix and 1 tablespoon of cornstarch in a small saucepan over low heat. Whisk in your favorite minced herbs or onion, remove from the heat, and add 1 cup of non-fat sour cream.

☞ PORK SAUCE

In a small saucepan over low heat, melt 1 cup of currant jelly with ½ cup of ketchup and 1 teaspoon of pineapple juice. Serve warm.

☞ VEGETABLE SAUCES

Melt 6 or more ounces of Velveeta with just enough milk to make a smooth mixture. Serve warm.

Slowly melt 6 or more ounces of regular or any flavored cream cheese with a small amount of milk on low heat in a small saucepan.

Whisk 1 pint of heavy cream and 1 cup of mayonnaise; blend well.

Low-Fat Cheese Sauce

½	cup white wine
3	cloves garlic, minced
½	cup scallions, chopped (light green and white parts only)
1	large red, yellow, or green bell pepper, seeded, ribbed, and finely chopped
2	tablespoons fresh Parmesan cheese, finely grated
½	cup part-skim mozzarella cheese, finely grated
¼	cup low-fat small-curd cottage cheese
	Salt and ground black pepper to taste

In a medium saucepan over medium heat, heat the wine to a point just below boiling, then add the garlic and simmer for 1 minute. Add the scallions and bell pepper and sauté for another 5 minutes, stirring frequently. Place the three cheeses in a blender and puree, then slowly add the puree and whisk. Makes an excellent low-fat pasta or vegetable sauce served warm.

Cornstarch Pancake Sauce

1	cup granulated sugar
2	tablespoons cornstarch
2	cups boiling water
2	tablespoons unsalted butter
2	teaspoons pure vanilla
⅛	teaspoon nutmeg

Whisk the sugar and cornstarch, then add the water a little at a time, stirring constantly. Cook the mixture for about 9 minutes, then add the butter, vanilla, and nutmeg. Whisk and serve.

LOWER-FAT SAUCES

ADOBO
A Philippine sauce made from vinegar, chilies, and herbs.

BARBECUE SAUCE
American-style barbecue sauce is made with tomato sauce, mustard, onions, garlic, brown sugar or molasses, and apple cider vinegar.

BORDELAISE
Prepared with wine, brown stock, bone marrow, shallots, and herbs.

BOURGUIGNONNE

A French sauce prepared with red wine, onions, carrots, flour, and bacon.

COULIS

Usually prepared as a vegetable puree.

DEMIGLACE

Prepared as a reduced stock made with either sherry or Madeira wine.

MARINARA

Prepared from tomato sauce, onion, garlic, and oregano.

SWEET AND SOUR

Prepared with sugar, vinegar, and seasonings.

VELOUTE

A stock-based white French sauce.

HIGHER-FAT SAUCES

ALFREDO

An Italian sauce prepared from cream, butter, and Parmesan cheese.

BECHAMEL

A white sauce prepared from butter, milk, and flour.

BEARNAISE

A French white sauce prepared from white wine, tarragon, vinegar, shallots, butter, and egg yolk.

BOLOGNESE

An Italian meat sauce prepared from meat, vegetables, wine, cream, and herbs.

HOLLANDAISE

Prepared with butter, egg yolk, and lemon juice.

MOLE

A Mexican sauce prepared from onions, garlic, hot chilies, and chocolate.

MORNAY

A white sauce prepared with milk, cheese, flour, and butter.

PESTO

An Italian sauce prepared from fresh basil, pine nuts, garlic, and Parmesan cheese.

RAGU

Prepared from tomato sauce, ground beef, onions, celery, white wine, and herbs.

SKORDALIA

A Greek sauce prepared from potato puree, garlic, lemon juice, olive oil, and nuts.

VINAIGRETTE

A French oil sauce prepared from olive oil, vinegar, and herbs.

TOMATO SAUCES

The French were the first to utilize tomato sauce in recipes after the tomato was discovered in Peru and brought to France by the Spanish Moors in the 1500s. If you are going to use fresh tomatoes in a recipe, be sure they are at room temperature for thirty minutes for the best results. Tomatoes can be refrigerated for storage, though they lose almost all of their aroma and flavor when cold.

☆ CHEFS' SECRETS ☆

- Since most recipes call for removing the skin and seeds of tomatoes, there is an easy method of accomplishing this. Just place the tomatoes in a large pot of boiling water for two to three minutes. This will loosen the skin. To remove the seeds, cut the tomato in half and squeeze the halves into a fine strainer. This will catch the seeds and allow the juice to be saved.
- Homemade tomato sauce can be stored in the refrigerator for two days and will freeze for three to four

Hot Garlic Tomato Sauce

2   tablespoons extra virgin olive oil (cold-pressed)
½   teaspoon canola oil
1   cup red onion, chopped
3   cloves garlic, finely minced
6   large ripe tomatoes, peeled and seeded (hothouse or homegrown if possible), or 1 16-ounce can peeled whole tomatoes
1   tablespoon finely chopped fresh basil or ½ teaspoon dried
1   tablespoon finely chopped fresh thyme or ½ teaspoon dried
     Salt and fresh ground black pepper to taste

Heat the oils in a large pan on medium heat. When slightly heated, add the onion and sauté for about 3 minutes or until the onions are soft, then add the garlic and stir for 2 to 3 minutes. Reduce heat and slowly stir in the tomatoes, basil, and thyme. Simmer the sauce while breaking up the tomatoes for 10 minutes if using fresh tomatoes or 6 minutes if using canned tomatoes. Add the salt and pepper. If you wish to spice it up a little, just sprinkle 1/8 teaspoon of powdered red pepper over the sauce as it is simmering.

The Ultimate Marinara Sauce

3   tablespoons extra virgin olive oil (cold-pressed)
½   teaspoons canola oil
3   cloves garlic, minced
1   cup red onion, finely chopped
½   cup fresh carrot, finely chopped
3   pounds Italian plum tomatoes or 1 6-ounce can tomato paste
½   cup Chianti (optional)
1   tablespoon fresh oregano or 2 teaspoons powdered
2   teaspoons fresh basil
¾   pound sliced mushrooms
     Salt and ground black pepper to taste

Heat the oils in a medium pan on medium heat and sauté the garlic and onions for 6 to 8 minutes. Add the balance of the ingredients, except the salt, pepper, and mushrooms, and simmer for 20 minutes. Add the final ingredients and continue simmering for 7 minutes.

Classic Old-Fashioned Spaghetti Sauce

4   tablespoons extra virgin olive oil (cold-pressed)
1   teaspoon canola oil
¾   cup red onion, chopped
1   large carrot, chopped
2   cloves garlic, chopped
1   large celery stalk, chopped
1   pound lean ground round
4   large ripe tomatoes, skinned, seeded, and chopped
½   cup Chianti (optional)
1   tablespoon fresh thyme
2   cups brown stock
     Salt and ground black pepper to taste

Heat the oils in a large pan over medium heat and sauté the onion for about 5 minutes; do not allow it to burn. Add the carrot, garlic, and celery and sauté for another 5 minutes. Add the ground beef and cook until the meat is well browned, then stir in the tomatoes, wine, thyme, and stock. Simmer for 50 minutes. Add the salt and pepper as desired.

BARBECUE SAUCE

Barbecue sauce is prepared to provide a particular flavor to the food and is usually brushed on meat and chicken. It is not designed to tenderize and does not penetrate very deeply into the food. Almost all barbecue sauces contain oil, which keeps the surface of the food moist and helps avoid burning. The sauce is applied a number of times during the cooking process with a natural bristle brush or a special barbecue brush.

Grandma's Barbecue Sauce

3   tablespoons extra virgin olive oil (cold-pressed)
1   teaspoon canola oil
5   cloves garlic, finely minced
½   cup red onion, finely diced
3   cups ketchup or seasoned tomato sauce
½   cup unsulfured molasses
¼   cup apple cider vinegar
1   teaspoon powdered cayenne pepper
1   tablespoon lemon juice
¼   cup quality mustard
1   teaspoon soy sauce

In a medium-size pan, heat the oils over medium heat. Stir in the garlic and onion and sauté for 6 to 8 minutes before adding the rest of the ingredients. Simmer for about 15 to 20 minutes. The sauce may be applied either warm or cold.

Old-Fashioned Rib Barbecue Sauce

3   tablespoons extra virgin olive oil (cold-pressed)
1   teaspoon canola oil
4   cloves garlic, finely chopped
¾   cup chicken stock
⅓   cup dark brown sugar
¼   cup seasoned tomato sauce or ketchup
2   tablespoons quality mustard
2-3 tablespoons soy sauce
1   tablespoon cayenne pepper (optional)

Heat the oil in a small pan on medium heat. Add the garlic and sauté for about 4 minutes, being careful not to allow it to burn. Mix the remaining ingredients gradually and simmer for about 15 minutes, which will allow the flavors to mix and the sauce to thicken.

Oriental Teriyaki Barbecue Sauce

½   cup beef or chicken stock
3   tablespoons low-salt soy sauce
1   teaspoon granulated sugar
½   cup dry vermouth (optional)
2   tablespoons lemon or lime juice
1   tablespoon minced ginger
¼   teaspoon red pepper (optional)

Combine all ingredients and whisk until blended. This lasts about 10 days in the refrigerator.

COMMERCIAL TERIYAKI SAUCE

Commercial teriyaki sauce should contain the following ingredients if the quality is superior: soy sauce, dried garlic, concentrated pear or grape sweetener, dried onion, sesame seed, garlic powder, ginger powder, onion powder, and natural vegetable gum. There should be no added salt.

MOLE SAUCE

This sauce is of Mexican origin and can probably be traced back to the Aztecs, who used chocolate to sweeten dishes. However, originally, a mole sauce was any sauce that contained hot chili peppers. The sauce is traditionally served with poultry dishes but can be found on almost any dish in a Mexican restaurant.

Mexican Mole Sauce

2	Poblano chilies, with seeds, ribs, and skin removed, cut up
½	cup roasted peanuts, finely chopped
4	large ripe tomatoes, peeled, seeded, and diced
¼	cup regular or seasoned bread crumbs
½	cup red onions, sliced
½	teaspoon ground black pepper
¼	teaspoon powdered cinnamon
	Salt to taste
2	ounces quality unsweetened chocolate, chopped
3	tablespoons extra virgin olive oil (cold-pressed)
½	teaspoon canola oil
3	cloves garlic, sliced
2	cups chicken stock
1	tablespoon toasted sesame seeds

Place the chilies, peanuts, tomatoes, bread crumbs, garlic, and onions in a blender or food processor and chop them up on a fine setting. Be sure not to make mush. Place the mixture in a medium bowl and stir in the pepper, cinnamon, salt, and chocolate. Heat the oils in a medium-size pan over medium heat for 2 minutes, then whisk in the bread crumb mixture and simmer for about 5 to 7 minutes or until the chocolate has melted and the mixture has thickened.

Add the chicken stock and simmer for about 15 to 20 minutes or until the mixture is very hot and thick but workable. Add the sesame seeds and the sauce is finished. This sauce should be served as soon as it is prepared for the best results.

FRUIT SAUCES

Fruit sauces go well with a large variety of foods, from desserts to meat dishes. When you make a fruit sauce, choose the best-quality fruits you can find. The resulting sauce will be more appetizing and flavorful.

Apricot and Lemon Sauce

20 fresh ripe apricots, pitted and sliced
1½ cup pure water
1   cup granulated sugar
2½ tablespoons lemon juice (fresh if possible)
⅔   teaspoon pure vanilla

In a large saucepan, bring the apricots, water, and sugar to a boil, then simmer for 15 minutes. Remove from heat and cool for 5 minutes before placing in a blender to puree. Beat in the lemon juice and vanilla.

Grandma's Cranberry Sauce

2   cups fresh or frozen cranberries
1½ cups granulated sugar
1½ cups pure water
1   cup dry white wine (optional)
½   cup dark rum (optional) or a small amount of rum extract
¼   pound unsalted butter, room temperature

In a large saucepan, simmer the cranberries, sugar, water, and wine over medium heat. Stop as soon as the cranberries pop. If they are cooked any further, they will be too bitter. Add the rum and butter and mix well. The heat should melt the butter and create an excellent sauce. The sauce should gel in the refrigerator in about 3 hours and may be served hot or cold.

SWEET SAUCES

☞ CUSTARD

One of the most popular sweet sauces is a custard sauce, which can be made in a number of great flavors such as chocolate, vanilla, raspberry, mint, blueberry, apricot, and lemon.

☆ CHEFS' SECRETS ☆

- When preparing custard, eggs are sometimes a problem if not handled properly. The eggs should be beaten first with sugar and set aside. The milk or cream must then be scalded until small bubbles form around the edges of the pot. Pour a small amount of the hot liquid into the eggs, mixing thoroughly, slightly cooking the eggs. Add the egg mixture into the hot milk and heat on low until it starts to thicken. The custard should then be strained into a bowl to remove any solidified egg or film that had formed.
- Custard must be stirred continually to prevent the bottom from burning. Chefs always use a wooden spoon when stirring custard since some of the eggs' minerals may react with certain types of metal spoons. When stirring, always stir in a figure-eight pattern to cover the complete bottom.

☆ CHEFS' SECRETS FOR CHOCOLATE SAUCE/SYRUP ☆

- If a liquid is used in the recipe, always melt the chocolate in the liquid, not separate, for the best results. Use low heat and stir continuously.
- The microwave is excellent for melting chocolate. Just place the chocolate in alarge measuring glass and cook until melted. Keep an eye on it to ensure that it doesn't cook too much.
- Most chefs melt chocolate in a double boiler over simmering (not boiling) water.
- Always use the type of chocolate called for in a particular recipe, and always use the highest-quality chocolate you can find.

☞ FINGER LICK'N GOOD

Ganache is one of the finest blends of chocolate sauce you will ever taste when made properly. It consists of melted semisweet chocolate, heavy cream, and unsalted butter. It is definitely not a healthy food since it is high in fat, cholesterol, and calories.

Ganache

1   cup heavy cream
2   tablespoons butter
12 ounce bag chocolate semisweet morsels

In a small saucepan, bring the cream and butter to a boil. Place the morsels into a medium bowl and pour the hot mixture over the chocolate; stir until smooth. When it is cool, it will remain somewhat soft and should not harden.

NOTE: Do not use vanilla purchased in Mexico for any of these recipes. The purity of this type of vanilla may be suspect and may affect the quality of the recipe.

Grandma's Hot Fudge Heaven Sauce

4   ounces bittersweet chocolate (4 squares)
2½ cups confectioners' sugar
12 ounce can quality evaporated milk
3   tablespoons salted butter
2   teaspoons pure vanilla

Heat the chocolate, sugar, and evaporated milk on the top of a double boiler with simmering water in the bottom. Stir occasionally until the chocolate has melted completely. Remove from heat and whisk in the butter and vanilla until smooth.

Chocolate Cherry Delight Sauce

¼ cup quality unsweetened cocoa powder
½ cup granulated sugar
½ sweet cream or half-and-half
⅓ cup corn syrup
¼ pound salted butter
2 ounces bittersweet chocolate (2 squares)
1 tablespoon quality cherry brandy (optional) or maraschino cherry juice
2 teaspoons pure vanilla

In a small saucepan, whisk the cocoa and sugar together over medium heat. Slowly add the cream, corn syrup, butter, and chocolate. Stir continuously until the mixture comes to a boil and is smooth. Remove the sauce and immediately add the cherry brandy or juice and vanilla. Serve hot or at least warm.

Chocolate Peppermint Cream Sauce

4   ounces bittersweet chocolate (4 squares)
½   cup granulated sugar
¼   pound unsalted butter
1   cup heavy cream
1   teaspoon quality peppermint extract

Heat the chocolate in a double boiler over simmering (not boiling) water. As soon as the chocolate is melted, add the sugar and butter. Add the cream and allow the mixture to remain on low heat for 3 to 5 minutes. Remove the sauce from the hot burner and add the peppermint extract slowly, while continually stirring.

☞ CONTROLLING YOUR TEMPER WHILE TEMPERING

Tempering chocolate is the process of melting it, cooling it, and then melting it again. This process produces a more lustrous, glossy, and stable mixture and is called for in many chocolate recipes. It is an exact science to obtain the right consistency and takes some practice. However, there is a quick-tempering method that utilizes a small amount of oil, which will speed the process up considerably. The end product will be a little thinner but will not make a difference in most recipes and decorations.

Use 1 tablespoon of vegetable oil (preferable a neutral oil such as canola or safflower). Clarified butter or even a solid shortening is used by some candy chefs. Stir 1 tablespoon of the oil into every 3 ounces of melted chocolate you use over low heat. Quick-tempered chocolate will hold up for only two to three days, but the candy is usually long gone before that.

☞ FINALLY, A LOW-FAT CHOCOLATE SYRUP

A new, low-fat chocolate syrup has hit the markets that has all the flavor and taste of the real thing and five times less fat. The product is produced by New-Market Foods of Petaluma, California, and consists of brown-rice syrup, honey, molasses, and cocoa. The syrupy, buttery topping can be found in health food stores.

VANILLA EXTRACT

The FDA has established guidelines for vanilla extract. If you use this in your cooking, you should know the differences in the various ones that are sold. To be called a "pure vanilla extract," the list of ingredients must include "extractives of vanilla beans in water and alcohol (35 percent)." This will probably be the more expensive brand. Other labels may read "water, alcohol (35 percent), vanilla bean extractives, and corn solids." The better brands may still use a small amount of corn solids, but they will always have the vanilla bean as the first ingredient.

To produce 1 gallon of pure vanilla extract it takes 13.6 ounces of vanilla beans, 35 percent alcohol, and water. The alcohol evaporates when you bake or cook with the vanilla. Sugar should never be listed on the label and may affect the product. Time will improve the flavor of pure vanilla extract.

Note: Vanilla sold in Mexico has been implicated in numerous studies as containing contaminants from the harvesting of the bean and the processing procedures. Since there is no way of telling which are good and which are bad, it is recommended that you not purchase any Mexican vanilla.

ORIENTAL DIPPING SAUCES

Peking Plum Sauce
3   tablespoon dry sherry
1   cup quality plum preserves
3   teaspoons ground anise
½   teaspoon ground fennel seed
½   teaspoon ground fresh cloves
½   cup dry mustard

Place all ingredients except the mustard in a food processor. While blending, add a small amount of mustard gradually, tasting the sauce at regular intervals until it is as spicy as desired. The longer you blend, the spicier the sauce will become.

Spicy Ketchup Sauce
2½ tablespoons chili sauce
3½ tablespoons ketchup
1   teaspoon pure lemon juice
2-4 drops hot pepper sauce
1½ tablespoons horseradish, finely grated

Mix all ingredients in a small bowl and serve. Adjust the hot pepper sauce and horseradish to your taste.

PUREE

Homemade Tomato Puree

½   teaspoon canola oil
3   tablespoons unsalted butter
½   cup red onion, chopped
3   cups whole peeled tomatoes
2   tablespoons lemon juice
    Salt and ground black pepper to taste

Heat the oil and 1 tablespoon of the butter in a large pan over medium heat. Add the onion and sauté for about 4 to 5 minutes, then add the tomatoes and simmer for 15 to 20 minutes. Remove the mixture from the heat, allow it to cool and the flavors to blend for 10 minutes, then puree the mixture in a blender or food processor. Place the pureed mixture back into the pan over a low heat setting and stir in the remaining butter and lemon juice. Add salt and pepper to taste.

Chapter 20
Liquid Substitutions

The following substitutions may be used for liquids that are not available at the time you are preparing a recipe. However, it is always better to use the ingredients called for in the recipe for the best results.

LIQUID INGREDIENT   ADEQUATE SUBSTITUTION

1 cup barbecue sauce . . . . .1 cup ketchup plus 2 teaspoons Worcestershire sauce

1 cup broth . . . . .1 bouillon cube dissolved in 1 cup of water

1 cup butter . . . . .1 cup vegetable shortening plus 2 tablespoons water

1 cup buttermilk . . . . .1 tablespoon lemon juice plus balance of cup in milk, allowing it to stand for 5 minutes before using; or add 1 tablespoon vinegar to 1 cup evaporated milk and allow to stand for 5 minutes before using

1 cup chili sauce . . . . .1 cup tomato sauce plus ½ cup sugar plus 2 tablespoons vinegar

1 cup corn syrup . . . . .¾ cup sugar plus ¼ cup water

1 cup crème fraîche . . . . .½ cup sour cream plus ½ cup heavy cream

1 egg . . . . .1 banana or 2 tablespoons cornstarch or arrowroot starch or ¼ cup tofu blended into liquid ingredients well

1 cup evaporated milk . . . . .1 cup light cream or half-and-half

1 cup heavy cream . . . . 1 cup whole milk plus ⅓ cup of butter

1 cup light cream . . . . 1 cup milk plus 3 tablespoons butter

1 cup ketchup . . . . 1 cup tomato sauce plus 4 tablespoons sugar plus 2 tablespoons vinegar plus ¼ teaspoon ground cloves

1 cup honey . . . . 1¼ cups granulated sugar plus ¼ cup water

1 teaspoon lemon juice . . . . 1 teaspoon vinegar

1 cup molasses . . . . 1 cup honey

1 cup whole milk . . . . 4 tablespoons dry whole milk plus 1 cup water or 1 cup buttermilk plus ½ teaspoon baking soda

1 cup nonfat milk . . . . 4 tablespoons nonfat dry milk plus 1 cup water

1 cup sour milk . . . . 1 tablespoon lemon juice or vinegar plus additional milk to fill 1 cup, allowing to stand for 5 minutes

2 drops hot pepper sauce . . . . .dash cayenne or red pepper

2 teaspoons tapioca . . . . 1 tablespoon all-purpose flour (more if desired)

1 cup tomato juice . . . . ½ cup tomato sauce plus ½ cup water

1 tablespoon tomato paste . . . . .1 tablespoon ketchup

1 cup tomato puree . . . . .6-ounce can tomato paste plus 6 ounces of water

1 tablespoon Worcestershire sauce . . .1 tablespoon soy sauce plus dash hot sauce

1 cup wine . . . . 1 cup apple juice or apple cider or 1 part vinegar diluted in 3 parts water

1 cup yogurt . . . . 1 cup buttermilk or sour cream

EXTRACTS AND ESSENCES

LIQUID INGREDIENT	ADEQUATE SUBSTITUTION
angostura bitters	orange bitters or Worcestershire sauce
anise extract	anise oil (use 50 percent as much)
cinnamon extract	cinnamon oil (use ¼ as much)
ginger juice	place minced ginger in cheesecloth and squeeze out juice
oil of bitter almonds	almond extract (use 50 percent more)
peppermint extract	peppermint oil (use ¼ as much)
rose water	rose syrup (2 to 3 drops)

OILS AND COOKING SPRAYS

LIQUID INGREDIENT	ADEQUATE SUBSTITUTION
almond oil	walnut oil or extra virgin olive oil
canola oil	corn oil or safflower oil
clarified butter	butter (foods may overbrown)
coconut oil	canola oil or corn oil
corn oil	canola oil or soybean oil
ghee	clarified butter or canola oil
grapeseed oil	avocado oil (very high smoke point)
peanut oil	corn oil or canola oil
schmaltz	no known substitute when prepared right
soybean oil	corn oil

VINEGAR

LIQUID INGREDIENT	ADEQUATE SUBSTITUTION
apple cider vinegar	wine vinegar
balsamic vinegar	sherry vinegar
champagne vinegar	apple cider vinegar
raspberry vinegar	red wine vinegar
red wine vinegar	balsamic vinegar
rice vinegar	apple cider vinegar
white vinegar	apple cider vinegar (canning only with at least 5 percent acidity)

Chapter 21
Miscellaneous Liquid Facts

IS THE LIQUID IN MY RARE STEAK REALLY BLOOD?

No! There is very little blood left in an animal after it has been properly slaughtered. The red juice that is released from a rare or medium-rare steak is really myoglobin, a red muscle pigment, which mixes with water and just looks like blood.

I CAN SEE A RAINBOW

Liquid food colorings are sold in small bottles since a little goes a long way. Food coloring is composed of water, propylene glycol, and artificial colors, many of which are suspect in relation to laboratory studies pertaining to cancer in mice. However, the small amount that is used should pose no health risk. A new addition to the colorings is decorative gels, which are composed of corn syrup, water, modified corn starch, salt, carrageenan gum, citric acid, preservatives, and of course those artificial dyes. Liquid food colorings have a shelf life of about four years if stored in a cool, dry location.

IT'S COMING ALIVE; LOOKS A BIT SHAKY—IT'S JELL-O MAN

In 1993 an EEGtechnician at St. Jerome Hospital in Batavia, New York, hooked up the electrodes to a bowl of lime Jell-O. The wiggling bowl of Jell-O was found to have identical "brain wave" patterns as that of an adult human. The EEG findings were confirmed by Dr. Adrian Upton.

POSTUM®

Postum was one of the more popular cereal beverages, which have lost most of their popularity since decaffeinated coffee came onto the scene. Postum contains wheat bran, wheat, molasses, and maltodextrin from corn.

WELL, EXCUSE MY INFUSION

Almost everyone is familiar with a simple infusion made by placing a tea bag in a cup of water and releasing the flavors and compounds. However, there are a number of other liquids that can be infused with essences, cinnamon sticks, vanilla beans, nuts, spices, dried fruits, and even flower petals. Hot liquids tend to cause the herb or essence to release its flavors and occasionally its colors more readily than a cold liquid.

Place the liquid you wish to infuse with the flavoring in a saucepan over moderate heat. The liquid may be milk, soup stock, sugar syrup, or cream. When the liquid is just about to boil, remove the saucepan from the heat, cover, and allow the mixture to steep until the flavor you desire is achieved. This process usually takes about thirty to sixty minutes. The mixture should then be strained to extract all the liquid, which is now ready to be used in your recipe.

LIQUID MAGIC

Supermarkets will soon have a section in the spice area for powdered food products that will be available to the general public. These products can be mixed with almost any liquid and made into a paste for thickening foods, consumed as a liquid drink, sprinkled on foods, and so on. If you want some tomato juice on a camping trip, just place some powder in a glass of water and you will have tomato juice. A few of the products will be tomato powder, spinach powder, beet powder, chickpea powder, orange juice powder, cheese powder, butter powder, cheesecake powder, peanut butter powder, and margarine powder.

CURIOUS LIQUIDS CAFÉ

Located in Boston, this café calls itself a "liquid lounge." It offers almost every kind of liquid imaginable, including chai, coffee, tea, fruit juice, hot apple cider, espresso, hot chocolate, and microbrewed juices.

POUR ME A COW—LIQUID COW—A REAL TREAT?

Bestfoods® sells a product called Bovril™, which is basically liquid cow. The product was originally sold in England and has made its way to Canada and the United States. The product is somewhat syrupy like molasses and very salty, and is usually used as a spread on toast, made into soup, or served as a hot drink. Many people drink liquid cow as a beverage before retiring to relax.

A NEW LIQUID FOOD PACKAGE

A new aseptic paperboard package will be found in the supermarkets very shortly called Cartocan. It will be used for liquid foods, will provide products with secure sealing, can be microwaved, and is relatively strong. When used for drinks, the top will have a newly designed pull-top opener and the drinks will not require a straw. It is environmentally friendly since the package is coated on only one side.

LIQUID ANIMAL FOOD—THE CAT'S MEOW

An excellent brand of liquid dog and cat food is produced by Liquivite®. The food is used only when the animal is unable to eat whole food. The food can even be used as a syringe-food and is tasty enough to tempt even finicky eaters. The food is produced from meat, whole eggs, and skim milk and is sold in cans. It is made from human-grade food and is very palatable, and can be used to rehydrate an animal. It is also commonly used during weaning as a puppy's or kitten's first "solid" food. Animals who have lost their teeth also find Liquivite® very satisfying. The animals I interviewed considered this product number one in overall satisfaction.

IT SURE IS FOGGY IN HERE

When you open any canned food, check the liquid and make sure that it is not cloudy. Cloudiness in many liquids indicates spoilage. If you have any doubts about foods, it is best to throw them out without tasting them. There are, however, a number of reasons that foods may become cloudy and still be good, such as different sizes of foods causing the breakdown of the smaller pieces, hard water, salt that contains impurities, and additives. Pickles may frequently become cloudy due to the fermentation process, and this is not harmful.

LIQUID LOVE BREW

Damiana Dynamite
1   shot quality rum
     dash triple sec
½   teaspoon granulated sugar
2   drops pure vanilla
1   tablespoon pure orange juice (no pulp)
½   teaspoon pure lemon juice (no pulp)
¼   ounce muira puama tincture
¼   ounce damiana tincture
1   tablespoon pure pineapple juice

Place all ingredients in a large glass and blend well. Pour over ice and enjoy. The key ingredients are the two aphrodisiac herbs muira puama and damiana.

BERRYPASTE

Strawberries can be mashed and used for toothpaste. They have just the right amount of abrasive action to remove yellow stains.

Approximate Metric Equivalents

¼ teaspoon	=	1	ml
½ teaspoon	=	2	ml
¾ teaspoon	=	3	ml
1 teaspoon	=	5	ml
1 tablespoon	=	15	ml
¼ cup	=	60	ml
½ cup	=	120	ml
1 cup	=	240	ml
1 pint	=	480	ml
1 quart	=	960	ml

1 oz.	=	30	g
4 oz.	=	120	g
8 oz.	=	240	g
12 oz.	=	360	g
16 oz.	=	480	g

325°F	=	160°C
350°F	=	180°C
375°F	=	190°C
400°F	=	200°C
425°F	=	220°C
450°F	=	230°C

GLOSSARY

A

ACIDULATED WATER

Water mixed with a small amount of citric acid from any citrus fruit such as lemon, lime, etc. Usually used to sprinkle on fruits that have a tendency to turn brown. The water is prepared by adding one part citrus juice to five parts pure water.

AL DENTE

Pasta that should be firm to the bite, not mushy.

ARROWROOT

A powder that is usually mixed with a cold liquid, then added to a liquid as a thickening agent.

AU JUS

Meat juices that are the result of a cooking process. Usually defatted before serving.

AU SEC

Until it is dry.

B

BAIN-MARIE

A pan of hot water used to keep foods hot.

BEARNAISE SAUCE

A sauce made from egg yolk, vinegar, tarragon, butter, and chives.

BECHAMEL SAUCE

A white sauce prepared from flour, butter, milk, and special seasonings.

BEURRE NOIR

Butter that is heated until the color is a dark brown, then flavored with vinegar.

BEURRE NOISETTE

Butter that is heated until the color is a light brown.

BISQUE

A creamy soup usually prepared from vegetables, meat, or shellfish.

BLANC MANGE

A thick, cornstarch type of white pudding.

BORDELAISE

A brown sauce with red wine, shallots, pepper, and herbs. Often garnished with marrow.

BOUILLABAISSE

A French soup/stew that has different types of fish and vegetables.

BOUILLON

A concentrated stock that has been clarified. Usually made from bones and meat or poultry.

BROTH

A clear soup produced from simmering meats, poultry, and vegetables in water.

BROWN SAUCE

Gravy that is prepared using onions, beef broth, butter, flour, vegetables, and seasonings.

BUD

The top unopened tender leaf of the tea plant.

C

CARMELIZATION
Browning of sugar by heating.

CHEVRE
Goat's milk cheese.

CHIBOUST CREAM
A vanilla pastry cream that has a very light texture produced by adding stiffly beaten egg whites.

CHINOIS
A cone-shaped strainer made of metal with a long handle that hooks to the edge of a pot. Mesh comes in different sizes.

CHOCOLATE LIQUEUR
Not real liqueur, but a liquid extracted from the cocoa bean, then used in the manufacture of chocolate.

CHOWDER
A thick soup prepared from cream, fat, vegetables, and a fish base.

CLARIFY
To remove solids from a liquid by heating until the solid materials fall to the bottom, leaving a clear layer. The clear layer is then removed. Butter is commonly clarified.

CLOTTED CREAM
Thick, scalded cream prepared by slowly heating and skimming the cream. The thick layer of cream rises to the surface and is skimmed after it cools. The process is used to destroy bacteria that cause cream to sour.

COAGULATION
Process by which proteins become firm when heated.

COCONUT CREAM
The layer that rises to the top of the milk when dried coconut meat is squeezed. Used in many Oriental recipes.

CONDENSED MILK

Canned milk produced by evaporation and then sweetened with sugar.

CONSOMMÉ

Strong brown stock soup that is clarified and usually prepared from two types of meat or poultry and meat combined.

CREAM

To beat a food until it becomes light and fluffy.

CREAM SOUP

Usually prepared using a vegetable soup base with the addition of cream or butter and milk.

CRÈME ANGLAISE

French for a rich custard sauce that is poured on cakes and fruit desserts.

CRÈME FRAÎCHE

The French version of heavy cream made by mixing 2 tablespoons of sour cream (or 1 teaspoon of buttermilk) with 1 cup of whipping cream. The mixture is shaken and left to sit at room temperature for twenty-four hours or until it is thick. It should then be covered and refrigerated.

CURDLE

To heat milk until it starts to separate and lumps begin to form.

CUSTARD

A mixture of milk and eggs, usually prepared in a double boiler or oven.

D

DASH

One-sixteenth of a teaspoon.

DEGLAZE

To add a liquid to remove and dissolve the residues on the bottom of the pan.

DOLLOP

A small amount dropped by a spoon. Usually refers to whipped cream or sour cream when only a small amount is added to the top of a dish.

DRIPPINGS

The fat and liquid that is released from meats and falls to the bottom of the pan.

E

EGG WASH

Prepared from a whole egg or portion of an egg, such as the yolk or white, and beaten with milk, cream, or water. Usually brushed on top of baked goods to produce an even browning.

ELIXIRS

Healing remedies usually concocted to alleviate the symptoms of specific diseases.

ETUVER

Cooking or steaming a food in its own juices.

EVAPORATED MILK

Whole milk that is very concentrated through evaporation.

F

FANNING

A leftover from the manufacturing of tea that is sometimes used in low-priced tea bags. If the color of the tea comes out quickly and is dark, the tea probably has some fannings or dust added.

FILE POWDER

Made from sassafras leaves and used as a thickener.

FLUSH

Also called plucking since it refers to the picking of the tea leaf, which is done several times each year. The first flush would be the first picking of the season and the finest-quality leaf.

FONDANT

A sugar syrup that is usually cooked until it is a soft ball, then kneaded until creamy.

FRAPPE

Frozen fruit juice that is usually mixed with a liqueur and used as a dessert topping.

G

GELATIN

A jellylike substance used as a thickening agent and derived from the bones and connective tissue of animals. Gelatin can also be derived from seaweed and is called agar-agar.

GLAZE

A sugar syrup coating for foods. Usually cooked to the "cracked" stage.

GRANITA

A coarse fruit ice similar to sorbet. Usually flavored with liqueur.

GUARANA

A berry that is cultivated in the Amazon and consumed by the Andirazes Indians of Brazil for thousands of years. Brazilians claim that the berry has the power to stimulate the brain and body, increasing thought processes and boosting energy. The Amazon natives revere the berry plant, which is used as a medicinal.

H

HOLLANDAISE SAUCE

A sauce prepared with egg yolks, lemon juice, and butter.

HYGROSCOPIC

Describes a substance that readily absorbs moisture.

I

INFUSE

To allow a flavoring or herb to remain in a boiling liquid.

INFUSER

A small metal ball used to hold loose tea when it is placed into a cup or pot.

J

JELLIED SOUPS

Prepared using the gelatin from animal bones or unflavored gelatin.

JUS LIE

Juices obtained from a roast that have been thickened.

K

KIRSCHWASSER

Also called kirsch. A fruit brandy distilled from morello cherries that are only grown in Europe, mainly Germany.

L

LEMON ZEST

Yellow part on the lemon skin without the white pith attached.

M

MINCE

To chop or cut up food into very small pieces.

MIREPOIX

A mixture of diced vegetables, usually carrots, celery, and onions, sautéed in butter.

MORNAY

A French white sauce prepared with eggs and cheese.

N

NAVARIN

Brown lamb stew.

O

ORANGE FLOWER WATER

A strong flavoring distilled from orange flowers. Used to flavor desserts and confections, it is very concentrated and a little goes a long way.

P

PEPPER SAUCE

A red sauce prepared from hot peppers and usually aged before being bottled.

PIPING GEL

A transparent substance prepared from sugar, water, vegetable gum, benzoate of soda, and corn syrup. Usually used to write on cakes and pastries.

POACH

To cook foods slowly using a small amount of liquid.

PUREE

To strain and blend cooked vegetables or fruits to produce a thick liquid. Usually done in a blender or food processor.

R

ROSE WATER

A pleasant oil distilled from rose petals. Commonly used to scent pastries and confections and frequently found in Turkish candies.

ROUX

A mixture of butter (or any oil) and flour that is browned and used as a thickener or flavoring agent for soups and stews.

S

SAUTÉ

To cook in a small amount of oil until the food has browned.

SIMMER

To cook food in a liquid at a temperature that is just below boiling. The liquid being simmered should be lightly bubbling.

SORBET

A frozen dessert that never contains eggs or heavy cream.

SOY SAUCE

A liquid seasoning prepared from fermented soybeans.

T

TONICS

These promote overall good health as well as fortifying your system. They give you a feeling of well-being.

V

VICHYSSOISE

A potato soup that is served cold.

VINAIGRETTE

A dressing made from vinegar, oil, and seasonings.

W

WAFTING

The process of waving your hand over a dish toward your nose in order to smell the aroma.

WHISK

To beat with a wire loop beater. Excellent for blending ingredients, especially sauces.

Index

Note: Entries with each word in capital letters are recipes.